I'm So
CONFUSED,
Am I Being
ABUSED?

I'm So
CONFUSED,

ISRAEL BOOKSHOP
PUBLICATIONS

Am I Being
ABUSED?

GUIDANCE FOR THE ORTHODOX JEWISH SPOUSE
AND THOSE WHO WANT TO HELP

Lisa G. Twerski, LCSW

Foreword by
Rabbi Abraham J. Twerski, MD

Copyright © 2011 by Lisa G. Twerski

ISBN 978-1-60091-142-2

Book design by Elisheva Appel

Distributed by:
Israel Bookshop Publications
501 Prospect Street / Lakewood, NJ 08701
Tel: (732) 901-3009 / Fax: (732) 901-4012
www.israelbookshoppublications.com / info@israelbookshoppublications.com

Printed in United States of America

Distributed in Israel by:
Shanky's
Petach Tikva 16
Jerusalem
972-2-538-6936

Distributed in Europe by:
Lehmanns
Unit E Viking Industrial Park
Rolling Mill Road,
Jarrow , Tyne & Wear NE32 3DP
44-191-430-0333

Distributed in Australia by:
Gold's Book and Gift Company
3- 13 William Street
Balaclava 3183
613-9527-8775

Distributed in South Africa by:
Kollel Bookshop
Ivy Common
107 William Road, Norwood
Johannesburg 2192
27-11-728-1822

Contents

Foreword

Rabbi Abraham J. Twerski, MD

It should not surprise anyone that during my training as a rabbi, domestic abuse was never mentioned. It simply never occurred among Jews. Non-Jewish mothers would advise their daughters, "If you want a husband who doesn't drink, beat you, gamble or carouse, marry a Jewish boy." How I wish they were right!

In medical school we were taught how to treat trauma. What was left unspoken was that the trauma might have been inflicted by an abusive spouse. You might think that in three years of intense psychiatric training we would have been alerted to domestic abuse problems, but again, nothing! I was in psychiatric practice for many years before my eyes were opened — and even then, not by the psychiatric profession, but by the lay media.

It became clear that there was a "conspiracy of silence" to avoid recognizing and managing domestic abuse, whether emotional, verbal, physical or sexual. In the Jewish community, where domestic abuse is considered a *shonda* (a terrible disgrace), the denial was hermetically sealed. Spouses denied to themselves that they were being abused; rabbis refused to believe that a person who was the pillar of the community, a philanthropist and benefactor, could be a vicious monster at home. Well-meaning but uninformed parents sent their daughters back to be tortured.

I felt it was my responsibility, as both a credentialed rabbi and psychiatrist, to blow the whistle and enlighten the Jewish community about the domestic violence in its midst. In 1996, I published *The Shame Borne in Silence*. The outrage at my exposure of the truth necessitated police protection at my lectures.

Yes, things have changed in the past fifteen years. I no longer require police protection. However, if you visit a Judaica store where many of my books are prominently displayed, you may not find *The Shame Borne in Silence* on the shelves. If you ask for it, they may give it to you from under the counter, or they may say, "We don't carry that book."

Lack of awareness of domestic violence among Jews still prevails. Many abused spouses suffer in silence and do not recognize that their spouse's behavior is also toxic to the children. Rabbis are often the first line of recourse in marital problems, yet they may not know how to elicit pertinent information or what to do when they suspect abuse. Parents may unwittingly become accessories to the abuse, because their lack of understanding keeps them in denial. And yes, even some therapists lack the required expertise in identifying and treating domestic abuse.

My dear daughter-in-law, Lisa Twerski, has had much experience in treating cases of domestic abuse and has provided training to therapists, rabbis, *rebbetzins*, *kallah* teachers and community members on the subject. This book, *I'm So Confused, Am I Being Abused?*, provides vital, detailed information on both identifying and addressing domestic abuse. This is a must-read, not only for a spouse in crisis, but also for community leaders, those who provide counseling for marital problems on the professional and lay leadership levels, and really, for every member of the Jewish community.

Domestic abuse can exist only in a community that tolerates it. It can be curtailed only if the community withdraws from the "conspiracy of silence," opens its eyes to reality, and gets educated about what is at the heart of the problem, so together we can do what is necessary to end domestic abuse in our midst.

Author's Note

This book is for *anyone* who is living in a painful marriage — and wonders if domestic abuse exists in that marriage. It is meant to be helpful, both in terms of figuring out if domestic abuse is the problem, as well as understanding the issues, choices and possibilities that exist in dealing with being abused.

In my experience, several issues often come up when I speak or do a workshop on domestic violence.

When Men *Are Victims of Domestic Violence*

Although this book is for *anyone* who is being is abused, and for those who seek to be helpful, it is written as if the wife is the victim and the husband the perpetrator. That is the population I work with and know. While it is true that the majority of victims of domestic abuse, as it will be defined and dealt with in this book, are women, it is also true that when someone is suffering and being abused, their gender is of little consequence. What causes a man to feel shame, to hesitate to reach out for help, may be different from a woman's experience. But the differences that exist are generally a matter of nuance. I therefore have not included separate material for men who are victims of domestic abuse. The similarities are such that *anyone* suffering can benefit from the information here.

Women Who Falsely Accuse Their Spouses to Gain Leverage in a Custody Dispute

I have been involved in a few different cases where the man has been falsely accused of domestic abuse in an effort by his spouse to gain the upper hand in a custody dispute. I truly don't know whether to be more saddened or disgusted. When even one woman is found to be making false accusations, it undermines the claims of the truly suffering. It is already so difficult to believe this type of behavior exists in our community — people would rather that it not be true. Any excuse or example of how it might not be true is jumped on, and then the veracity of the claims of the truly suffering is undermined.

Additionally, I am truly saddened for the good and caring husbands and fathers who are accused falsely. This is done occasionally out of mental illness, but more often out of spite, selfishness and a sense of entitlement. The husbands suffer terribly, but ultimately, the ones who truly lose are the children. When a woman who is abused *has* to relate information or behave in ways that expose her children to the claims of abuse, it can be agonizing for her. The women who make false accusations seem to have no problem sacrificing their children and the stability of the children's relationship with their father, purely for their own gain. I have to believe that nothing good comes of this — certainly no more than the good that comes to the man who extracts a price for giving a *get*.

Differentiating between Dysfunction, Disorders, and Domestic Abuse

It can be very confusing to people who feel abused in their marriage, or are trying to help someone having problems in his or her marriage, to distinguish between a dysfunctional relationship that may have some abusive features, and domestic abuse. In fact, if in two different marriages there is name-calling, demands about how time and money are spent, and demands about housekeeping and childrearing — in one case, these inappropriate behaviors may be part of the larger context of a dysfunctional relationship or spouse (particularly if one's spouse has a personality disorder), while in the other, these behaviors are part of the larger picture of domestic abuse.

To effectively examine what might be going wrong, it's best to begin by exploring what a marriage looks like when things are going right.

A healthy relationship is one in which *each* spouse feels responsible for enjoying, considering, and caring for the other — emotionally, spiritually, physically and psychologically. This dynamic is at the heart of the most fulfilling and healthy marriages. This is not to say that everyone always gets what he or she wants, or that there are not some areas that are deferred to the husband or to the wife, even exclusively. What it does mean is that in a healthy marriage each spouse acts in consideration of the needs, feelings, opinions and perspectives of the other. In this way, both are getting their needs met, but from a position of giving. When this dynamic is present, we can refer to this as a functional marriage, because both partners are functioning in their intended roles, and the marriage works in the way it was intended.

In a dysfunctional marriage, one or both spouses is not abiding by this guiding principle. Even when one spouse is functioning in his or her proper role, if the other is not, the marriage can still be dysfunctional.

This may occur for a variety of reasons. There might be mental health issues that are getting in the way of the couple's having a functional, healthy relationship. One of the spouses may have a serious mental illness, an addiction or an anxiety, mood or personality disorder. In some cases, that mental illness affects the person's ability to consider the needs of his or her spouse: the emotional needs consume him or her and make it extremely difficult to be attentive to someone else, except to get his/her own needs met.

Sometimes, one or both spouses in the marriage may have the right ideas and is even trying to consider and care for the other spouse — he/

she just doesn't know how. Sometimes a couple has poor or different communication styles, which leads to misunderstandings and discord. Sometimes the couple doesn't have a mechanism for healthy conflict management, acceptance or resolution. Sometimes one or both spouses will act out of misunderstood or inaccurate assumptions or expectations, leading to disappointment, anger and frustration. There are countless areas of misunderstanding that — if a couple does not have the ability or mechanism to reconcile or manage their differences — can lead to *shalom bayis* problems.

Another major cause of dysfunction in a marriage can be viewed as a basic lack of understanding of the role of a healthy, caring spouse. One or both spouses may be overly focused on him/herself and on what the spouse or the marriage, as a new chapter in life, can provide for him or her. That focus can permeate many, if not all, aspects of the marriage and cause tremendous tension and discord. This may be due to a lack of *chinuch* regarding the proper role of a husband or wife.

In cases of domestic abuse, on the other hand, the abuser's focus on himself is not due to a mental illness, lack of proper *chinuch* regarding his role, or a lack of understanding of how to fulfill that role. An abusive spouse firmly believes that he is entitled to have his needs met by his wife and sees no place for the concept of considering hers. He expects to make all decisions he feels are important and to have the home and his spouse comply with exactly the way he wants things done. For the abuser, it's all about him. The abuser believes this so strongly that he is willing to instill fear by utilizing a variety of tactics to gain and maintain the control that will ensure that his needs, including the expectation of power over his spouse, are met.

In a dysfunctional relationship, the spouse who is not being cared for, thought about or considered has a variety of options. This is because the neglect (or active exploitation) stems from some sort of deficiency in the ability, understanding, and emotional availability to care about the spouse. This is in contrast to the abusive spouse, who is convinced that this standard of being cared for without caring for his spouse is his entitlement in marriage.

What this means on a practical level is that someone who is married to a dysfunctional spouse may be hurt, disappointed or even intimidated by her spouse's disregard or demands. However, she could assert her needs, disagree or make decisions without fear of escalating repercussions.

Not that it would be easy. She would have to step out of the role of the caring, concerned spouse who puts her spouse's needs ahead of her own. This may be incredibly upsetting, because the healthy spouse in a marriage has always wanted and expected to fulfill that role in an appropriate way. Indeed, this intentional role change may be frightening, because the anger, or perhaps the fragility, that the unhealthy spouse displays seems difficult to challenge.

In fact, a challenge to the dysfunctional spouse's self-centeredness may at first make the marriage seem even more dysfunctional, because it increases discord, as both spouses are now "fighting" for their own needs. However, in a dysfunctional marriage it is possible to stop assuming the caretaking role and assert one's own needs. Often when this shift takes place, especially with professional help, that couple can experience profound change and improvement.

This is very different from being married to an abusive spouse. The abusive spouse lives with the conviction that the marital relationship is all about him, and he will do whatever it takes to make sure that conviction is fulfilled. His spouse doesn't have the option of fighting to get her needs or her opinions considered, because if she did try to stand up for herself, she would have to contend with much more than just discord or unpleasantness. In an abusive relationship, the abuser will continue to escalate the consequences, making things increasingly unbearable or frightening for his spouse, until she feels she has no choice but to comply with his expectations. She is often too frightened to get help from an outside source because of the consequences the abuser is willing to impose in order to get his way and maintain his control.

In a dysfunctional marriage, there is a lot of pain, hurt and maybe even worry over a spouse's reactions. Ultimately, however, when the spouse of someone dysfunctional stands up to him or puts his or her foot down, there is a limit to how far the dysfunctional spouse will push for his way.

In an abusive marriage there is fear. This fear is based on the knowledge that the abuser will continue to escalate his tactics. It is a fear born of seeing that when things are not the way he insists, the consequences escalate until the abused spouse feels it is no longer worthwhile to assert her opinions or her needs. Alternatively, it may be fear for her own safety or well-being, or that of her children.

This is an extremely important distinction. For the dysfunctional couple, couple's counseling and other similar approaches may be the intervention of choice. But those same interventions, in the case of domestic abuse, could be anywhere from useless to unsafe.

The information, precautions and suggested interventions in this book are meant for the case of domestic abuse only.

Chapter One

Am I Being Abused?

Why Is This Such a Difficult Question to Answer?

Perhaps you've been feeling that things aren't quite right in your marriage. In fact, much of it is not at all how you imagined it would be. On the other hand, you were told somewhere along the line that a good marriage takes a lot of hard work, so perhaps that's why things seem so difficult. But you've reached a point when you've been much more miserable than seems normal. You've started to wonder whether this is more than the expected "hard work" that marriage requires. You're just not sure.

> *Sheryl sought help because she was feeling very "down," and someone told her she was probably experiencing postpartum depression after the birth of her third child. She reported feeling overwhelmed*

and despondent, certain that she would never be able to manage, and didn't see the point in even trying.

In exploring these feelings, it emerged that Sheryl had been feeling overwhelmed and incapable for quite some time — years, in fact. These feelings were not due to postpartum depression, though her depressive feelings had increased during this most recent pregnancy. What took a long time to discover was where these feelings were coming from in the first place.

Sheryl talked a lot about how her feelings of despondency over her incompetence were based in reality. She explained that she never got the housework done sufficiently because she was so disorganized. The children were always missing something: enough clean clothing to last the week, healthy food for their lunches, and so on.

But as Sheryl continued to explore her feelings, it soon became clear that in her opinion, she was doing okay. Life with several young children can be unpredictable, and she was actually juggling her responsibilities fairly well. Her husband, on the other hand, was very definite that she was not measuring up. He would berate her constantly, make her come back and repeat tasks if they were not done to his liking, and endlessly compare her to his sisters, whom he felt were the perfect wives and mothers.

Sheryl kept vacillating between feeling that "she" should have some say in the household, and her husband's right to "have needs," be particular and ask for things to be a certain way.

At the end of the day, she knew she wasn't happy. But why?

Though you may be unhappy — even very, very unhappy — it is not unusual to be somewhat confused and ambivalent about what is happening in your marriage. You can't quite define what's wrong, though you sense something is off. Even if you have toyed with the idea that something is drastically wrong, it can be difficult to define the problem.

To some extent, this is because no one wants to be having "marriage problems." Even harder to face is the possibility that the problem is abuse. Complicating matters is the fact that "marriage problems" can mean many different things. How is it possible to know if it's actually abuse, or something else?

Answering that question is just one of many things that may get in the way when a woman tries to face the disheartening possibility that she is living with an abuser.

You can't/don't want to imagine that **this** *could be* **you.** When she thinks about her upcoming marriage, a *kallah's* focus is on how she is going to build her happy home. She is getting married because her *chassan* is the right person for her; they share the same goals and have the same expectations and hopes for a healthy, fulfilled married life. This is true of *kallahs* who are young, and those who are a bit older, having waited for some time to find the right person. This is true of *kallahs* who are remarrying, hoping that, "*This* time, things will be good." This is true of *kallahs* who had a wonderful first marriage that ended due to a premature death, and would never dream that a second marriage would be any different. They are all happy at their *chasunahs*, convinced that they will be happy with their new husbands. And even if a *kallah* has some misgivings or concerns that she has pushed aside, she certainly did not think her concerns equaled abuse!

How and when things start to get difficult differ from situation to situation. Perhaps during the *sheva brachos,* or maybe a few weeks or months later, things begin to happen that make you uncomfortable. Perhaps the concern for you that he had shown previously has disappeared. Perhaps he ceases to show any interest in your wellbeing or your opinions. He may become more demanding — perhaps unreasonably demanding. Your husband expects more and more from you, and he is not satisfied with your efforts. Perhaps he begins to complain about your inability to satisfy his wishes. Perhaps he begins to yell at you or to insult you. All of this comes as a shock to a new wife, and the possibility that your dreams of a happy home are falling apart is very hard to accept.

Under these circumstances, many new wives minimize the problem, make excuses for the behavior, choose to believe that what's going on is only temporary, didn't really happen the way they thought, or was just a misunderstanding. When I speak to women about the earliest instances of abuse, they often report that their initial reaction was, "That couldn't have really happened," or, "He didn't mean for that to happen."

Rochel had been married for twelve years when she came in for help. She started describing an abusive marriage, focusing primarily on what had been happening in recent years. Then she abruptly stopped. "You know," she admitted, "I knew during sheva brachos *that things were not headed in a good direction."*

During one of the days of sheva brachos, *Rochel's husband had gone out while she was in the bedroom getting dressed for the day, without telling her that he was leaving. Five hours later, without calling her once during that time, he walked back in as if what he had done was perfectly normal. Rochel told herself that he was planning a surprise for her, and even though his behavior was a bit unorthodox, that would make it okay. But when it became clear that he had disappeared without any reasonable excuse, Rochel told her new husband how she felt: "I feel hurt that you just disappeared for hours without telling me anything. I was so worried." The hurt inside was strong enough that she actually started crying.*

Her husband's response? "You're such a baby." Then he went to take a nap.

This was Rochel's second marriage. At twenty-four years old, Rochel had already gone through a brief marriage that ended in divorce when her husband had a psychiatric break. Her immediate thought was, "Uh oh, what kind of man have I married?" But she immediately quashed that response with her second thought: "This can't be happening to me again!" Rochel refused to think about the implications of his behavior — it was too much for her to handle. So she shoved her thoughts aside and rationalized this incident.

As time went by, more and more incidents occurred, going from inconsiderate to overtly abusive. Because Rochel couldn't bear to think about being in another bad marriage, it wasn't until years

later, when she just couldn't take it anymore, that she finally sought
help.

This disbelief can center around several sentiments, such as, "I work so hard on myself to be a good person, to improve my *avodas Hashem*. Why do I deserve this?" Another common reaction: "I dated so many guys; there were so many people I could have married. How did I wind up marrying the one who is abusive?" An inability to reconcile your assumptions about life with your current reality can lead to rationalizing the inappropriate behavior — sometimes for years.

There hasn't been any physical violence — can it still be abuse?

We tend to think of domestic abuse as manifested in violence, that only a woman who is being physically assaulted and injured seriously by her husband is the victim of abuse. If this is your definition of abuse and you are not being physically abused, you may be assuming that whatever it is you are going through does not constitute abuse.

The truth is that there are many women being abused and controlled by their spouses who have never been physically assaulted.

In fact, domestic abuse has been defined as "a pattern of coercive control that one person exercises over another in order to dominate and get his way." Abuse is behaviors that physically harm *or* use other tactics to arouse fear so as to prevent a person from doing what she wants, or to coerce her to behave in ways she does not freely choose.[1]

What this means is that in the case of domestic abuse, the abuser will use a series of escalating tactics to gain and maintain his control. If his initial tactics of control are challenged, he will employ increasingly severe and fear-inducing tactics until the woman feels there is no choice but to acquiesce to his demands, whether big or small.

Generating sufficient fear to gain control over one's spouse does not necessarily require physical violence. The abuser may use other tactics,

---

1.   Susan Schecter, Guideline for Mental Health Practitioners in Domestic Violence Cases, Washington, D.C. The National Coalition against Domestic Violence, 1987, p. 4

or may include a combination of tactics along with physical violence, to achieve and maintain control. Sometimes his efforts have a sudden onset with an immediately obvious goal. Tactics aimed at control may also emerge gradually, almost imperceptibly, over a period of time.

The essential dynamic of the abusive relationship lies in the abusing partner's efforts to gain and maintain power, and his feeling that he is entitled to assume that right in the marriage. He may use a variety of tactics. Fear is a thread that runs throughout. But physical violence is not always present.

Marriage is hard work. So you assume you just have to work a little harder.

Women who are abused often don't perceive it as abuse because they have so many messages about having to just "work a little harder" on their marriage. They spend so much time doing just that that they don't catch their breath, step back, and see the big picture: that the effort is completely one-sided. Her spouse may also be exceptionally good at making her believe that *his* effort and hard work is putting up with her deficiencies.

> *Lilly* knew *that marriage is hard work. She heard this at different times both from her mother and her kallah teacher. So the fact that Henry was very particular and became frustrated easily didn't concern her at first.*
>
> *Henry couldn't handle it if the food didn't taste a certain way, if she spilled something, or if the children were not kept neat on Shabbos. It bothered him to the extent that if any of those (or many other things) were to happen, he would not only berate her about them at that moment, he would also bring it up countless times. He often punished her for being incompetent by denying her money, or privileges such as going out with a friend or agreeing to go to her parents for Shabbos. Lilly kept reminding herself that "marriage is hard work," and she would just work really hard to keep Henry happy.*

One Shabbos they went to a neighbor's house for lunch, and two things happened. Everyone started eating the cholent and it was clear that it had too much salt. The host started laughing, kidding with his wife about how she really did like to "spice things up." Then, a little later, the hostess knocked over a water glass. Her husband calmly got a towel to help clean things up, joking that she had done that because "you are such a tzaddekes, you wanted to make sure that if anyone else spilled, they wouldn't feel bad about it."

That got Lilly thinking. Yes, it's true that marriage is hard work. But maybe there was a deeper problem if it was this *hard. Plus, she wondered, "Why do* I *have to do all the hard work in this relationship? Where's* his *hard work?"*

When we prepare for marriage we learn how to have good *shalom bayis*. Some of these concepts include putting in effort, caring for the other person and considering his needs, making allowances for the differences between husband and wife while figuring out how to reconcile them, and so on.

The first reaction to the concern that something is not right, therefore, may be going to a lecture on *shalom bayis*, or reading books and listening to tapes on this subject — all of which emphasize the need to work on our marriages. It's no surprise that the natural tendency is to assume that *we* should take responsibility for making things work. And if things don't seem right, our first inclination is to work harder to make them right.

For certain types of marital difficulties, books and lectures of this kind can be quite helpful. Sometimes, however, the spouse who is healthy and functional tries to fulfill her role, losing sight of the fact that her spouse is not fulfilling his. So when demands are made, the initial response is usually an effort to satisfy the demands. And if those first efforts are unsuccessful, the next response is to redouble these efforts. It is easy to fall into a pattern of behavior where a woman spends so much time and energy trying to satisfy her husband's demands and to make things better that she loses sight of whether these demands are reasonable or fair... whether it's really possible to make *shalom,* if the other person is making *milchamah.*

He has such good qualities — he can't be an abuser!

Alison often really enjoyed Seth's company. He was funny and so helpful at times, and they could have so much fun together. They had gone on a trip just recently, and had a great time.

But when they weren't having those fun times, he was on top of her about everything. He didn't like her friends, he thought her relationship with her family was childish, he told her she was careless with money and restricted her access to it. But he was also so popular with everybody as the shul youth group leader. It was so confusing.

There was another really confusing aspect to Seth's behavior. It wasn't just that he could be so horrible and so great, it was the juxtaposition of these two extremes that could make Alison doubt her sanity. Sometimes, right after being horrible to her, Seth would tell Alison that he had made plans for them to go to a great new restaurant. Or after a horrible night, he would get up and cheerfully wish her luck on the test she was having in one of her classes. His complete switch into the normal or even caring mode could sometimes make Alison doubt her sense of reality. She would find herself wondering, "Did that really happen? He's acting so normal. Maybe I misinterpreted or overreacted earlier."

It can be *very* confusing for a woman to be mistreated by her husband and yet respect or enjoy him for his accomplishments, for how he treats others, or for the good times she does have with him. The degree to which there are positive aspects to your husband and your relationship may vary, but in almost every situation that I have seen, women who are grappling with whether this or not this is abuse will say, "But he's not all bad. He can be good!" Yes, that's true — that's what keeps you confused about what is going on, and uncertain about what to do about it. It is *also* true that his ability to be good, or your ability to have good times with him, does not diminish or make his bad behavior a figment of your imagination.

Women want to believe that the good times are the "real" him, and if you could just figure out what to do to keep *that* guy around, things would be great. The reality is that it's all him. The him that mistreats you is confusing because it is interspersed with good experiences, but it is still who he is. It does not eliminate the possibility that he is an abuser.

This ability to switch from abusive to caring — oblivious of any wrongdoing or bad feelings on your part — is commonly reported by women in these situations. It does not diminish what you know has happened. It's hard to know if this switch is itself a tactic, designed to make you doubt reality and sometimes even go so far as to make you feel crazy. Alternatively, perhaps for the abuser, once he's done putting you in your place, he's done. He can just move on. Deliberate or not, either way leaves most women feeling very disturbed and confused.

The people you've talked to say such different things — you don't know what to think! Maybe you *have* talked to people about what's going on. But most people don't understand the nuances of abuse. Their reactions usually fall into one of two very rigid categories and often don't hit the mark in terms of making you feel understood.

Chances are you've run into those who tell you he doesn't mean it, or it will get better with time and effort, or he's a good/smart person and you should just talk to him. You've probably already tried that. You know it doesn't help, but this person doesn't seem to get it. He or she thinks you must not have explained yourself well enough, or really listened to him well enough. The problem is, this perspective just doesn't fit the picture you have of what's been going on.

Conversely, you may talk to someone who makes a quick pronouncement and starts pushing you to take steps you don't want to take. This category of person may say that he is just plain terrible, even evil, and you need to get away, no questions asked. This doesn't work for you either, and doesn't quite answer your questions about what's going wrong. Ultimately, you're left feeling confused and alone.

What Does Abuse Look Like?

As we explore some of the most common tactics that abusive husbands use to control their spouses, it is important to keep in mind that domestic abuse consists of a *pattern* of coercive control. If one of these tactics of control exists in a relationship, that does not necessarily define it as abusive. In an abusive relationship, there's a general sense that you cannot freely make decisions or choices; express or get your needs met; or have a say in any of these if your spouse decides that you should do it his way. There is also an awareness that if you try to disagree or express yourself or do things differently in a situation where he has a definite opinion, there will be negative consequences that make you afraid. In addition, in an abusive relationship, a closer look reveals that the core dynamic of power and control is present in good times as well as bad.

This is in contrast to a dysfunctional marriage, where many similar tactics may also exist. But while there is a lot of pain, hurt and even worry over a spouse's reactions, when the spouse of someone dysfunctional stands up to him or puts his or her foot down, there is a limit to how far the dysfunctional spouse will push for his way.

Here, again, the conceptual definition of an abusive relationship bears repeating: "A pattern of coercive control that one person exercises over another in order to dominate and get his way." Abuse is behaviors used to instill fear so as to prevent a person from doing what she wants or in order to coerce her to behave in ways she does not freely choose.[2] The core elements are coercive control and fear. There need not be physical violence present for it to be an abusive relationship, only for a woman to be afraid of escalating tactics should she fail to back down or comply with what the abuser's expectation is at any given time.

---

2. Susan Schecter, Guideline for Mental Health Practitioners in Domestic Violence Cases, Washington, D.C., The National Coalition Against Domestic Violence, 1987, p. 4

The confusion felt by a woman who is being abused often surrounds those times when there is no physical violence. In those situations, when she does confide in someone, they often ask, "Why do you take it?" What the questioner doesn't understand is that while physical violence is one way an abuser might reinforce his spouse's powerlessness, it is by no means the only way he can make this point.

Emotional Abuse

Emotional abuse is when your spouse attempts to control you by verbally attacking you, undermining your positive sense of self.[3] He attempts to make you question and doubt your worth or even your sanity. You become more dependent on him, and less likely to reach out to others, because of how worthless and hopeless you feel. This may include humiliating you, calling you names, putting you or your efforts down, making you feel crazy so you begin to doubt your every thought and action. As an escalating tactic, emotional abuse is used to punish non-compliance, usually with a form of harassment that diminishes your self-esteem and fosters your dependence on him.

> *Paula said that at first her husband Jason just seemed to be particular. He wanted his dinner ready when he got home. He wanted the towels in the linen closet folded and lined up in a particular manner. Paula did not question these demands. In fact, Paula worked very hard to satisfy them and make her new husband happy. But whatever she did never seemed to be enough.*
>
> *At first Jason indicated his disapproval simply by muttering to himself, making some sarcastic remarks, and withdrawing from her. In time, however, he began to attack Paula with barrages of outright insults.*
>
> *On one occasion, he thought that she had said something "stupid" when they were visiting their neighbors for Shabbos lunch. He told her that they needed to "talk." When they got home, he told her to*

---

3. Definitions in this section are adapted from "Education Groups for Men Who Batter: The Duluth Model," Ellen Pence and Michael Paymar.

stand in front of him and explain to him why it was that she was so incompetent, why she didn't feel that it was important to please her husband, and why she couldn't correctly perform tasks that any "retard" could do. When he had finished berating her, he made her stand where she was and "think about" what she had done and what she would do differently in the future.

These verbal assaults became longer and more vicious over time. They began to happen in front of their children. Jason also started to include humiliating accusations of infidelity. He called her stupid, ugly, and lazy.

Finally, after one particularly bad incident, Paula told a friend what was happening, who then encouraged her to seek help. As Paula began to talk about all that went on, she realized how skewed her perspective had become. She used to be such a happy, confident person, perceived by others as capable and accomplished. And now she questioned everything she did. In fact, when she looked at the big picture, she could see that she accomplished the majority of what her husband asked of her. He would find the minor thing she had not, focus on that, and she would accept his assessment that she was incompetent. She had even started to rationalize his tirades in front of the children. She didn't understand what had happened to her.

There are a variety of ways an abusive husband can make you feel bad about yourself. The abuser may humiliate you by criticizing your physical appearance, your intellect, or your devotion to him or to your children. He may blame you for things that go wrong, regardless of your involvement in them. He may accuse you of various misdemeanors, ranging from inadequate care of the home to inadequate mothering.

He may ignore your comments in discussions, criticize your knowledge or logical reasoning in public, or tell others to "pay no attention to her." Usually, though, that only happens in front of people he doesn't care about. More commonly, even after severely damaging behavior, he will treat you well in public, perhaps even acting loving, caring or solicitous, in order to protect his reputation. His tactics will be reserved for the privacy of your home, demeaning you in private — or in front of the children.

He may insult you and call you names. He may pretend that the things you say make no sense. He may even imply that you are not completely in your right mind, or go to specific efforts to make you think you are crazy.

If you complain about his behavior or accuse him of being unkind or insensitive, he may claim that you are imagining things or that you are ungrateful. The possibility of evoking his anger will tend to make you afraid to speak up. You will be walking on eggshells all the time. He will focus intently on things you do not manage to do, even if the things you do get done are far greater and those you did not were unrealistic requests.

Women in this situation often find themselves endlessly thinking and second guessing all of their actions and decisions, fearful of how he will react. Often women also start to fear that others will "find them out" — in other words, see them as their husbands do.

What makes this particularly confusing is that there is nothing wrong with trying to fulfill your husband's initial request. But when he isn't satisfied, you work harder, trying to make things better. That's when you lose sight of the line and when it gets crossed. It's not until something extremely egregious happens that you get shaken into realizing that your life is out of control — *your* control, anyway. At this stage, however, many women have already been isolated from potential support people, and so much has happened that it is hard to figure out how to reach out for help.

Isolation

Abusive husbands seek to isolate their wives from anyone who might point out the abuse or suggest to the wife that she needs to take some action. Isolation involves any attempt to control who you see, what you do, what you want for yourself, what you think, or what you feel. The abuser may subtly or directly prevent you from seeing family or friends, or restrict the circumstances under which you do see them, so private conversation is difficult or impossible. He may prevent you from going to work or school. He may restrict you from going out of the house for recreation or shopping. An abusive husband may insist that you ask his permission to go anywhere, see anyone, or do anything. He may check up on you incessantly, calling you multiple times while you're out, investigating your whereabouts and activities. He may review telephone bills and credit card statements in an effort to prove that you are doing something that he would not approve of, thereby making going out not worth the hassle.

> A colleague called for help regarding a situation with a referral she had received of a woman who reported being in an abusive marriage. The woman said that she really wanted to come in for help, but didn't know how she was going to make that happen because her husband monitored where she went. She didn't know how to get out to see the therapist without putting herself at risk.
>
> The colleague called because she couldn't tell if this was for real or not. She didn't have much experience with abuse and she was having a hard time evaluating the situation. If this situation was real, she wanted help in coming up with strategies to enable this woman to get out to see her. If it wasn't real, and the woman was possibly delusional, maybe she should call in the local visiting psychiatric services.
>
> We strategized possibilities for this woman, creating a scenario where she could come to a session safely without her husband finding out. The woman agreed to the plan and did make it to the session. The therapist called me to follow up, feeling terribly guilty over having doubted the woman. The colleague reported that during the course of this one session, the woman's husband called four times to check where she was and what she was doing. Each time he called she had to pick up the phone and talk with him for a few minutes, keeping up the pretext that she was out grocery shopping and taking the baby for a walk.

Some abusive husbands isolate their wives by accusing them of infidelity. In this situation, the woman herself may start restricting her outside activities to avoid these accusations.

More subtle behaviors may also be used to accomplish the isolation of the abused wife. An abusive husband may start a fight just before you are ready to go out to see someone. He may become ill and require you to stay home with him. He may imply that certain individuals aren't good for you or are potentially bad influences on your marriage. He may simply tell you that your plan to see this person or go to this event is so repugnant to him that if you go he will be unable to feel close to you. You may find that he allows you to go out, but then interrogates you mercilessly when you get back, asking what went on, what you talked about, and whether or not you mentioned him, so it simply isn't worthwhile to go out too often.

Although the following case is not an example of overt isolation, it is an example of another type of isolation that women suffer as a result of living with an abusive spouse. Although it's a slight departure, it's worth addressing because it is a common occurrence.

Tehila is a highly intelligent and articulate woman whom I heard speak at a domestic violence workshop. She told the story of her twenty-five-year marriage in which she had been abused in almost every way imaginable. She described a different form of isolation that she went through.

Tehila was not isolated physically from family, friends, or community members. In fact, she was quite active in her community. She was even the president of her neighborhood shul, and she was an active member of another woman's group.

Nevertheless, she was isolated by the fact that she never told anyone of the abuse she experienced, simply because she was firmly convinced that no one would believe her. Her abusive husband was a prominent and well-respected physician who was a big baal chessed. *People would regularly come over to her and tell her how much they respected her husband and how proud she must be of him. They would describe him as an incredibly talented and caring doctor who had done wonders for their father or brother or son.*

Tehila stated that in the face of such an avalanche of favorable opinion regarding her husband, she felt compelled to simply smile and agree, unable to share with anyone the abuse she experienced when at home with him alone.

This case illustrates how hard it is for most women to confide in someone for fear of not being believed. Keep in mind that you can always report your situation to a helping professional who is unfamiliar with you or your spouse. Such a professional will be able to hear about your situation free from preconceptions based on public appearances or your status in the community. Make sure, though, that the professional you go to understands abuse (we will explore this further in a later chapter).

Isolation is a particularly pernicious tactic of control, because the victim is cut off from external sources of validation for any feelings she may have that she is being controlled and abused. Without an objective outside perspective on the abuser's behavior, it is very difficult for the abused wife to be certain that her feelings are valid. In addition, external validation is an important source of self-esteem. The abuser's efforts to isolate his spouse work in conjunction with other forms of emotional abuse, such as humiliation and criticism.

Intimidation

Intimidation is the use of actions, words, and/or looks that are meant to frighten. These tactics can be the most difficult to quantify and describe both to yourself or others. Often I'll hear from women, "I'm just afraid of him." The look he gives you, or the angry way he walks around the house — getting in your way without actually doing anything — can be hard to describe or define. But you know the clear message: If you do not comply with his demands, there will be serious negative consequences.

> *When Shaindy first decided to go for help, she was extremely fearful that somehow her husband was going to find out. He had warned her explicitly against telling anyone about their marriage, and she knew that whenever she did anything contrary to his wishes, he would become extremely "scary."*
>
> *Her husband employed intimidation whenever he was displeased with her. Sometimes he would just stand in her way or trap her in a corner, much the way a schoolyard bully blocks the escape of the hapless child he has targeted. Sometimes when he had her trapped he would insist that she explain why she was attempting to do something*

that he did not want her to do. Although he often rationalized this behavior as "just getting in her way" so he could talk to her, his size and angry demeanor made these encounters frightening as well as unwanted.

As time went on, he took to destroying things to emphasize how angry he was. Sometimes he would throw things in her direction to convey the message that any attempt she might make to defy him could result in unpleasant consequences, including physical punishment. But since he hadn't actually physically harmed her, Shaindy found it difficult to explain the cause of her fear.

Because intimidation is so hard to describe, women who experience this are concerned that if they did try to explain, no one would understand the problem. "So he yelled — ignore it." "So he gave you a look — what's the big deal?" You *know* it means more, is dangerous, and your fear is justified, but it doesn't translate well into words.

Threats and Coercion

While intimidation is threatening, it involves an *implied* threat that produces fear. *Actual* threats are explicit. They take the form of statements such as, "If you ever do that again, I will..." or "If you don't do this the way I like it, I will..." You can fill in the blanks with any number of harmful acts, including hurting you or killing you, hurting your children or other family members, or destroying possessions of which you are particularly fond. The abuser may also threaten to file false charges against you, report you to child protective services as a neglectful mother, or to immigration services in the case of a woman who is not a citizen. Another twist on the tactic of coercion is to threaten to commit suicide or otherwise harm himself.

Threats and coercion often occur as a response to the decision of the abused spouse to leave the marriage or take other action to disrupt the abuser's control.

After living with her abusive husband for many years, Fraidy finally decided that she had to talk to someone about it. She began by confiding in a friend. When her husband found out about it he responded with a threat, telling her that if she continued to discuss their relationship with "outsiders," he was going to leave her.

He then proceeded to discuss their marital problems with others whose support he sought to co-opt — his rav, members of his family, and some of his friends. He told them that he was worried about his wife because she was taking new medication for a condition that seemed to be making her imagine things. He said that he wanted to get help for her, but she was not cooperating.

Having had these conversations, he then returned to Fraidy and told her that she had better stop talking to her friend about him, because he had already made everyone believe that she was "losing it." If he chose to do so, he could use this against her to obtain a divorce and take the children.

This case also illustrates one way in which an abusive husband can use the children to insure that a woman will comply with his demands. I consider that tactic of abuse next.

Using the Children

An abusive husband may use children in his tactics of control in a variety of ways. We have already noted the possibility of threatening to harm the children or take them away. A more general definition of this control tactic is any attempt to control you by threatening to damage the children or threatening to damage your relationship with your children.

Within the behaviors encompassed by this definition are efforts to turn the children against you, perhaps by making you seem inept, foolish, or unreasonable, or by making the children believe that you have been unkind to them. Perhaps you have observed or found out that your husband tells the children things about you that are not true. Perhaps he attributes his impatience with you to your inability to control the children or make them do the things he wants them to do.

Often abusive husbands will demand that their wives do a better job getting the children to work hard at school or behave better, yet at the same time will undermine the authority of the wife, telling the children to "pay no attention to her," or telling them, "If you want permission to do something, ask me, not her." A very different form of this tactic is when your spouse compromises your function in the household by creating a system where requests for things, favors, and errands that come from you are ignored, while requests of the same nature from the children are acted upon. This leaves you at the mercy of the children, a clear diminishing of your status in the family.

> *While Donna suffered much abuse and humiliation in her marriage, there was one incident she found particularly humiliating. The day before, unable to bear the heat anymore, she found herself begging her ten-year-old son to ask her husband to turn on the air conditioner. Anything she or her daughters asked was routinely denied. Her son was the only one her husband gave anything to. In fact, he gave him everything, spoiling him and encouraging bad behavior. Worst of all was Donna's sense that her son was enjoying the power he had over her.*

Sometimes an abusive husband will do more than threaten the children. Some abusive husbands enforce their control of their wives by actually mistreating the children when they are displeased. In this situation, a woman will very quickly pull back and comply with the abuser's demands out of concern for the children.

> *Each chol hamoed, Carol's husband would plan a big family trip. He talked about it weeks in advance, elaborating on the special treats they were going to have. Privately, however, Shimon let Carol know that if she didn't keep him happy in the bedroom they were not going to go.*
>
> *When Carol couldn't cope with his demands, she told herself that it would be fine. Yes, the children would be disappointed, but her husband would be the bad guy. Unfortunately, that's not how it worked out. Not only did her husband cancel the trip, he told the children it was because their mother could not keep the house*

appropriately clean. He forced everyone to spend the day of the special trip cleaning the house instead.

Using Male Privilege

This control tactic in the Orthodox Jewish community refers to an abuser who uses his superior knowledge of halachah to convince his spouse that it is her obligation to behave as *he* wishes. The husband demands that she obey him regardless of what he is demanding, how he is treating her, or how he goes about getting his expectations met. The abuser may employ a twisted or inappropriate interpretation of the halachah to bolster his demands, and he may restrict her access to halachic authorities to keep her confused and compliant out of fear of transgressing halachah if she doesn't listen to him.

Rikki's husband refused to shower, brush his teeth or use deodorant. She was completely repulsed by being with him and she couldn't bear going to the mikvah. *Her husband told her he showered when he felt it was necessary and she would have to deal with that.*

Rikki told him to ask a she'eilah *regarding whether she was obligated to go to the* mikvah *and be with him if she was so repulsed. Perhaps it was reasonable for him to be more accommodating to her olfactory senses.*

When Rikki came home from work, her husband said that he had called their rav, *who ruled that Rikki did have to be with her husband, and his hygiene was not a factor. Her husband also told her that the* rav *said that she should always be compliant with her husband's wishes.*

Rikki was devastated. She couldn't believe the insensitivity of the rav. *Her husband would come to her filthy, at midnight every night. Even if she were asleep he would wake her up and tell her she had to be with him.*

After a few months, Rikki felt she couldn't endure it any longer. Though she was terribly embarrassed, she spoke to her kallah *teacher, crying at how horrible things were in her private life. When the* kallah *teacher told her that what she was describing was not acceptable, and that she should speak to a* rav, *Rikki became hysterical. "My husband asked his* rav *and he completely supports this behavior!"*

"Did you actually hear your husband ask the she'eilah, *or what the* rav *answered?" the* kallah *teacher gently asked.*

At that moment, Rikki realized her resentment of the rav *could very well be totally misplaced.*

Women whose husbands use halachah to justify their efforts to enforce their control may suspect that the abuser is interpreting the law in a self-serving manner. Or, you may suspect that he told you he asked a *she'eilah* — and got an answer that conveniently supports his demands — but you have no way of knowing what he actually asked, what the *rav* actually said, or whether he asked at all.

At times, this alienates a woman from halachic authority. A woman who assumes that her husband did ask, and that the *rav* was insensitive or completely dismissed her concerns or needs, may then hesitate before contacting a *rav* herself, because she has a negative impression of how he will answer. This may all be based on her husband's lie, but it will be very real for this woman.

Another form of this tactic occurs when a woman tries to obtain an independent halachic interpretation. If you suggest seeking your own confirmation from the *rav*, your husband may discourage you by pointing out how bad that will make you both look. Or you may hold back on your own, feeling embarrassed about contradicting your husband in front of the *rav*. If you are allowed to accompany your husband on a visit to the *rav* to either ask a specific *she'eilah*, or talk over "the situation at home," you may find that you are too intimidated by your husband or his seemingly close relationship with the *rav* to explain the situation fully. Your husband may distort his report of the situation in such a way that guarantees a response that *he* finds favorable, and you may be too intimidated by your husband to point out the inaccuracies.

Economic Abuse Economic abuse is controlling the family income or limiting the spouse's access to money to keep her dependent on the abuser, or to get his way.

Since the beginning of her marriage, Miriam had been severely restricted financially by her husband. She became pregnant right away and was so sick she had to quit her job. Howard's attitude about the finances was that he made it, so he got to decide how it was spent. There was an "approved list" of items that Miriam could buy, such as groceries or other household items. But if she spent more than her husband thought she should, he would berate her and sometimes cut her off from money altogether. If she wanted to buy something not on the approved list, she would have to earn the privilege sexually.

When she was finally able to, Miriam got a job. In turn, Howard started refusing to pay for the household items, so she was still left in a very restricted financial situation. When Miriam started to earn enough to be able to afford necessities as well as some extras, he worked very hard to sabotage her job. He would hide her car keys so she would be late, and he would call her incessantly to undermine her while she was at work.

Some abusive husbands will not allow their wives to work, because they know that access to a paycheck will give the wife the economic wherewithal to resist control. If a woman insists on working over the objections of a controlling husband, he may find ways to sabotage her employment. Other abusive husbands allow their wives to work but insist that she hand over her paycheck to him.

A husband who employs economic abuse may insist that his wife account for every penny that she is given. This prevents her from putting aside any funds that she might someday use to enable her to leave him.

Husbands who use money to control their wives may accuse their wives of incompetence if they exceed the budget. They may cut off money as a form of punishment for other acts of defiance.

Physical Abuse The existence of physical violence is when most people, including the woman herself, have an easier time defining a situation as abusive. It should be clear by now, however, that there is a whole host of tactics that men use to abuse and control. An abuser who wants to control his spouse has many ways to engender the fear that will help him accomplish his goal. Physical violence is just one of these tactics.

The abuser who uses physical violence may do so anywhere from frequently to extremely sporadically. Whatever the situation, when a woman knows that her husband is willing to be violent to make his point, it becomes a very effective tool to keep her afraid of defying him.

> *Mindy reported that her husband began pressuring her and attempting to control her life almost from the very beginning of their marriage. She wasn't allowed to have contact with her family. She was denied privacy, even to the point where she could not lock the door to the bathroom. She wasn't allowed to go out shopping unless she gave her husband the specific amount of time that she would be gone, and she agreed that there would be a penalty for each minute she was out longer. Whenever Mindy appeared as if she might question one of these rules, her husband told her that it was her job as a wife to listen to her husband: "Isha kesherah osah retzon ba'alah."*
>
> *Mindy finally went to a* rav *to ask if this was indeed what the halachah meant. Her* rav *told her, "Your husband is not allowed to forbid you from speaking to your mother, and he isn't allowed to forbid you from speaking to your sister." Mindy went home bolstered with the knowledge that she wasn't "bad" if she didn't follow her husband's dictates in these areas.*
>
> *The next time her husband asked her who she was talking to on the telephone, she told him, "I'm talking to my mother. The* rav *told me that I am allowed to talk to my mother." Her husband's response to this challenge was to slap her. This was the first time that he had actually been physically violent with her.*

Following this assault, Mindy not only hesitated to call her mother, but also hesitated to discuss her marital situation with her rav, because now she was afraid for her personal safety.

Escalating Tactics Women who are abused quickly learn that if they try to stand up to a lesser tactic of control, an abusive husband will keep going, piling consequence on top of consequence, until the price a woman has to pay for defying him just isn't worth it or is too frightening. Physical violence is one escalating tactic, but there are many more available to an abuser. Husbands can do or threaten many things that engender fear in their spouses which force them to comply with their demands and tell no one what is happening.

After having divorced her abusive husband, Susan needed to seek relief for symptoms of post-traumatic stress disorder, including persistent fears, flashbacks, and negative emotional states.

Susan talked about how confusing it had been for so long. She had felt abused, but both she and her previous therapist had questioned it because her husband was never physically violent. Susan then related an incident in which her husband had responded when she challenged his control over her. It illustrated why she feared standing up to him even though he never physically hurt her.

While working with a previous therapist, Susan had described her husband's Erev Shabbos ritual. Her husband would come home from work one hour before Shabbos. He would take a shower, and he insisted that Susan lay out his clothes while he was in the shower, so they would be ready when he came out.

Susan usually complied with this demand. But there was a lot that had to get done so close to Shabbos and it was really very difficult for her. She told her therapist that she wanted to be able to lay out his clothes earlier, when she thought of it, and not necessarily while he was in the shower. She also thought that when she was very busy downstairs she could have one of her older children run upstairs and lay out the clothes.

However, her husband absolutely insisted that the clothing be laid out while he was showering, by her. He wanted to come home, go upstairs, see that the clothing was not laid out, and get into the shower, secure in the knowledge that she would come upstairs to lay out the clothes during the five minutes that he was in the shower.

Susan's therapist knew that her husband had never assaulted her physically. She had told her therapist that she was not afraid of being assaulted. So her therapist told her to stop doing it. "What's he going to do if you don't lay out the clothes? You're not afraid of him. So what if he yells and screams? Call his bluff! Stop allowing yourself to be controlled by him."

After a good deal of pushing on the part of her therapist, Susan decided to try it. One week she simply didn't go to lay out her husband's suit as he expected. At first, she thought that she had won the point. Her husband had obviously found his own suit, because she saw him come downstairs after his shower. He said nothing.

Susan couldn't believe it. All this time she had allowed him to control her, when all she had to do was simply refuse!

But two minutes before Shabbos, while Susan was bentching licht, her husband took all of the Shabbos food that was on the blech for Friday night and all the food in the refrigerator for the next day. He unwrapped the food from its containers, pans, and plastic, then threw all of it outside, straight into the filthy garbage cans, so it became completely unsalvageable.

In attempting to understand why an abused woman has not stood her ground or sought outside help, we must recognize that she may fear any number of negative consequences that might result from her refusal to be controlled, including knowing that he will keep upping the ante.

Blimie was married to a man who would harass her mercilessly if she chose to spend time with anyone other than himself. If she wanted to get together with friends, or if she wanted to spend a Shabbos with her family or walk over to her sister's house, he would come after her and complain. He would say things like, "I don't understand.

Aren't I enough for you?" or "You want to go out with friends? I'll
take you out. What do you need them for?"

He would try to make her feel guilty. He'd say, "I can't go on like
this. I feel like I'm sick. I don't know what I'm going to do. I don't
understand why you don't love me. Tell me why you don't. Tell me
why this is important to you. Why aren't I enough?"

Blimie's husband would go on and on like this for hours. He would
keep her up until the wee hours of the morning. If she didn't cancel
her plans to see her friends, he would start in again first thing in the
morning, no matter how busy she was taking care of young chil-
dren. He would behave this way even if there was an infant waking
up every few hours to eat. Anytime he was upset about something,
he would pursue her relentlessly into sleeplessness until she backed
down. This behavior went on for many years.

To stick to any plan that she made, Blimie had to be willing to
suffer the exhaustion that came with enduring his onslaughts. Her
strategy for dealing with this abusive situation was to give up her
plans most of the time, and to pick just a few incredibly important
events each year where she would be willing to hold her ground. She
made a conscious decision to save her energy to be able to withstand
the onslaughts that were invariably associated with these few occa-
sions.

Blimie's husband had many ways to maintain control in their re-
lationship. The loss of the regular visits that women have with their
families, and the simchas *that were ruined because her husband*
never wanted to go anywhere, took much of the joy from Blimie's
life. It eventually reached the point where Blimie became depressed
just contemplating the possibility of a visit with friends or family.
She grew more and more isolated, and her isolation was psychologi-
cally debilitating. As I pointed out previously, isolation is one of the
abuser's most effective control tactics, in that it cuts the victim off
from a normal, healthy perspective on life and marriage. The victim
loses the reality check normally provided through sharing experi-
ences with family and friends.

Eventually, Blimie confided in a friend about her husband's behavior. Predictably, Blimie's confidant was outraged, and she urged Blimie to "live your life." Blimie's adviser suggested that she ignore her husband's crazy demands for exclusivity and his efforts to keep her at home and alone with him. She suggested further that if he continued to badger her until late at night, she should simply go to another room to sleep.

Again, the absence of physical violence misled someone into thinking that it's the victim's problem; that if she would "just stand up to him" her life would be so much better; that she has spoiled him by letting him get his way for too long and has to be strong and change things. This can be very frustrating to a woman who is reaching out for help, knowing in her heart that the person's analysis just isn't right, but not knowing how to make the other person understand — except by taking his or her bad advice, and then suffering the consequences.

Blimie was actually encouraged by this advice and put it into effect. She began to tell her husband that she was going out and he couldn't stop her. She also told him that she was planning to take a job outside the house.

Blimie's new assertiveness was met not with violence, but with suicide threats. Instead of just asking Blimie why she needed to do these things, he now said, "I can't go on like this. Maybe I should just kill myself." Then he would continue with, "I'm so depressed. I can't eat when I think about how you're rejecting me. I'm sure that I'm getting seriously ill from all this."

When her husband realized that these complaints and veiled threats were not working, he began to make more direct suicide threats. For some time, this escalation of the threat level had the desired effect. Even though Blimie was pretty sure that her husband's suicide threats were just another tactic to control her, she still thought there was at least a possibility that he would carry out his threat, and she knew that if he killed himself she would feel guilty for the rest of her life. Accordingly, she once again reduced her contacts with family and friends.

These are but two examples which illustrate how an abuser has at his disposal a broad range of escalating behaviors to intimidate his wife into submitting to his control. He does not necessarily need to use physical violence to threaten and instill fear. Many of the tactics themselves are consequence enough to stop a woman from challenging her husband's bad behavior.

Coerced into Compromising Your Standards

There are instances where, over time, the abusive husband's insults and diatribes have succeeded in destroying his victim's self-concept to the extent that she no longer considers herself worthy of love or even consideration. But more insidious and less talked about are the times when an abuser coerces his wife into behaving in ways that are contrary to her most fundamental beliefs, making her feel compromised so she no longer deems herself worthy of being treated well. This also inhibits her from going to anyone for help for fear that she'll have to report what she's done.

Women who are victims of domestic abuse are sometimes so desperate to make things right that they do things that ultimately make them feel bad about themselves. It may be a religious standard that she compromises, or a moral or ethical one. Whatever the compromise, when it is significant to her self-image, the guilt that is felt often obliterates the nature of the compromise and works toward making the woman feel unworthy of help or better treatment. The fact that the compromise wasn't actually a compromise at all, but was really a capitulation after much coercion — usually in an attempt at self-defense or self-preservation — often gets lost, and much damage is done.

> *Dahlia's husband controlled and degraded her, he berated her constantly for being ugly, dumb, and incompetent. He made her beg for money just to buy groceries to feed the children, even though he made a very good living and took pride in owning a beautiful home that all the neighbors admired.*
>
> *Her husband made Dahlia scrub the floors with a toothbrush while he stood over her to make sure she did an acceptable job. He*

told her that this was necessary because she was "such a slob" and she "needed the discipline."

When the children were old enough to understand what was happening, he would humiliate her in front of them. He would point out all her mistakes to the children, and he would ask them if they could see how stupid she was. Then, if they agreed with him and said yes, he would turn on them and yell at them for being disrespectful. In this way, he made both Dahlia and the children doubt their own sanity.

Dahlia explained that he had behaved in this way from the very beginning of their marriage. As she recounted the abuse, Dahlia got lost from time to time, almost as if there was so much to report that she didn't really know where to go next.

At one point, Dahlia looked at me and said, "You are probably thinking that I am not very religious because I don't cover my hair. You don't know who I was. I grew up in a Yeshivishe *family and I always felt close to that world. I believed in being* frum, *and I certainly always believed that when I got married I would cover my hair."*

At first Dahlia did cover her hair after her marriage. But as her husband mistreated her, he would say, "If I could be attracted to you I wouldn't get so angry at you, and I wouldn't have to treat you this way. Maybe if you didn't have that awful thing on your head we could have a normal marriage."

Dahlia thought that her husband's demand that she uncover her hair was ridiculous, and she refused to compromise something that had always been so important to her. However, after trying to get him to treat her the way a husband is supposed to treat his wife, after begging him to go to therapy with her, and after consulting with some rabbanim *who couldn't reach her husband and get him to stop harassing and abusing her, Dahlia finally relented. She could not bear to be mistreated any longer, and she decided to stop covering her hair.*

Following this change, things were better with her husband for a short time. But it wasn't long before he returned to his vicious and controlling behavior. Dahlia told me that when this happened she felt completely betrayed. She even confronted him on his behavior. "I don't understand. You said it would be better if you were attracted to me, and you said you would be attracted to me if I didn't cover my hair."

His response was, "Suddenly, you are such an aishes chayil? *What did you really expect?"*

And from that time until Dahlia came to see me, fifteen years later, her husband continued to mistreat and abuse her in every possible way.

Why did Dahlia wait fifteen years before she came for help? One reason is that the decision that she made to uncover her hair made her feel as if she were a bad person. She had compromised an important standard in an effort to satisfy her abuser, and the compromise she made had the effect of making her feel undeserving of better treatment — possibly even making her feel deserving of his treatment. She was convinced that anyone who she might reach out to would view her as the bad one. It wasn't until she felt completely desperate that she decided she may as well reach out, because at that point, she said, she "had nothing to lose."

Sexual Abuse

Sexual abuse is one of the most difficult for women to talk about. It is frightening and demeaning. It's also a subject that in general *frum* women don't freely discuss, even in terms of a healthy sexual relationship.

Sexual abuse may include being forced into having sex when you don't want to, being forced to do things that you are uncomfortable with or cause you pain, or sometimes having affection withheld from you. An abuser may demand relations after a fight, he may be unfaithful, or he may compare you to other women, pointing out the various ways you don't measure up.

It can be very confusing for a *frum* woman with no previous experience or real understanding of healthy marital intimacy to know where the line is. Yes, there is an expectation in marriage of an intimate physical relationship. And yes, it is something that can be less comfortable or even a little painful at first. Even in a happy, healthy, respectful marriage, couples need to get used to each other and negotiate differences that may exist between them. However, there is a difference between sharing this experience with someone who is concerned for you and your pleasure, as is his halachic obligation, and someone who is demanding or forces you into things for his personal pleasure.

Sometimes women are confused about where the line is, and sometimes they are completely unaware.

Rochel was a truly frum *girl, with no awareness of the outside world. When she got engaged at eighteen she had no inkling regarding what went on between husband and wife "in the bedroom." Her* kallah *teacher taught her the practical halachos, and by way of education about relations between a husband and wife, told her, "Your husband will know what to do."*

Years later, Rochel reflected that this might have been okay if her husband had been the frum, *innocent* ben Torah *that she thought he was. Unfortunately, he was not. He seemed to be mainly concerned with his own gratification in general, and even more so in the bedroom.*

Rochel remembers being woken at all hours, being told all sorts of things that she was to do to him, and being kept locked in the bedroom doing them until her husband was ready to stop, which could take hours.

Because she didn't know where the line was, Rochel told herself that this must be what happens in marriage. She wasn't happy, didn't enjoy any of it, often was in pain, but figured that if this is what a wife is supposed to do, then she needed to deal with it. And she worked very hard to convince herself of this.

When Rochel started sinking into a depression, she convinced herself that she *was the issue. It wasn't until months later, when her* kallah *teacher called to check in and asked how things were going intimately, that she actually got the education she needed to recognize how far over the line her husband had gone.*

As painful and abusive as situations like that are, one of the most painful forms of sexual abuse is when it comes in a form that compromises your religious standards, leaving you feeling undeserving in much the same way Dahlia did. An abusive husband may demand that his wife engage in sexual behaviors that she considers inappropriate. He may browbeat her into engaging in a sexually intimate act that she has understood to be *assur.* She gives in, either because he physically forces her to do so, or because she hopes that by acceding to his demands, things will get better. But by giving in, the victim feels complicit, guilty, and not worthy of better treatment.

An abusive husband may also coerce his wife into sexual intimacy when she is a *niddah.* In this case, even though the woman was coerced into this, she feels tainted by the enormity of the *aveirah,* and she may be unable to differentiate his responsibility from her own. This leaves her feeling guilty, emotionally depleted, and unworthy. It contributes to the feeling that she deserves to be abused, and makes it almost impossible for her to reach out and tell anyone what is going on — she is just too embarrassed. She feels caught up with her abusive spouse, feeling bound to him by his tactics, rather than viewing what he has done as his responsibility — and that she is deserving of help and better treatment.

Denial, Minimization, and Blame

When a wife confronts an abusive husband regarding his behavior, instead of resorting to threats or physical assaults to enforce his control, he may choose to use one of these tactics: denying that it ever happened, minimizing his abusive behavior by discounting the effects of his actions, or blaming his wife — shifting the responsibility for the problem to her.

In denial, the abusive husband insists that he doesn't understand what the problem is, or that the thing she is complaining about never happened. He may tell his wife that she was injured when she fell down as she was running away — he didn't actually strike her. He may tell her that she has completely misinterpreted the remarks that she took to be threats. He may even tell her directly to her face that she is making up stories to justify her angry feelings.

> *Shifra's husband was an intelligent and well-liked psychologist. He abused her with outbursts of angry and degrading insults and destroyed the things that she loved. He prevented her from spending time with friends and family members, usually by demanding that she not leave the house unless it was neat — and then creating a mess, so it was almost never possible for her to go anywhere.*
>
> *After she had missed the event she wanted to attend, he would invariably act as if nothing had happened. If she tried to talk to him about it he would deny any fault, adding insult to injury by talking to her in a seemingly supportive manner, asking if there was anything he could do to help her deal with her extreme sensitivity.*
>
> *Shifra reported that her husband was an expert at denying fault. "My only concern is that you should feel good about yourself as a wife and mother," he would say. "I know you would not be happy with yourself if you didn't fulfill that role." He would use his best caring, sensitive persona in these exchanges. Listening to him, Shifra would sometimes question her own sense of reality.*

When minimizing his abusive behavior, the abusive husband may tell his wife that it really wasn't anything to get upset about. He may tell her that she just scares easily or tends to get hysterical. Or he may explain to her that she has been depressed, and when women are depressed any little thing will upset them.

> *Leah and her husband had been going to couple's counseling for several months with another therapist, when she called and asked to see me individually. When I saw her alone she told me that during the couple's counseling her husband would always act cooperative and report various changes that he had made in his behavior to improve their relationship.*

But while her husband was putting on a good show in counseling and even making a few real changes, he was also continuing with the same forms of abusive controlling behavior. Out of fear, she did not mention the continuing abuse during their joint sessions.

On top of all that, her husband could not understand why she was not giving him greater credit for the small changes that he had made, and why these changes did not offset the other forms of abusive control he continued to use. He minimized his ongoing abusive behavior and focused on the few changes that he had made in an effort to convince both his wife and the therapist that things were getting better, and it was her lack of responsiveness to this that was the problem.

In blaming his wife for the problem, he may tell her that it's her fault for "pushing his buttons," and that she should have known better. He may tell her that he *can't* allow her to go out with her friends because of how she behaves when she goes out. He may accuse her of telling stories about him or staying out longer than agreed upon. He may blame her for going out with friends that she knows he disapproves of, and who are not a good influence, which is why he has to restrict her actions. He may tell her that the problems she seems to have with him must be her own fault, since no one else ever has any problems with him.

When denial, minimization, and blame are not sufficient to stifle complaints regarding his behavior, the abusive husband may resort to the next tactic: apologizing.

False Apologies

Sometimes an abuser maintains control by acting remorseful, but without actually ending the use of his tactics of control. Remorse is used most often as a tactic when the abuser believes that the abused spouse is about to take some real action, such as calling the police, an important community member (perhaps his *rav*), a family member, or walking out of the marriage. In an attempt to reassert control and restore the status quo, he may tearfully apologize, buy a gift or flowers, plan a trip, or just become charming or solicitous.

When is this considered a tactic of control? If the abuser goes back to his controlling and abusive behavior as soon as things have calmed down. Alternatively, the apology may be used as a way to send the message, "Stop talking about it — it's over. Time to move on."

> *Joan tried to cope with the demands her husband made, the accounting he expected of her actions, her spending, her child care decisions, and so on. She was upset about it, but rationalized that most people did not live in some sort of "fairy tale." But there were times when he would physically assault her over some perceived infraction of his rules or expectations. It was at those times that Joan, though terrified, knew with absolute certainty that he was abusive. It was then that she would come close to telling someone, or even leaving for a while.*
>
> *It almost seemed as if Barry could read her mind. Each time Joan would get really upset, ready to actually do something about it, he would plan an amazing trip or give her a gift. The first time this happened, Joan thought it meant that Barry felt remorseful, and she tried to tell him how she felt. Barry's response: "This is nice now — don't ruin it for yourself."*

A challenge to the sincerity of the abuser's apology may be met with the question, "Isn't there such a thing as *teshuvah*?" The answer is yes, of course — but one of the criteria for *teshuvah* is change. Assuming that your abusive husband has apologized, the question remains whether his tactics of control will cease. If the abuse stops with the apology, then the apology is real, and your forgiveness is warranted. If you forgive and the abuse does not stop, then the apology or apologetic gestures are just a tactic of control. It will be a tactic used either to dissuade you from any move you might make, or as a way of telling you, "It's over. Time to get off the subject, no need to discuss it further" — whether you feel finished or not.

Summary of Tactics of Control

This chapter contains the most common tactics of control to which abused women are subjected, as well as the tactics and circumstances that keep you fearful and unable to resist his demands. Depending on the particular relationship, over time the abusing partner may use some or many of these tactics in combination or separately. Generally, the tactics will escalate with time. If you have been a victim of domestic abuse, you have likely identified with a number of the cases that I have presented. However, just to avoid any ambiguity, take a look at this list of indicators of domestic abuse.

Examples of Emotional Abuse:

- Does your spouse put you down, call you names?

- Does he blame you for everything that goes wrong, including when he abuses you?

- Does he destroy things that you care about in order to punish you?

- Does he try to make you think you're crazy, accusing you of things you know you did not do, mistreat you and then act as if everything should be normal between the two of you, making you doubt your sense of reality?

- Does he tell you that everything that is going wrong is because of something you did or did not do?

- Does he accuse you of everything that he himself does wrong?

- Do you feel that you never know what will make him angry — in fact, something that once made him happy can make him furious another time? Does it feel like you are walking on eggshells?

Examples of Isolation:

- Does your husband (try to) prevent you from spending time with friends or family, by either aggressively getting in your way or punishing you for seeing them; or by subtly making it difficult (picking a fight, acting miserable when everyone gets together, embarrassing you so you don't feel it's worth it, coming up with other things you need to do when it's time to spend time with your family)?

- Does your husband try to intimidate you into isolation by accusing you of infidelity?

- Does your husband try to get you to give up certain friends, family members or activities by putting them down, telling you how bad they are, and that you are negatively influenced by them?

- Does your husband tell you that if you pursue a relationship with someone he doesn't approve of, he won't be able to feel close to you?

- When you do go out with friends he doesn't approve of, does he call you an excessive number of times?

- Does your husband scrutinize every moment of your day, questioning where you've gone and what you've done?

- Does your husband check up on who you call, listening in when you're on the phone, checking the cell phone bill, and so on?

Examples of Intimidation:

- Does your husband scare you by punching walls?

- Does your husband drive recklessly with you in the car, though he knows it scares you?

- Does your husband get very loud, screaming in your face, scaring you to the point where you're not sure what else he might do?

- Is there a look that he gives you that lets you know you're in for it?

- Does your husband physically get in your way so you can't get out of the room or get away?

- Does your husband give you the angry silent treatment, so you never know when something might happen?

Examples of Threats and Coercion:

- Does your husband threaten to harm you, your children, your family?
- Does your husband threaten suicide as a consequence to making him unhappy?
- Does he threaten to cut you off financially?

Examples of Using the Children As a Tactic of Control:

- Does your husband threaten to take the children away or turn them against you if you talk to anyone or try to leave?
- Does your husband tell the children things that are untrue about you?
- Does your husband blame his behavior on your inability to control the children?
- Does your husband undermine your authority with the children?
- Have you noticed that if your husband gets upset with you he mistreats the children to get back at you?
- Does your husband withhold money for things the children need in order to punish you or get you to do what he wants?

Examples of Using Male Privilege:

- Does your husband use halachah to justify his mistreatment of you? Have you explored whether this is a true interpretation of the halachah with a halachic authority (not your husband)?
- When you *do* have a differing of opinion and he agrees to go to a *rav*, do you take an active part and speak to the *rav* yourself? Or does he ask the *rav* by himself and tell you what the *rav* said? Does the *rav's* supposed response usually follow your husband's opinion?
- If you want to speak to a *rav* yourself, does your husband refuse to let you or discourage you from doing this? Does he warn you

that it will make one or both of you "look bad"?

- If you are part of the process of asking the *rav* a question, are you able to give all the details that are relevant, or are you intimidated by what your husband might do?

- Does your husband lie to the *rav* in order to get an answer he likes?

Examples of Economic Abuse:

- Are you on a strict budget but your spouse is not?

- Does your spouse harass you over every expenditure, questioning you endlessly?

- Does your husband tell you that you can't be trusted with the finances, that you are incompetent and spend too much on everything, as an excuse for limiting your access to the family funds?

- Do you have to hand over any money you make, but don't actually have access to money, except for what your husband decides to give you?

- Does your husband sabotage your ability to keep a job?

- Does he discourage you from getting the education you would need to get a job?

- Does he cut off funds as a punishment?

- Does he tell you there is no money and limit your spending, yet there's always money for the big purchases he feels are important?

- Do you find yourself lying about or hiding money because you're worried that you might not have any when you need it?

Examples of Minimization:

- He dismisses what he has done with statements such as, "I didn't really do anything", "you just scare easily", "you're overreacting", "you do get hysterical sometimes" or "I think you're just depressed, no matter what I do it's no good."

- He won't discuss something he has done that has upset you — he feels it wasn't a big deal and therefore you shouldn't be upset.
- Once a fight is over and *he* is over it, he expects you to be too.

Examples of Denial:

- He denies that he has done anything. "I didn't do what you're saying I did. You lie all the time."
- When commenting on non-violent abuse, he makes statements such as, "You don't mind when I joke around like that" or "I didn't do anything. You're misunderstanding," or misinterpreting, or lying.

Examples of Blame:

- He says things like, "You pushed my buttons", "you should stop when you know it's going to push me too far", "I was drunk" or "you know that upsets me but you did it anyway, what did you expect?"
- He tells you if you keep insisting on doing things that upset him he's going to kill himself and it will be your fault.
- He tells you that obviously his behavior is your fault because everyone else thinks he's a great guy; no one else makes him this angry.
- He tells you that if you were a better mother, a better wife, more attractive to him, less busy with so many other things, things would be good between the two of you.

Examples of Physical Abuse:

- Punching | Pushing | Shoving | Choking | Slapping Burning | Kicking | Biting | Using a weapon | Pinching

Examples of False Apologies:

- Does your husband apologize for his abuse when he sees that you are on the verge of doing something about it? Is this successful in weakening your resolve? Does it undermine your decision to reach out for help?

- Does your husband write apologetic notes, cry about what he's done, send flowers after a fight, or buy you a present as an apology, but you get the feeling it is another way of telling you, "Stop talking about it, it's over"?
- Does he expect that you will be "over it" because he is "over it"?
- Does he proceed to do the same things all over again?

What you might be feeling:

- Afraid of your spouse much of the time
- Avoiding certain topics for fear of arousing his anger
- Feeling that no matter what you do, it will not satisfy or please him
- Catching yourself thinking that you have done something that you deserve to be punished for
- Wondering if you are going out of your mind
- Realizing that you have become emotionally numb, that is, you have stopped experiencing spontaneous feelings.

If you have found yourself in this chapter you are probably feeling relieved about being understood, overwhelmed with all of the feelings that it has produced, and frightened about what it all means. Know that all it means is that you are understood. And that understanding yourself usually is a great comfort.

The next two chapters deepen and expand this understanding to illuminate other common struggles that women go through when they are being abused.

Chapter Two

Excuses
and Questions

You've gone through the initial stages. The confusion and the disbelief have started to dissipate, and it has become clear that what's going on is abuse. What happens next?

Most women just want to make things better, and their first step in making things better is trying to figure out why their husbands are treating them this way. There must be a reason, an excuse for the abuse. So they find something they can focus on fixing that will make the abuse stop.

As tempting as this is, the excuses or reasons women come up with aren't helpful, because they aren't the true reason an abuser abuses. Instead, this method usually has the opposite effect — they keep a woman working at making things better in a completely ineffective way, instead of gaining the clarity that will help her make better decisions about her situation and seek solutions that at least have some potential.

Understanding the common hesitations that women have about facing their situation head on, and why you might hesitate to reach out, is an important step in clarifying your own circumstances and deciding on a course of action.

The Excuses

It's Stress You can recognize this excuse with the thought that accompanies it: "If I can find a way to alleviate the stress, he'll be different."

Financial stress is often blamed for the abusive behavior — stress experienced due to job pressure, trying to be successful in business, or stress associated with not having a job. You may hope that if the financial situation improves, the abuse would stop as well.

But while the abusive husband may be experiencing stress — whether it is financial, health related, or issues with his personal relationships — being "stressed" is just an excuse for abusive behavior, not an explanation. Stress is a feeling, and feelings do not dictate actions.

Domestic abuse is not a response to stress-related discomfort. Domestic abuse is about control.

If I am working with an abused wife who uses the excuse of stress to explain her husband's abusive behavior, I ask her if she can recall times in the marriage when there was less stress, or when this particular stress didn't exist at all, and I ask her if he behaved differently then. Invariably, if she can recall less stressful times, she will recognize that her husband was just as controlling and abusive then.

Mental Illness A woman may wonder if her abusive spouse has an impulse control disorder, depression, anxiety or personality disorder that keeps him from behaving respectfully as a husband.

There are certain disorders or dysfunctions which, to the untrained eye, can be confused with domestic abuse. Hopefully, this book will give you clarity about whether you are living with domestic abuse or dysfunction of some sort. If not, perhaps further research or a consultation with a professional who understands domestic abuse as well as other mental illnesses is in order.

He Can't Help Himself

Perhaps, you think, he really can't control himself. He just *can't* keep this anger from boiling over and expressing itself in insults or physical aggression. You may even hope that this is the case, because it may be possible to get help for this — getting him to counseling, or even easier, finding the right medication that will help him control himself.

Here again, this excuse is superficially plausible, but most often incorrect as an explanation for abuse. There are traumatic brain injuries and some forms of psychosis that can account for uncontrollable outbursts. But abuse consists of a *pattern* of systematic exertion of control. That is very different from spontaneous outbursts which may be scary, but are clearly without the goal of control.

When I see a woman who wonders if this is the reason her husband flies into rages or physically assaults her, I typically ask her to consider two questions. First, is your husband abusive to *anyone* who angers him, in any situation that frustrates him? Or is it only you whom he treats this way? Second, does your husband react in the same way, and to the same degree, whether you are out among other people or in the privacy of your own home? Or are you only subject to this treatment at home, and he would never do it in front of others?

If his behaviors are in fact erratic, spontaneous, and uncontainable, regardless of the circumstances, then you might be dealing with something that is not abuse. But if the latter examples are true, then this is part of the pattern of control that is typical of an abusive spouse.

He Is Insecure — Low Self-Esteem

It is tempting to think that your husband's controlling behavior is a reflection of his insecurity. If you bend over backward to build him up and show him how important he and his needs are, he will no longer need to be abusive.

This misguided strategy not only doesn't work, it becomes very difficult to extricate oneself from this dynamic once it's been set in motion. It may be true that her husband's insecurity contributes to his need to be in control. But the abused wife cannot rectify the situation by catering to him and making him feel good about himself. This is because catering to him is exactly what he expects and demands. It is an underlying goal of his tactics of control.

Since he is convinced that this is exactly what she should be doing, there will be no end to this cycle. In fact, catering to his demands may actually result in an escalation of his demands, along with an increase in the frequency and severity of his abusive control tactics. Since he needs to feel that he is actively asserting his control, when the abused wife anticipates his demands, he instead changes his demands and expectations, so he can always remain in control.

After several years of marriage, Melinda felt completely despondent and heartbroken that she had not been able to "keep her marriage going in a positive direction." She expressed feelings of failure that she wasn't able to make her husband happy and anticipate his needs.

In exploring this with Melinda, a pattern became apparent. Her husband would expect things to be a certain way. But that "certain way" changed constantly, making it impossible for her to know what to do to make him happy. Nevertheless, Melinda always felt that she should be able to figure it out.

For example, he liked to have potato kugel with the Friday night meal and lukshen kugel on Shabbos day. But Jeremy only liked potato kugel that was made fresh on Friday. When Melinda finally figured out how to fit that in with her job and her many household chores, Jeremy declared that her kugel wasn't good because it didn't taste exactly like his mother's.

Then came the Friday when Melinda finally perfected his mother's recipe. Instead of expressing his appreciation, Jeremy exploded in anger. "You make the same things every week. Is there ever going to be some variety around here?"

What Melinda came to understand was that Jeremy's expectation of control in the relationship meant that she could *never* get it right. No amount of making him feel special and important and good about himself would stop the abuse, because his ability to control her actions was, to him, what marriage was all about.

Poor Communication Skills

Perhaps he simply does not know how to communicate his needs through normal conversation. You may reason that as a result of his poor communication skills, your husband becomes frustrated, and his frustrations spill over in the form of angry verbal outbursts or physical assaults.

But consider the net result. Does he end up getting exactly what he wants? Are his tactics designed to insure that his wife will comply with his demands? If so, the problem isn't really in *how* he asks for things. In fact, most abused women report that their spouses are perfectly capable of speaking politely and appropriately when they feel the need to impress. The problem is *what* he wants — which is control.

His Addiction Is Causing His Behavior

Here again we have an explanation for abuse that has an element of truth in it, but is nevertheless counterproductive when used to excuse the abusive behavior. It is certainly true that abusive husbands are disinhibited when they are under the influence of alcohol or other powerful addictive substances. However, "for batterers who drink... the majority (76 percent) of physically abusive incidents occur in the absence of alcohol use."[4]

Consider the pattern of control. The many tactics that are part of this pattern are in no way connected or associated with addictions. The reality is that if the abusive husband gets clean and sober, you will then have a clean and sober abuser.

---

4. Kantor & Straus, 1987

Difficult Childhood/ Absence of Positive Role Models

There are a few specific ideas that are commonly suggested for this excuse:

"His parents divorced when he was very young, and he never had any role models to teach him about a stable marriage."

"He lived in a community where there was no *yeshivah gedolah*, so he went away to yeshivah at a very young age. He was around boys, they're a lot rougher than girls, so he just doesn't know how to treat a wife. He's still acting like boys do in yeshivah."

The implication is that because the abusive husband didn't have positive role modeling of how to have a good, healthy relationship, he only knows how to act in a controlling manner. While it's true that the absence of good communication, problem solving, conflict resolution or any of the other skills necessary for a good marriage may cause difficulty, this is very different from the person who is abusive.

If someone is hurting your feelings, or doesn't know how to appropriately consider you and your needs out of ignorance, you can talk to him about it. As long as he is willing to listen and learn, this person may be dysfunctional — but not an abuser. An abusive spouse, on the other hand, acts out of entitlement, rather than ignorance. With or without positive role modeling, this person doesn't care to hear or consider you and your feelings, and is often not willing to listen to you or anyone else in an effort to make things better. In fact, you might have to hide that you went to talk to anyone about the problem for fear of his reaction.

He didn't just miss out on positive training on how to have a good marriage. He wants his marriage to be exactly the way *he* wants, feels entitled to this, and is willing to escalate his tactics as much as necessary to get it that way.

He Witnessed Abuse/Was Abused As a Child

It is true that someone who has witnessed abuse, or was abused as a child, is more likely to be abusive than those who never experienced abuse. Yet this is not a forgone conclusion. Several studies show that 65-85 percent of people abused as children do not grow up to abuse their children.[5] The way an adult chooses to behave is exactly that: a *choice.*

Simply not having good role models or experiencing positive treatment does not define a person's future treatment of those he loves. On the other hand, if his attitude has been shaped so he feels entitled to certain treatment in his marriage, he will act accordingly. Understand, however, that recognizing the wounds he suffered as a child will not alter the choices he makes in how he treats you.

The Questions

In addition to trying to figure out "why" he is the way he is — and trying to find ways to "fix it" — many women also get tangled up in some very common questions. This can be both positive and negative. Sometimes women dwell too much on these questions and have a hard time extricating themselves. On the other hand, addressing them sufficiently to come to some sort of understanding — and perhaps even a conclusion — can often be helpful in moving a woman along in her process of determining what she can do.

"Why me?" This and a host of other *hashkafic* (philosophical) questions often arise for people when something this distressing happens in their lives. Some women will wonder whether their situation is not perhaps a *tikkun*, some sort of reparation for unspecified transgressions. Others wonder if the treatment they have been receiving is their *nisayon*, a challenge in life that they have been destined to bear.

The answers to these questions are, of course, far beyond human comprehension. They are also completely irrelevant to your current situation. If you had a physical illness or tragedy, G-d forbid, you would not tell yourself that, "Everything is from Hashem, so we must accept the situation and wait to see what will happen." While it is true that

---

5. WLGW chapter 3 cite1

everything is from Hashem, and we have to have *emunah*, it is still necessary to explore the best course of action, the best source of help, or the best specialist to seek out and consult.

Just as this is understood to be necessary for a physical problem, it is also true in the case of an abusive marriage. It doesn't lessen your *emunah* to seek out someone to consult with and talk to, and to get support from people who understand the problem. Doing nothing but telling yourself that this must be your *nisayon* would be much like someone who was out of work or needed *parnassah* doing nothing, telling himself, "I guess I was just meant to be poor and living on the street."

"Why didn't I see this?"

Liba was widowed as a young woman, and she remarried much later in life. At the time she remarried, she was a mature woman very active in the community, with a large social network. She had been set up several times over the years, but she had never felt that it was the right time or the right one.

The man she eventually did decide to marry turned out to be very controlling. He often made it difficult for her to pursue the friendships and community activities that she had cultivated and enjoyed over the course of her adult life. He was jealous and constantly checked up on her. He wanted her to spend all of her time with him. He successfully manipulated her by "developing" various psychosomatic ailments that seemed to come up whenever she wanted to do something with a friend or her grown kids. He belittled her outside activities by calling them shallow and petty, even though they had been part of her life before they were married. When belittling and ailments weren't enough to stop her from going out, the threats started.

Liba knew this wasn't right, but she was plagued by self-doubts. She kept asking herself, "How could I have gotten into this mess? Why didn't I see this coming? How could it be that I didn't recognize what he was really like when we were dating? I went out with other men and turned them down, and said yes to him — why? Maybe it's really me, and I'm not seeing things right."

Liba couldn't get over the fact that she was a grown woman with some experience with relationships, and yet had made such a mistake in judging her future spouse. It caused her to doubt her good sense and undermined her ability to focus on what her options were, what might work, and what she could try. All she could think about was how silly and stupid she felt.

When a woman asks herself this type of "why" question, it only serves to weaken her. Questions like this undermine her self-esteem, making it more likely that she will believe the things he says that are designed to weaken her and gain control.

On a practical level, looking behind you always interferes with your ability to move forward. You can't drive a car looking in the rear view mirror. Constantly looking back and questioning yourself impedes your ability to see where to go.

The fact is that there may be very good reasons you didn't see this. Perhaps the cues that hinted at his controlling nature were so subtle that only with specific training could you possibly have seen it. Most girls and women are not given that training beforehand. Were there really such clear signs while dating that you just ignored? Usually, that's not the case.

If in hindsight you feel that there were clear signs that you ignored, there were probably any number of reasons you chose to ignore them. You might not have realized how important those signs were, and what they really signified about your spouse. Sometimes, ending the relationship and having to start over again seems worse than the potential problem. This may happen to a woman who is under strong family or community pressure to get married. Perhaps your family was not a strong source of support — if there was negative treatment at home, then what your spouse was doing didn't seem that bad in comparison.

You may have thought to yourself, or you may have been told, "Don't worry about that so much; he'll change, you'll change him, marriage will change him." Perhaps he had all the wonderful qualities on your "list," and this one thing you don't like… well, it couldn't be the "real" him.

"He's so considerate, he can't really be nasty." "He's *frum*, he wouldn't be dishonest." "He's so attentive, so he's a bit demanding."

In some situations, the potential spouse has already managed to convince his future wife to compromise one of her standards for him, making her feel that she already "belongs" to him and leading naturally to their marriage.

After all is said and done, whatever the reason you didn't see this coming, your attention now has to be on your current situation.

"Doesn't he want to have a good, rewarding, mutually satisfying relationship?"

The abusive husband wants power and control. This is extremely hard to comprehend when it is so far from who you are and what you want. You can't imagine wanting to be in control of your husband. You don't want to be out of control of your life, but you're not looking to boss someone around.

Most people, men and women, are looking to love, support, share life with and care for their spouses. If you are one of those people, you see life through those glasses, so you can't understand that your husband doesn't want the same. If you would stop looking for what you think *should* be there, and start looking at what actually *is* there, things would probably be a lot clearer.

"He says he loves me — is he lying?"

He isn't necessarily lying when he says that he loves you. He's simply speaking a different language. Whereas most of us define love in marriage in terms of respect, dignity, and mutual satisfaction, the controlling, abusive husband defines love differently. You are loved the way a cherished possession is loved: as an object to be guarded jealously, an item from which enjoyment and gratification are to be taken, but not a partner with whom to share one's life.

When *you* think about loving a person, you probably think a lot about what you give. You love your children and your parents, even your husband, and to you this means thinking about what they need and what you want to give them. It is only in regard to an object that you could use the term love and be referring only to what *you* gain from it: "I love the way that dress looks on me," "I love my dining room chairs." You aren't concerned that the dress doesn't want to be worn, or if the new chairs would prefer to be placed somewhere else. Unfortunately, this is the type of love that the abusive husband is referring to, assuming that he uses that term at all with his wife.

"Why is he 'good' with everyone else?"

What is the underlying concern behind this question? If he's treating others well and everyone else thinks he's a great guy, maybe it's *me*. The abuser will often compound these self-doubts by telling his spouse, "No one else makes me angry like you do." Or, "I get along great with everyone else. I'm not the problem — you are."

The truth is that you probably also don't have any other relationships like this. But don't expect your husband to highlight that fact. Instead, he will focus on how well he gets along with others, how helpful he is to other people, and how he's willing to go out of his way for others. You are left wondering how you can just get a little piece of that treatment — and why he would want to give it away to strangers, and treat his own wife so badly.

There are two separate pieces of the puzzle here. Why does he treat others well? Because the abuser is very much focused on himself and making himself feel good. The way to get positive reinforcement, re-spect, and power from outside people is through positive types of public displays and actions. Being abusive and controlling won't get him what he wants from this group of people, and he knows he can't get away with it for the most part.

Then there is the implied second half of this question:

*"Why does he treat me *this way?"*

This is one of the hardest things for women to face. He treats you this way because he has a specific expectation of marriage — to have power and control over his wife. He expects to be able to dominate and get his way. He treats you this way because he wants to, since it allows him to fulfill his expectation of marriage.

To gain some clarity, change this question and instead ask yourself, "What does he gain by treating me this way?"[6] What happens when he treats you in ways that are hurtful, demeaning, controlling or abusive? You will probably be able to find a pattern: his abusive tactic or treatment gets him power and control over you, your actions, your decision making, your time, your spending, and so on.

When you look at it that way, it's clear that both his outside behavior and his behavior toward you are deliberately designed to get him power and control. Outside the home, the way to that prestige and power is though treating people well — so that's what he does. Inside the home, his feeling of entitlement will lead him to using controlling tactics, and eventually to abuse, so he can feel that power in the marriage.

Cycling Through Denial and Reality

There is a certain comfort in denial, in the hope that somehow, an abused spouse can find the elusive key to making things better. Yet even after debunking the excuses and facing the truth of the situation, many women hesitate to reach out for help. Going to someone for help with a marital problem, whether it is a professional or lay person, makes the problem seem official and more real. While suffering in silence is extremely painful, the thought of exposing this situation to others — and herself along with it — is a huge mountain for a woman to climb. The act of reaching out feels like a ton of reality coming down on top of her.

Still, eventually many women do reach out, albeit hesitantly and often with trepidation. Even after reaching out, though, the denial doesn't end. The realization that your husband is abusing you because he expects to have power and control in his marriage, that *he* is making a choice to abuse, may leave you feeling relieved — because you are now absolved from all the guilt and responsibility you feel for the abuse. On

---

6. WLGW p. 72

the other hand, it also leaves you feeling more powerless. When you thought it was your fault, or you thought there was something underlying the problem that you could change or work out, there was more hope. If in fact your husband is abusing you because he wants to control you and he feels entitled to control you, then you alone can do very little to alter this reality.

This realization produces despair. You recognize that he will not change without outside intervention, and you do not know where this intervention is going to come from, or if it is safe to seek it out. After all, if it's my fault, I know I'll work on it. But if it's all up to him, I'm pretty sure he won't. And then where are we?

As a result, many abused wives will vacillate back and forth between despair and denial. Even though you now know that your husband's abuse is within *his* control, you will occasionally once again fall into thinking that he cannot help himself, it isn't as bad as you think, if you only do X or Y or Z things will be different. Many women have to go through many rounds of this back-and-forth cycle, switching between seeing his actions clearly and then doubting that clarity, because the implications are difficult to face.

When you have faced these questions and concerns and are ready to reach out for help, the next chapter will guide you through the process. Recognize, however, that these questions cannot be answered quickly. Many women need to think about them over and over again. Each person has to come up with satisfactory answers in her own way, and in her own time. No one can or should push you to go through this process any faster than you are ready to go. This process of deciding when to reach out for help or what kind of help to seek ultimately needs to be your decision.

Chapter Three

Reaching Out for Help

Clarifying Your Fears

There are a number of issues that might stand in the way of a woman asking for help, even after she has recognized and faced the fact that she is living in an abusive marriage. It is important to name the things you may be worrying about. If you can clarify your fears or hesitation, you can address it and move forward on getting the help and support you need.

Anger and Disloyalty Sometimes a woman is afraid that her husband will find out she has told someone what he's been doing, and she knows this will make him furious. And when he's angry, it inevitably means she will be abused. The fear of his anger makes her hesitate to tell. To address this fear, recognize that while there are no guarantees in life, there are ways to plan as you reach out for help that will optimize its privacy.

This raises another concern which is often at the heart of the matter when a woman says she has been afraid to go for help. A woman may be afraid that she is doing the wrong thing by going for help if she has to do it behind her husband's back. She feels it is disloyal, or a betrayal, to talk about him in a negative way to an outside person.

Many people find this confusing — and not just the woman in the situation. Consider Eta, a therapist, who found herself troubled by this.

Eta asked to consult with me briefly about a situation she had on her hands. She had been seeing a couple in counseling for several weeks when it emerged that the husband was abusive to the wife (more about the issue of couples seeking therapy together when there is abuse later in this chapter). Eta, not really sensing the pitfalls and possible danger, started trying to deal with the abuse in the sessions. Although she was very good at not being complicit with his excuses, deflections or minimizing, Eta did not foresee the natural outcome this would have with a controller. At some point, the husband told her that she was obviously not helping them and that they would not be seeing her any longer.

About two weeks later, the wife called Eta and asked to see her alone, without her husband's knowledge. Eta's question to me was, "Would that be ethical?" to which I responded, "What would be the ethical basis for dropping a client in need?"

If it could feel confusing and uncomfortable to a therapist to go behind this man's back, even though she knew how desperately his wife needed her help, how much more true this is for the wife, who is caught between her pain and her assumptions of loyalty and marital responsibility.

It is also quite common for an abusive husband to explicitly forbid his wife from telling anyone about the "problems" they have in their marriage, and actually describe doing so as "disloyalty." She can be confused by this characterization, manipulated into questioning her own judgment in spite of the self-serving nature of these accusations.

He may say, "You need to be loyal to me," or, "Why won't you listen to me and trust what I tell you — isn't that what marriage is all about?"

or, "Shouldn't I be the one you believe/rely on?" You are left feeling that talking to someone about your husband, even if it's to improve things, is "going against him," and you certainly don't want to be guilty of that!

So consider this: Why are you speaking to someone without your husband's knowledge? Aren't you trying to make things better? Isn't it true that you *would* tell him, but you are afraid he will stop you or that it will be unsafe? Aren't you hoping that this person will help you overcome this obstacle and create a plan for change? And if this is your goal — is it really a betrayal, or is it actually the best thing you could do for your marriage?

Concern for the Children

Maybe you're concerned about the effect this might have on the children. Perhaps your husband has made direct threats aimed at the children if you tell anyone about the abuse. Or, if he controls you by using the children, his anger at your initiative in reaching out for help will worsen that situation.

Mothers are also constrained by the realization that what is known about the family affects the children. Children are embarrassed when there is obvious conflict between their parents. They can be stigmatized for being part of a "family with problems." Older children might directly express their desire for their mother to keep things calm and quiet, because if this issue "gets out" it would be embarrassing.

Mothers who try to protect their children from knowing about the abuse may be afraid to bring the subject up with friends, because the children might overhear. They won't make an appointment to see a therapist, because the children will ask where they're going. Some mothers hesitate to tell anyone what's going on because they don't want to be told that they should leave for the sake of the children — they simply aren't ready to make that choice.

And finally, there are those who avoid saying anything out of fear that it will ruin their children's chances for a good *shidduch*.

> *A colleague told me about a woman who called for help after thirty-five years of suffering tremendously and in silence in her marriage.*

When my colleague asked her gently why she had waited so long to seek help — and what prompted her to finally call now — the woman responded, "Last night was the last sheva brachos for my youngest child." When I repeated this story at a workshop, a woman came over to me to let me know that she had been in exactly that situation, except that it had been forty-five years until her youngest was married.

No One to Tell
A significant obstacle is the belief that a woman has no one she can go to for help. For some, the abuser has been successful in isolating his wife from family and friends, so she never has the opportunity to sit down with a concerned individual in private and share her experiences. Alternatively, she may have given up on going out with friends because her spouse made it so difficult. Now, when she needs help, she feels she can no longer call on them for assistance. This is particularly true if the friendship was affected by rifts created or fueled by her husband, as a way of keeping her away from support.

Soon after Yocheved got married, her husband told her that he didn't want to be one of these typical couples who always go to their parents for meals or even on Shabbos. He wanted to be more independent. Yocheved's parents grew concerned, as not going too often became practically not going at all. Finally, the parents decided they wanted to talk things over with the couple.

When they got the couple to sit down with them, Motti, their son-in-law, told them that he and Yocheved were going to Eretz Yisrael for a while. When the parents asked Yocheved what she thought about this plan, she said that she had always wanted to go for a year after she got married, so she agreed with the plan.

After Yocheved and her husband moved, her parents had almost an impossible time reaching her. They found out through the child of a friend who lived in her building that Yocheved's apartment didn't have a phone, they had only one cell phone, and that her husband kept it with him.

At one point, Yocheved's sister moved to Eretz Yisrael and con-
tacted her. She told Yocheved that their parents were very upset that
they couldn't reach her. Yocheved told her sister that her husband
had told her what her parents really think about her: They didn't
want her to go to Eretz Yisrael because they considered her incompe-
tent and unable to manage without them nearby. Try as she might,
Yocheved's sister was unable to convince her that their parents had
never said any such thing.

After years of abuse, Yocheved was finally ready to confide in
someone. But she had been isolated from family, had not been al-
lowed to make any real friends, and found she couldn't think of
anyone to turn to. It wasn't until a few more years went by that she
finally happened upon a hotline number.

If you find yourself in this situation, think for a minute. Imagine that someone you love came to you for help. Is there anything she could do that would make you reject her? Chances are if that person needed you, no matter what had transpired you would want to be there for her. Your friends and family members will respond the same way. Consider that carefully before writing off the possibility of reaching out to a family member, even one from whom you have become alienated.

If you still can't imagine reaching out to your own family members and don't have a close friend to fill that role, there is still the possibility of reaching out to a professional. This will be discussed further in this chapter.

Not Being Believed

You may simply fear that you will not be believed. Recall the case of Tehila from a previous chapter. Her abusive husband was a well-respected physician whom many in the community admired; he was perceived as a *baal chessed* who helped many people. Tehila hesitated to bring up the subject of abuse with anyone in the community, because she could not imagine that anyone would actually believe that of her husband.

If your husband is important, well-respected, well-liked or a community or public figure, you might be particularly worried that you simply will not be believed.

Some years ago I was asked to conduct a workshop in a Jewish community for professionals and community leaders about domestic abuse. The expense of this domestic violence training workshop had been underwritten by a man who was considered a big philanthropist in this small city.

When I described how women hesitate to come forward, and specifically their fear of not being believed, I thought of a perfect example — though I kept the thought to myself. Imagine if the wife of the underwriting philanthropist came to one of the people attending the training with the claim that her husband was abusive. Would any of them believe her?

During a break, the philanthropist came over to me in the hallway. "My wife says I used to have this abuse problem," he told me, "but I've worked on myself and I don't have it anymore." Whether he currently did or did not, certainly at the time that his wife was experiencing the abuse, she undoubtedly found it very difficult to imagine that anyone in the small community would believe this of her husband.

Most abusers confine their worst actions to when they are alone with their wives. While some men might criticize or even insult their wives in front of others, they tend to reserve their most egregious tactics of abuse for private moments. And physically abusive men almost never hit their wives in public, because they know that their public respect, admiration, and status will be seriously tarnished. (They also don't want to be arrested!) It is therefore not at all unlikely for an abusive husband to be a respected member of the community.

This is why it is important to know how to present your situation in a way that is likely to be believed.

Being Blamed

A woman may be apprehensive that the person she discloses her situation to will blame her for failing to create a happy home, and attribute her husband's abusive behavior to his frustration regarding these failures. Such misgivings can represent a particularly powerful impediment to disclosing the abuse, particularly to one's parents. You have already suffered a severe blow to your self-concept, based on the mistreatment that you have received from your husband. If you were to disclose your distress to your parents, only to be saddled with blame for creating the situation — the effect could be devastating. Many women therefore hesitate to reveal their difficulties to their parents.

It is also distressing to have a friend either blame you for the situation or minimize what you're going through or its effect on you. When the person is someone you look up to and particularly respect, such as a former teacher or *rav*, it can be even more difficult. This is particularly true because the abuser often tries to blame you for the way he treats you. When a friend agrees with that opinion it is tremendously undermining, sinking you into despair. Most women know instinctively that they can't handle being invalidated like that, so they hesitate to share.

> *Debra had been married less than a year when she revealed to her sister, with whom she was quite close, that things were not right in her marriage. She told her sister that her husband was terribly obsessive, and that if anything was ever out of order he became agitated and resorted to calling her names. He also engaged in compulsive spending that left the family without adequate money to pay regular bills. Finally, he often engaged in sexual behaviors that Debra considered inappropriate and abusive. When she asked him not to do these things, he would apologize. But he didn't stop despite her protests.*
>
> *Debra's sister suggested that she enlist the help of her husband, Debra's brother-in-law, because he had been involved in many* shalom bayis *issues with different couples. After much back-and-forth about what should be done, the brother-in-law set up a meeting including both Debra and her husband.*
>
> *Debra had assumed that he would confront her husband at the meeting and insist that he change his objectionable behaviors (though she wasn't sure that would work anyway). What actually happened, though, was far worse. Debra's brother-in-law gave*

them a long lecture about the fact that no one is perfect. He said that everyone makes mistakes and that Debra shouldn't be so upset if her husband occasionally lost it and called her some names. He also advised Debra not to be so overbearing.

After the meeting, Debra was tremendously distraught, feeling betrayed and hurt. She felt that her brother-in-law had virtually given her husband permission to continue his abusive behavior.

This case illustrates how hard it is to have your disclosures met with blame. It also indicates the importance of not allowing an untrained friend or relative to become an amateur therapist. Friends and relatives can be great for validating the feeling that you're being abused, but you probably want to avoid allowing them to step into the role of counselor.

The degree to which you should fear that you will be blamed for the abuse you disclose to a parent, friend or authority figure will depend upon your past history with that person. In most cases, you do have something on which to base the decision regarding whether it's a good idea to confide in that person. In the case of someone with whom you have no history, there are ways to test the water without jumping in all the way. This is a topic we will discuss later in this chapter.

Shalom Bayis *Is Your Responsibility*

This is connected to the fear of being blamed, but instead of being blamed by others, you are blaming yourself! You may be assuming the blame for failing to make your home a happy one, and that causes you to be embarrassed to reach out. *Frum* women are taught that it is the responsibility of a good wife to make the home a place of peace, beauty, Torah, and *mitzvos*. While this is in fact our goal and our hope for our homes, this is often misinterpreted by an abused woman in several different ways.

Thinking the home is your responsibility as the *akeres habayis* may lead you to assume that the abuse is the result of your failure to live up to your responsibility. When the abuse starts, you may assume that it is your responsibility to figure out how to stop it. And if you can't, that is also a failure to live up to your responsibilities.

The latter misconception is particularly dangerous, because experience shows that women involved in abusive relationships don't have the power to stop the abuse without outside intervention. Abused women who struggle mightily to stop the abuse and fail not only subject themselves to continuing danger from the abuse itself, but also tend to feel worse about themselves because of their failure to change things for the better.

Shulamis endured many miserable years with her abusive husband. She tried everything she could think of to make him happy, including ideas that she had read and others she had heard in shalom bayis *discussions. Nothing made the slightest bit of difference.*

Shulamis finally decided that she was simply going to have to get over her humiliation at what she thought was her failure to create a peaceful home. She worked up the courage to reach out, even though she knew she would be revealing her perceived inadequacies.

Shulamis went to speak to the rav *of her shul. Although she was terribly embarrassed, she told him in detail about everything that had been going on.*

The rav *was horrified at the abuse she described. Almost in tears himself, he asked, "Why did you suffer for so many years without talking to someone? Why did you think that you should suffer this in silence?"*

"I always learned that an aishes chayil *stands with her husband, not against him," Shulamis responded. "We were taught* Isha kesherah osah retzon ba'alah. *I remember my* kallah *teacher talking about how the woman sets the tone of the house, and it is her responsibility to shape the house and infuse it with Torah and* mitzvos. *I thought it was my fault — and I was embarrassed."*

"These principles and ideas are true in a real Torah marriage," the rav *said. "But they are not meant to hold you solely responsible for the relationship and for* shalom bayis. *And they are certainly not meant to be applied in the face of abuse."*

Shulamis told me that she did not wish to seem chuzpadik, *so she didn't say anything to the* rav. *But all she could think was, "No one ever told me that."*

Messages that are appropriate and desirable under normal circumstances may be dysfunctional if applied by the victim in an abusive relationship. It is both sad and ironic that these important and well-intentioned dictates that help us build strong, beautiful homes can also lead an abused wife to feel that she is the one who is responsible for her plight. When misused and manipulated by an abuser, these principles can extend a woman's suffering and the suffering of the family — because this sense of responsibility, and the resulting shame at not "measuring up," may keep her from reaching out and getting help. It can be dangerous or even tragic if the misinterpretation of such directives leads you to fail to seek the help you require.

Embarrassment

Some women recognize that they are being abused, but they are too embarrassed to talk about it. This might be out of a sense of blame and responsibility, as mentioned previously, or you may feel that it is inappropriate to "wash your dirty laundry in public." This feeling often arises when a woman is sure that the profile of an "abused wife" describes someone who is incompetent, unsuccessful, beneath her... but certainly not *her*.

Deena: "I couldn't imagine telling anyone that I was living with this. I wasn't so sheltered growing up, I knew things went on, but in my mind it was those people I sometimes saw on the subway who could be abused."

Esther: "I always imagined that if I ever tried to tell anyone, they would wonder how a successful, educated woman could let herself be abused."

Lynn: "I hesitated in going to a support group because I didn't think I would see anyone who looked normal. I thought you had to be a real case to be abused, and if I go to a group or even individually to talk to someone, it'll confirm that I'm a real case."

Sometimes embarrassment comes from worrying about things that you've done to survive the abuse. We mentioned how women may compromise their standards to try to make things better. This precipitates a tremendous amount of embarrassment when you contemplate telling someone about what's going on, because you worry about their reaction to what *you've* done. Abuse also creates a situation where a woman is so exhausted from dealing with it that she can't be the mother she wants to be, or maintain her home as she would like, or handle other areas in her life. Most people have details about their lives that they would rather not broadcast. If you feel that in order to get help you need to lay bare not only the abuse, but also your own personal shame, it may be too much for you to consider.

> *Susan's son Donny was quite a handful. She had him evaluated and got him the services he needed. She even went to parenting classes. There were times, however, that she had to restrain him for his own protection.*
>
> *One time when she was restraining Donny, Susan inadvertently scratched his face. Her abusive and demanding husband took pictures, then told her if she ever tried to talk to anyone about his abuse, he would show the world what an abusive mother she was. He also threatened that he would let everyone know that all she did was yell at their disabled son.*
>
> *Susan certainly did not yell at her son "all the time," but she was terrified of what her husband could get people to believe about her.*

Losing Control Another major consideration is the possibility that once you open the door and confide in someone, you lose control of it. Because of how controlled you are by your husband, you may be particularly resistant to giving away more control by confiding in someone and not knowing what he or she might do with the information. You may worry about confidentiality, that your situation will become common knowledge in the community, or that the person you confide in will take steps without your knowledge. This makes a lot of women hesitate.

> *Debbie was suffering terribly in her marriage but never told anyone what was going on. One of her neighbors in her apartment building could hear everything through the walls and went to talk to Debbie's father. Her father asked her what was going on and Debbie reluctantly told him about the abuse. Reluctantly, because she didn't know how he would react.*
>
> *Her father immediately confronted her husband, who apologized and said he was going to change. What he actually did was take a job and move the family out of the country, away from everyone who had a close relationship with Debbie. Debbie found herself with an infuriated husband, still being abused, but now far from any family or friends. Confiding in anyone else seemed a pipe dream. It took almost another decade and total desperation before she actually did so.*

This is an extreme example. A more likely possibility to be concerned about is that the friend/family member will — perhaps even unconsciously — behave differently around you and your spouse. Will the telling make your life worse? Will it change things in ways you can't control?

These are legitimate concerns. Fortunately, there are choices you can make, including who and how you confide in someone, so the process will be helpful and supportive to you.

Fear In some instances, your husband has so isolated you, controlling your every move — possibly monitoring or even recording phone calls — that the idea of reaching out simply terrifies you. Perhaps you are not allowed out unless you can account for everything you do. Maybe your husband has convinced you that if you ever reach out to anyone, he will know, and the consequences will be dire: He'll leave you or hurt you or worse.

If you are in this position, reaching out can in fact be dangerous. Still, it's important to reflect on whether your husband actually knows your every move, every hour of the day. Perhaps there are places or times when he would not know you had spoken with someone. Consider the possibility that he plays up the times he does know things, or talks up his seeming omniscience, but does not really have much to back it up.

> *Talia hesitated to reach out because her husband seemed larger than life. He always knew what she was up to without her telling him. She would go somewhere and there he would be, often with a calm but smug look, as if to say, "You don't even have to tell me where you're going, I'll always know anyway." He told her that he always knew where she went, whom she spoke with, and even what she's thinking.*
>
> *Talia knew it sounded crazy. But there were so many times that it seemed true.*
>
> *He also told her that he could place curses on people, that he had powers based on kaballah that made him invincible. She knew this sounded even crazier. But still, there was evidence to back it up. For example, he cursed her sisters, who were encouraging Talia to get help, that they should be unsuccessful and have a difficult time with parnassah. "Since then," Talia reported, "my sister Layala hasn't been able to keep a job, and she's in terrible trouble financially."*
>
> *When asked about her other sister, Chani, Talia reported that Chani was still in the same basic job she had for years. In exploring further, she said that although it's true that Chani's job isn't the biggest moneymaker, Chani herself is happy with the job.*
>
> *Talia's husband had discovered the tactic of leaning heavily on his "successes," and minimizing the times he didn't know things or was incorrect in his predictions. By playing up the times he was right, he maintained control through belief and fears.*

It's important to think clearly about what's real, and what is actually the abuser's ability to capitalize on your fears so you end up helping him in maintaining your isolation. There are, however, abusers who do in fact follow their spouses or tape them or their phone calls. They really do monitor their spouse's movements to keep control. This makes it very difficult to reach out for help.

The task then becomes thinking of those situations or times, which admittedly may not be often, when you can reach out to someone. Perhaps you are able to go to a neighbor if you need to borrow something, and then you can make a call from her or his house. Perhaps there is an outing he would approve of that you could use as a cover for when you're really going to talk to someone. Remain cautious, but do begin to think about opportunities you may have to reach out for help.

Illness or Disability

If a woman is ill or disabled there are multiple details that make it difficult to reach out for help. There is the practical matter of getting somewhere or getting in touch with the person or resource you have chosen. There is also the increased psychological and emotional difficulty. Under these circumstances, although the woman is being mistreated, there is also an increased dependency on the abuser — more so, if she lacks an outside support system or family.

Women who are healthy hesitate to talk against their husbands for fear of what will happen if he finds out. When ill or disabled, the fear of retaliation is compounded by this sometimes very literal dependency. Alternatively, depending on the condition, but especially if the illness is a mental illness, you may have an increased fear of not being believed. This is particularly true if he has a very upstanding public persona, as described previously.

> *Regina had been married and miserable for five years when she was in an accident that left her paralyzed from the waist down. She was still pretty functional around the house and with the children, which she was grateful for. But her husband, who had been demanding and demeaning before the accident, was only more so afterward. He told her that if she was too much of an invalid to get things done around the house, then she was too much of an invalid to go out.*
>
> *Going down in their building was possible for Regina on her own in the elevator, but then there were stairs to the street that she needed help with. When Regina wouldn't or couldn't comply with her husband's expectations, he would refuse to help her out of the building.*

She reported that this could go on for weeks if her husband got particularly angry, or if he wanted to make a strong point.

She was worried about reaching out for fear of her husband discovering what she had done. He had made it clear to her that getting him angry would have grave consequences. He also told her that if she ever tried to leave, he would sue for custody and get it, because "she's a cripple."

Halachic Concerns An abused woman may think that confiding in someone could be construed as speaking *lashon hara* about her husband. If you feel unsure, you can ask a *rav* if you are permitted to speak to someone about problems you are having with your spouse, for the purpose of getting help for the situation.

Disclosing the Abuse

Let's assume that you have concluded that there is something "not right," or even definitely abusive, going on in your marriage, and that you really need to talk with someone so you can get help. To whom do you go? Some women choose to discuss the problem first with their parents. Others might want to speak with a support person, such as a *rav*, their *kallah* teacher, or a close friend. And there are those who immediately decide to go to a professional.

Deciding who might be the best person to approach can be very difficult. This is true whether you are deciding to tell someone for the first time, or if you have told someone from the support person category and you are contemplating seeking professional help. Fortunately, there are ways to maximize the possibility that when you do reach out, you will have a positive and helpful experience.

Why is it important to spend so much time addressing this issue? Trying to handle abuse by yourself makes life much more difficult. Going it alone lessens your chance of succeeding in whatever plans you make for change. On the other hand, women have had negative experiences when reaching out for help, to the point of almost wishing they hadn't. If you choose the people you go to wisely, and understand the best way of approaching those people, you have a much better chance of getting the help *you* want. This is why we will spend the rest of the chapter figuring out your best options for reaching out.

Some women have had bad experiences when they confided in a support person, while others have had bad experiences with professionals. In most cases, however, where a woman has had a bad experience reaching out to either a support person or a professional, this was because there was no guidance beforehand. Complicating this issue is the fact that although you may be ready to share with someone what is going on, you might not be sure what you want to do. Perhaps reaching out is about figuring out what to do. And there is the fear, as described previously, that reaching out will cause you to lose even more control over your life. But if you are well prepared, your sharing experience will be a positive one, instead of making things feel worse.

Gathering Your Thoughts

Once you've decided you are going to reach out, it's a good idea to prepare for that conversation. As a side effect of the trauma of being abused, many women report that thoughts and memories come up unbidden, sometimes at the most inopportune times. You remember the details of the incidents of abuse so clearly that the pain is palpable. On the other hand, you probably spend most of your time trying not to think about the abuse. There are things you need to do; you need to go to work, you have to take care of the children. And you hope that things will be better and prefer dwelling on the times that are good.

If you talk to someone when you are in touch with the memories and the terror of the abuse, you may be so overwhelmed that you have trouble getting calm enough to really express what you want. If you talk to someone when you are in the "push the abuse away" mode, you may find it hard to think of what to say, because you can't just push a button and call up whatever you want in perfect order.

Because of both of these realities, it is important that you organize your thoughts and determine the goals for your upcoming conversation, as well as your goals for what you want that person to help you with. Without that preparation, it often is an experience that doesn't initially go well for women.

> *Rosie often mentioned her disappointment in the* rav *she had chosen to speak with about the abuse. She had gone to him before choosing to go to a professional and fell apart in his office. The* rav *told her that he was sure that everything was going to be okay, that he knew her husband, this was all probably just a misunderstanding, and that she should go to him and talk it out.*
>
> *Rosie was devastated at how dismissive he had been of what she was going through. "I was being abused and he was so cavalier about everything."*
>
> *One day, while discussing how difficult it can be to recall all the details, Rosie stopped talking in mid-sentence. "I've been so upset at this* rav *for so long," she admitted, "but I just realized that I've been very unfair."*
>
> *Looking back, Rosie recognized that when she had shared her distress, she had been so overwhelmed by the memories that she hadn't really told him any specifics. She had given virtually no details, probably leaving the* rav *with the impression that she was a very emotional person, but it would probably pass. From his perspective, there was no real reason for her distress.*
>
> *While Rosie added that she wished he had drawn her out, she had to take responsibility for the fact that she really hadn't told him anything.*

When organizing your thoughts as a preliminary step to reaching out, the first thing you can do is go back to the first chapter. Look at the different categories of tactics and use the definitions to organize your own experiences. In addition, below is a list of questions that you can use to recall and organize the abuse that you've suffered. Put into words *exactly* what has been going on.

- What do you consider to be the beginning of the abuse?
- What did you notice first?

- In hindsight, were there earlier incidents of control that you initially didn't recognize as such?
- What has the progression been?
- What has happened during some of the bigger blow-ups?
- What are some of the everyday ways he controls you?
- In what ways specifically has he been abusive: emotionally, physically, financially, psychologically or sexually?
- What are some examples of these things in your life? Including dates, times, and duration will be beneficial, if you can recall them. If not, start keeping track now.
- Are you afraid to challenge his control?
- What incidents/consequences have you suffered in trying to stand up to the abuse?

Obviously, writing things down in a journal or other form of written record has to be safe for you. If there is nowhere in your house that you can safely keep your notes, try to keep them elsewhere.

Bring along these written notes to your conversation, and perhaps a checklist of topics to be covered. Keeping notes on the abuse will help make sure all the important details get conveyed. Sometimes these details are embarrassing or painful to describe. Having the details in writing and reading them when necessary may make it easier to describe the events, because it helps you feel a little distanced from them. Sometimes a woman will even ask the person to read the notes, so she doesn't have to repeat every detail herself. What is important is that the person you go to for help has all the facts.

Sometimes a woman isn't clear with the person she is reaching out to due to the nature of the abuse she has endured.

Shira was completely overwhelmed by her husband's incessant tirades and his demeaning treatment. He insisted on approving her every movement, including where she went, what she did, and with whom she spent her time. Each night he interrogated her endlessly about what she had done that day, insinuating that she was involved in immoral activities, and even implying that she was unfaithful. If she resisted his demands for accountability or was the least bit vague or uncertain regarding an activity or a period of time, he demanded that she "prove" her love for him by engaging in certain sexual behaviors with which she was uncomfortable, and which could go on for hours.

Finally, when she could suffer this abuse no longer, Shira went to the rav *to complain and ask for his intervention. But when she actually spoke with him, she found that she was only able to tell the* rav *a small part of what was so distressing to her. She was too embarrassed to tell him about the accusations of infidelity or the sexual degradation.*

The story of Shira indicates how important it is for an abused wife who is contemplating disclosure to carefully think through what she is willing and able to report. In considering what needs to be said, keep in mind the particular individual to whom you plan to disclose. If you are planning to speak to the *rav*, your *kallah* teacher, or anyone else by whom you might feel somewhat intimidated, or with whom you might be reluctant to share the most embarrassing elements of your husband's behavior, you need to figure out in advance how you are going to convey those more embarrassing details. Having those details could make all the difference in getting you the help you are looking for. In this case, it's a good idea is to bring your notes to any meeting you have, in case you get flustered. You might want to ask the person to read the parts you are too embarrassed to say, to make sure you relate everything that is important.

Setting Goals An equally important part of preparing to reach out is deciding beforehand what your goals are. Many women, when they finally confide in someone, *sound* like what they want is for that person to take over and tell them what to do. Some women even feel or think that that *is* what they want: someone to just rescue them and take over. However, my experience working with abused women suggests that in reality, most want that person to respect their own choices about when to act, what to do, and what not to do.

If you do think that you want the person to whom you disclose to take over or to tell you what to do, ask yourself: What would you definitely *not* want to hear? Then imagine that the person in whom you confide says that this is precisely what he or she is going to do, or starts pushing you to do.

If you find that you have opinions about the situation, then you really don't want someone to rush in and take over, however overwhelmed you might feel. You would be running the risk of hearing exactly what you don't want to hear.

What, then, might be some of your goals for disclosing your abuse?

Goals are tricky because they can keep changing. You can't know what your goal will be in a month. What you can be relatively certain about is what your goal is for right now.

Keeping goals clear for yourself and for the people in your life will be a fluid process. If in the course of pursuing one goal, you realize that you have other goals as well, or that you've changed your mind, make sure you are clear with the people you've reached out to on how your thinking may have changed. Take the time to be clear.

The following list contains possible goals you may have with your situation. Use it to pinpoint what you are looking for if you decide to reach out.

- Are you looking for a listening ear, someone who will just let you vent, without pushing you to make a move?
- Are you looking for someone who can give you resources?
- Do you have a general hope that the person you're going to can make your husband stop?
- Is the help you're looking for financial?
- Are you considering legal measures and need a referral?
- Are you looking for help regarding the children? (They are acting out and you need help, they need something like tutoring or

braces and your husband is refusing, you see they need a positive environment and don't know how to help them?)

- Are you looking for help convincing your husband to go for help (something we will discuss in more detail in the next chapter)?
- Do you need information? Halachic or legal?
- Do you have a halachic question and need to know what to do?

There are any number of specific things you may be looking for when you decide to confide in someone. It is up to you to be clear in your expectations and in your presentation.

Getting the Help You Want   When a woman confides in a non-professional, the more desperate and out of control she sounds, the more likely the person is to try to rush in and take over. If you can reassure the person that however upset you are, you want to remain in control of what happens next, it is more likely that he/she will respond by respecting your request or decision.

Unless someone is a trained professional with a specific expertise in domestic abuse, he or she is very susceptible to "overhelping." Keeping this in mind, you may serve your cause best by carefully monitoring the level of desperation that you communicate, and by prefacing your disclosure with your specific wants, with an additional request to please not do anything without your input and permission.

It may be hard to think about keeping things on such a rational level, especially when you're feeling so desperate. In fact, the goal is not to be completely unemotional. It probably wouldn't be possible, and if you were completely unemotional, it might be hard for someone to believe you are going through something so terrible. The goal of being prepared in this way is to keep you in just enough control to get the results you hope for. When you can express yourself clearly and provide the other person with a clear sense of what you want, it will lessen the instinct to jump in and take over. If you sound in control, you will remain in control.

Keep in mind the other person's likely response. When someone discovers that a person he/she cares about is going through a hard situation, the natural reaction is to want to *do* something and see change. If things continue to stay the same, your support person will probably have a hard time staying supportive without getting pushy at some point. The clearer you remain about what you need, while gently letting the person know what is and is not helpful, the better off you will be.

We will discuss how to maintain a relationship with a support person in the case of your long term choice to stay in the marriage in the next chapter.

YOUR POSSIBLE SUPPORT NETWORK

Once you have gathered your thoughts and determined your goal, consider whom you are reaching out to. Although you are going to this person for help because you perceive him/her as being able to support and focus on you, it is worthwhile to focus on that person for a bit, too.

Sometimes when I encounter a woman who has been disappointed when reaching out, it's because she didn't take into account what this disclosure might mean to the other person, and where he/she might be coming from. Taking a moment to do that will make it possible to accommodate these details and maximize the possibility of having a really positive experience.

Parents   Your parents have spent their lives caring, intervening, advocating, and problem-solving for you in a variety of situations: school, teachers, friends, extracurricular activities. It has been their long-standing role to be actively involved in this parenting endeavor. Laying everything out for them in a way that sounds desperate and miserable will likely jumpstart a loving parent's proactive, protective instinct.

Even if you sound relatively in control, you need to think about whether your parents are going to be able to let *you* determine your goals and your pace. There are women, often younger married women, who don't reach out to their parents because they know if their parents knew what has been going on, that would be it. No questions, no discussions: Their parents would pack them up and take them home.

That may be what you want, and there are those who tell their parents for exactly that reason. However, you may want them to do something *with* you rather than do something *for* you. This may be a very different role for your parents, and it could be difficult for them to adjust to this new role. It may also be an adjustment for you.

Being clear about what you actually want, as difficult as that might be when you are in a crisis or overwhelmed, will be to your benefit, so you can get the help *you* prefer.

On the other hand, there are women whose parents have never been particularly supportive. You may be hoping that, under these circumstances, they can't help but be supportive. It's important, however, to consider what you will do if they don't rise to the occasion. Have a backup person you can go to now that you're ready to reach out, in case you don't get what you want from your parents.

Some women hesitate to reach out to their parents out of a desire to protect them:

> *Rivka had tried everything to make her husband happy and create a relationship between the two of them, but all she got were putdowns and dismissals. Rivka finally decided that she was going to tell her parents and ask for their support.*
>
> *Then her father called. Before she could tell him what was on her mind, Rivka's father let her know that her mother was sick and was going to be undergoing treatment. At that point, Rivka knew that she couldn't burden her parents with this. She would need to get help from a different source.*

Other women hesitate because although they know their parents will be a tremendous source of support, they have been cautioned not to confide in them. Perhaps the abuser has told his wife that if she tells her parents anything about their relationship, the marriage is over. Perhaps she received messages from a *kallah* teacher, or from someone who has already gotten involved in her marital difficulties, that it would be a big mistake to involve her parents: they meddle, make things worse, and so on. You will have to evaluate this to determine if they are the best source of support for you.

A Rav Typically, one goes to a *rav* to ask a *she'eilah* or get an *eitzah*. Consequently, a *rav* will generally expect to give a *psak* or an *eitzah* to someone who comes to talk with him about a difficult situation.

Many *frum* women, when they finally decide to reach out and break their silence, will seek out their *rav* first. They consider their *rav* to be smart, caring, safe, and an authority figure, all of which are true. The issue that arises, however, is that if you're only looking at this point to break your silence, and not really interested in a *psak* or *eitzah*, you may find that you will get one anyway, because that's what a *rav* assumes someone is coming for.

Before choosing to go to a *rav*, ask yourself, "What *she'eilah* do I have? What do I want an *eitzah* for — specifically?"

> *Rosie was reaching out for help in getting out of her twenty-five-year marriage. As an aside, she mentioned that when she had been married for five years, she had gone to her* rav *in desperation, wanting to unburden herself about what had been going on in her marriage. He was the first person she had reached out to, and she told him everything.*
>
> *The* rav *was horrified and told her that she needed to get out. "But I was young, with three children five years old and under, and I just couldn't imagine getting divorced. Now I have nine children, and I must leave."*

If you have a specific *she'eilah*, then the process of consulting with a *rav* can be fairly straightforward, as we will discuss in a later chapter. However, if you are going to a *rav* for support, you need to understand a *rav's* perspective and respectfully clarify the reason you are coming to see him.

Some women feel that it is appropriate to give the decision making over to a *rav*. If that is your plan, make sure you are really ready to listen, no matter what. Believing it's the right thing to do, and being able to follow through when you hear something you don't feel ready to do, can be two different things. If ultimately you find that you can't follow through, you may end up losing the connection with the *rav* because you are too embarrassed to face him afterward. It's prudent to think through this process before going forward.

A Friend   If you're thinking about reaching out to a friend, consider what you want from that friend and what qualities that person should have in order to meet your needs. Your first thought might be to turn to your best friend. But perhaps she often repeats things to others, which would make you uncomfortable regarding your privacy. Maybe she's very busy and overwhelmed and you're not sure if she'll have the time or patience to listen to you. Maybe she's very judgmental.

Think clearly about the qualities you need in a confidant and who in your life might fit that bill.

> *Nina's husband Ray thought well of himself, his ideas and his decisions, to the exclusion of everyone else's — including hers. Everything had to be his way, and he derided and forbade anything she thought or wanted that he disagreed with. There was only one person Ray looked up to: his older brother. But Nina was hesitant to tell Ray's brother about what was going on, because his brother was also his boss. Nina was worried that if she told Ray's brother, it would somehow impact his job, and she just couldn't see "doing that" to him. And as Ray's brother, could she really expect him to believe ill of Ray, or would he be more likely to blame her?*

A Mental Health Professional   Disclosing abuse that you have been experiencing to a professional has a number of unique advantages, but also raises some concerns. Among the advantages of going to a professional is that this person can be an objective outsider. He or she should be able to listen nonjudgmentally, and is free from possible hidden agendas. Because the professional is outside your social circle, and maybe even outside your community, you will be able to begin to get help without feeling like you are airing your family's "dirty laundry" for all to see.

There are also a number of reasons women hesitate to go to a professional to seek help. Finances can be an obstacle, either because the family has a low income, or because an abusive and controlling husband has effectively limited his abused wife's access to finances. Some abused women can take advantage of a low cost mental health facility or a no cost or low cost domestic violence service. To see what options may be available to you in your community, consult the Resource Appendix in the back of the book.

Another concern is a woman's perception that consulting with a professional implies that *she* is "the problem." Your husband may reinforce this stereotype by telling you that you are crazy. If you ask your husband to go with you to a professional for help with your marriage, he may respond that *he* is fine, but you can go because *you* obviously need help. Your reluctance to go for help then becomes twofold. First, you know he's the one being abusive, so you may be thinking, "Why do *I* have to go for help?" Second, you worry that in the event of a separation or divorce, your husband may use the information that you went to therapy to demonstrate that you are mentally unbalanced and therefore incapable of caring for the children.

The reality is that trying to seek help to make your marriage better does not count against you. It is also not an admission that *you* are the problem. You aren't going because you have a problem. You are going to find out how to deal with his problem, and what help there might be out there for getting him to end his abuse.

If the idea of talking to a professional still makes you nervous, but there is no one else you can speak with, perhaps try calling an anonymous hotline. That might be a good way to get your feet wet in terms of seeing what it feels like to reach out, without making too much of a commitment. If you don't like the experience, you never have to call back and they aren't able to call you back.

Disclosing abuse to a professional mental health worker is potentially a very good route to follow, *provided* you choose a therapist who has expertise in the area of domestic abuse and experience working with abused women. Because it is so important to choose the right professional, I have included a discussion of the qualifications and characteristics that one should look for in choosing a therapist.

CHOOSING THE RIGHT THERAPIST

While a therapist can be an extremely useful resource for the abused woman struggling to find a way to improve her situation, it is very important to choose the right therapist. Obviously, expertise in the area of domestic abuse, experience working with abused women, and experience working with Orthodox women are all important. The expertise and experience of a particular therapist may be determined by word-of-mouth, by obtaining a referral from someone who has worked with the therapist in the past, from a general referral line or from counselors at domestic abuse hotlines. In some areas, it may be hard to find a therapist who is both Orthodox and has an expertise in domestic violence. Use the list of important characteristics below to guide you in finding a therapist.

A good therapist should...

- **Have an expertise in domestic violence:** If you seek help at a domestic violence program this is more likely. If you go to see someone in a general mental health clinic or in private practice, it is perfectly okay to ask about his/her training and experience working with abused women. You can also assess this yourself by looking for the following characteristics.

- **Not confuse abuse with other issues, such as:**
  a. co-dependency: There are many different terms that are thrown around to refer to a woman who stays in an abusive relationship. They may include, "she is co-dependent" or "she is a love addict" (so addicted to love, she is willing to put up with anything). Some of the

details you read about these terms may seem to apply to your situation.[7] However, in an abusive relationship, the dynamics are very different, even though some of the defining characteristics might apply in a tangential manner. An experienced and competent therapist should help keep you from getting caught up and confused by those terms, which can lead you to wrongly blame yourself for the abuse that you have experienced.

b. masochism: I had a therapist refer a woman to me to whom he called a "masochist." When I inquired further about the case, I discovered he was referring to a woman who was staying in an abusive relationship. Your counselor should be very clear about all the rational and complicated reasons some women stay in abusive relationships. She should not attribute this decision to a mental illness on your part. In my experience, women do not want or enjoy being abused, and if they choose to remain in the relationship it is for other reasons. An experienced therapist will not make you feel ashamed because you are in an abusive relationship. She will not ask questions such as, "Why do you stay?" or "What do you get out of his violence?"

c. marital problems: A therapist who doesn't understand, validate and work in a way that recognizes the difference between marital dysfunction and domestic abuse does not have enough expertise in domestic violence to help you. Your advocate should be clear that a woman who is abused is not in an equitable marriage. Your advocate shouldn't make you feel responsible for your husband's abusive behaviors by asking things like, "What did you do to make him so angry?" Your advocate should understand that your situation is not the same as someone with general *shalom bayis* problems, and it cannot be dealt with in that manner.

- **Understand issues of safety:** Whether a woman decides to stay, leave, or has left and decided to return home, a professional will be able to

---

7. *When Love Goes Wrong,* Ann Jones and Susan Schecter, Harper Perennial, 1993

help her strategize around issues of safety, whether or not there has been physical violence in the past. She will take issues of safety seriously without making both of you more anxious. Additionally, if your counselor has contact with your spouse, she should understand that an abusive or controlling spouse can look and sound very different to others compared to how he treats you at home.

- **Strictly adhere to confidentiality:** A professional will keep a client's information confidential. If it is determined that it isn't safe for a woman's husband to know she's in therapy, she'll support your decision not to tell him. If others try to interfere with your counseling, she will not allow it. This may include having to withstand pressure from various community members, or even community leaders, when your work with her is not proceeding how they or your husband would like.

- **Have an understanding of resources:** Your counselor should understand the different resources that are available to you: legal, shelter, housing, public assistance, and so on.

- **Follow your lead:** Although your counselor knows what's available to you, she should adhere strictly to a policy of following your lead with respect to decision making. The therapist should be familiar with the pros and cons of various alternative courses of action and should be able to provide you with support and advice on how to best follow through with the path *you* choose. She should believe that she has an expertise, but only *you* can decide on the best course of action for you.

- **Have an understanding of and consideration for religious issues:** A good counselor who has an understanding of *halachos* that may come up will respect what you decide to do without trying to influence you or pressure you based on *her* religious adherence. If she is not from the community and is not knowledgeable, she will respect your adherence to *halachos*. She will not try to tell you to "do away with those antiquated ideas."

- **Understand that you know your situation best.** A good therapist will not think that she can tell you how the abuser is doing. Although she knows that she has some information that you don't, she also knows that in terms of information about the abuser, *you* are the expert.

- **Lighten your load:** When you start working with a counselor or advocate, things might not change right away or quickly. In fact, how much things are likely to change is hard to determine. Nevertheless, seeing someone who understands domestic abuse should make you feel better. You should feel validated and understood, and you should experience relief for having shared your feelings.

A good therapist should not...

- **Jump to conclusions** about your situation without hearing you out.
- **Think for you:** She should not assume that she knows what you would want and what choices you would make. Sometimes therapists assume women want to leave, when they don't. Sometimes they assume women want to go to court, when they don't. Sometimes they assume that women want to stay when they don't. Sometimes they assume women shouldn't go back, when they want to.
- **Be closed minded or difficult to tell things to** because she does not fully believe the details of your situation or that your spouse could do "such things."
- **Have a personal connection to you or your spou**se.
- **Have an agenda:** She should not think that successful work with an abused woman means that you *leave*, or think that all marriages should be preserved no matter how badly you are suffering and want to leave. An appropriate therapist will respect your decisions.
- **Minimize his abusiveness** while telling you that she/he has to build rapport with your spouse to be able to help him. This is usually code for collusion with his abusive behavior.
- **Disbelieve you.**
- **Excuse your spouse's behavior** as due to stress, childhood trauma, your behavior, and so on.

- **Place the responsibility for his change on you.**

- **Make non-violence contracts**, where the therapist tells the abusive spouse that he is going to *agree* to not be abusive. There are therapists who have a false sense of their own influence on the abuser.

What follows are examples of situations where the counseling experience was not what it should have been for the women seeking help. This is not meant to be discouraging. It does demonstrate that simply being a trained professional is not enough to make a therapist effective in dealing with domestic abuse. If you are unfamiliar with the mental health system, you may mistakenly assume that a professional is a professional, and that one is as good as any other. In fact, when dealing with domestic abuse, as with other serious issues, seeing someone with a specific expertise in this area is quite important.

I hope these case examples make it clear that if you are feeling uncomfortable with the professional you are seeing, it is not necessarily your issue. It could well be that your professional does not have an appropriate level of expertise in domestic violence. That's why it is important to check that out ahead of time.

> Bella realized she was uncomfortable with the therapist she had been seeing. The therapist had been referred to her as someone who was very experienced, but Bella found that she was not comfortable with her approach. The therapist told Bella at the start that she had a very specific way of working. She operated on the assumption that domestic abuse and domestic violence thrive on isolation — a very accurate belief. Based on this assumption, she always began by breaking down the isolation the husband had created. She would bring in the husband and the husband's rav, along with the abused wife. She would get everything "out into the open" by enumerating the abusive behaviors and stating that these behaviors must end if the relationship is to continue. This therapist told Bella that by using this approach, she makes the husband accountable to both the rav and to her, the therapist.

Bella did not dispute the correctness of the therapist's assertions regarding the role of isolation in maintaining the abusive relationship, but she was uncomfortable with the plan. In talking it through, she realized that she was uncomfortable with the therapist's assumption that this would be a safe course of action. Bella felt that the therapist should have asked her if these actions would be safe.

Bella wasn't sure that her husband's rav *would be the best person to bring in. She just didn't know how he would react to this information about his talmid. They had seen the* rav *many times over the years and she had never given a hint of what was going on in her marriage. She was also concerned about what would happen when she went home with her husband, after his behavior had been revealed to his* rav.

In determining whether she could continue to work with this therapist, Bella needed to discuss these concerns and ascertain whether that therapist would work *with* her, at *her* pace and direction. Could the therapist provide information and remain non-directive with respect to specific steps to be taken?

It turned out that the therapist was quite set in her ways, as she had suggested when they first met. The therapist reiterated that her approach was very effective in ameliorating abusive and particularly violent behavior. The therapist remained so sure of herself and her approach that she did not fully appreciate Bella's safety concerns. Bella therefore decided that she needed to make a change in therapists.

Mimi had been married for about ten years, and had suffered from her husband's angry outbursts from the start. Whenever her husband would get angry, which was often, he would call her degrading names, throw things at her, and hit her. He would often do this in front of their children, and he would sometimes terrorize the children as well. She also described financial abuse and being isolated from her friends and family.

At some point, Mimi was able to convince her husband to go to couple's counseling. The therapist told Mimi and her husband that his goals were to help Mimi understand her husband's frustrations, anticipate impending outbursts, and help her husband understand that he could not act out in the way that he did.

Mimi said that things seemed worse, and she also felt worse, because the implication seemed to be that it was her responsibility to sufficiently understand her husband's frustrations and anticipate them, so he wouldn't keep having angry outbursts. In desperation, Mimi went to a rav *and told him what was going on. The* rav *told her that she was being abused and that she should speak to someone who had an expertise in domestic abuse. Mimi told me that even though she knew that her husband's outbursts were a problem, she had never really thought of them as abuse. The* rav's *statement came as a bit of a shock — but was also like a burst of sunlight.*

When Mimi went back to the therapist and told him what the rav *had said, his response to her revelation was, "You weren't supposed to find that out yet."*

Apparently, this therapist's approach to saving the marriage was to keep Mimi ignorant of what was happening to her. Although Mimi was also seeking to save her marriage, she didn't want to be blamed for behavior that was beyond her control, and to leave the therapy process feeling worse instead of better. This therapist apparently thought that if he told Mimi that she was being abused, she might decide not to work further on her marriage. He made the determination that it would be okay for her to suffer in the dark in order to keep the marriage going, assuming as well that pandering to the abuser works — which it does not.

This role of "deciding what's best for her" is not appropriate. Therapists are not supposed to take control of your life; they are supposed to respect you. If you find that your therapist insists on promoting his personal agenda for you, rather than allowing you to decide on goals for treatment, you should consider switching.

Another point to take away from this vignette is that you must decide whether couple's counseling is really the most appropriate forum in which to attempt to resolve your situation. If you are married to someone who is abusive and controlling, the abuse and control is *his* issue. It's something *he* has to change. You are not responsible for changing his attitudes and behaviors. In fact, you aren't even capable of it. So it is reasonable to ask, what are you doing in therapy together?

If you decide you need, want, or are encouraged to go into couple's counseling, ask yourself the following questions:

- Can you be honest with the therapist about what really goes on at home in front of your spouse? If not, what do you hope to accomplish with a therapist who has a partial picture?
- Regardless of whatever assurances the therapist might make about how it will be fine for you to tell the truth, do you feel safe?

Therapists who have an expertise in domestic violence usually work by seeing one spouse in counseling and conferring with the other spouse's therapist unless or until it is safe, both physically and emotionally, for the couple to be seen together. This will not be the case until all tactics of abuse and control have stopped.

When women ask themselves the above questions about the safety of being in couple's counseling, they usually come to the conclusion that it is *not* safe to be honest. If you can't be honest in your therapy, then what is the point? Someone with expertise in domestic abuse will understand this and will refuse to do couple's counseling if there is abuse.

Sometimes women go to couple's counseling because it is the only type of counseling that the abusive husband will agree to. The reason abusers often limit therapeutic options in this manner is that they refuse to take responsibility for their behavior. They will only participate in a setting where they can lay blame for their behavior on the abused spouse. You may understand this, but you may still think to yourself, "Some therapy is better than no therapy." Unfortunately, that isn't how therapy works.

On numerous occasions, women have reported being in couple's counseling, sometimes for years, without the therapist having any idea about the husband's abusive behavior, simply because the wife was too scared to tell. Instead, the therapy was focused on what *she* was doing wrong. Such an orientation can only serve to further oppress and wear her down emotionally. Alternatively, an abused woman can be lulled into a false sense of safety. She may disclose what her husband is doing, only to find out later that her disclosures may have dangerous consequences. Furthermore, a woman may leave couple's counseling after realizing how unsafe or pointless it was, only to be later accused by her spouse or his supporters of not wanting to work on the relationship.

To sum up, in respect to selecting a therapist, feel free to ask direct questions that will provide you with the information you need to determine whether that therapist meets the criteria listed above. The therapist may be an expert and have advanced degrees, but you should not allow that to intimidate you. Shop around for a suitable professional if need be, and do not be afraid to tell candidates what you are looking for. This will be especially important if you decide that you want to build a plan to try for change.

Chapter Four

Understanding Change

Women who are victims of abuse usually want to know one thing: How do I keep my marriage, but end the abuse?

Women often contemplate taking action to end the abuse for a long time before they actually do anything. An abused woman may hesitate to act because she fears for her own safety or the safety of the children, or she may simply wish to avoid precipitating a crisis that could have unpredictable and disastrous consequences. Because the decision to act carries with it substantial risks, the woman who does decide to reach out and seek change should do so with a clear understanding about the process of change: what's true, what's not, and what has the potential to work.

Change is a complex process. The first thing to recognize is that hoping for change is not the same as making a plan for change. Next, it's important to understand the various principles of change. Then you can begin to craft a plan that has the potential to stop the abuse. You will also need to determine sources of support and leverage to enlist in helping with the plan for change.

It will be necessary to identify the abusive behaviors that must change and become familiar with the tactics an abusive spouse might use to avoid real change. You will need to know how to monitor and evaluate changes in his behavior, and how you might respond to true change.

This chapter will step you through this complex and necessary process.

Understanding the Principles of Change

Take a minute and ask yourself: What do you hope the process of change will look like? What are your assumptions, beliefs, and wishes regarding the change process? It is important to know the truth about the possibility of change so your plan will have the best chance of working.

WHAT WOMEN OFTEN WANT TO BELIEVE IS TRUE ABOUT CHANGE

- The *real* him is the nice person I sometimes see. Though he is often abusive and controlling, I think deep down he really is the nice, fun guy that I enjoy. I just need to figure out how to keep *that* guy around.

- Once he begins to listen to me, **if I can just explain things the right way, he'll understand** the way he should behave, and things will be pleasant all the time.

- He would change if he understood how he hurts me. I must not be communicating well enough. After all, **I'm sure he wants a mutually satisfying relationship — doesn't everyone?**

- If I can just **get the right person to talk to him**, he'll understand how he should act, and he will become a loving and supportive husband.

- Now that I have told his father (or mother, *rav*, grandfather) **he will be motivated** to become the husband that he should be. Such a drastic measure will certainly change him.

- **"Going for help" will change everything**. The therapist will make him understand his "issues" that have made him behave badly.

- Since this is his problem, **I won't have to do much work.**

- Once the right plan is in place, **change will come easily.**

These beliefs are for the most part unrealistic. If you examine them closely, you will discover that they all keep the onus on someone other than the abuser himself to do the work. It's *you* with the right words, or it's the influence of a family member or a professional. Bringing someone else into the picture feels so huge to you that it's hard to imagine that it won't have a significant, long-lasting impact. In fact, however, things rarely work themselves out as a result of action you have initiated to get him to change.

Remember the description of the characteristics of an abusive relationship. Domestic abuse is about *control*. Abusive husbands do not simply or easily see the error of their ways and transform themselves into partners who can share responsibility, compromise, and embrace the concept of a mutually satisfying, give-and-take relationship. Certainly they do not change just because someone tells them that they ought to.

The fantasy expectations for change listed above should be compared to the more realistic counterparts presented below.

REALISTIC BELIEFS AND ASSUMPTIONS ABOUT CHANGE

- All the behaviors that you have experienced in your husband, **both the good and the bad,** are reflections of his whole personality.

   Abusers expect to have to control in their marriage, and the abuse you have been experiencing stems from this expectation. The "good times" may be a tactic to keep you unsettled or to stop you from going for help. Even if they are genuine, his expectation of having control remains the essential underlying dynamic of the abusive relationship. It is important for you to understand that he *is* like other abusers, many of whom have this "good side," and the principles and realities below apply to him.

- **Explaining things to him in itself is not likely to change anything.**

    Abusive husbands change only when they *must* change. Change is most likely to occur when it is impossible for him to continue his abuse, because you establish and enforce *negative consequences* for these behaviors that sufficiently outweigh his desire to control you. Don't think he would stop if he understood how badly he was hurting you, and do not assume everyone wants a mutually satisfying relationship. Abusers don't want mutuality; they don't see or feel the need for that. They expect and want to dominate and control. They know what they are doing, although they might claim not to understand as a way to confuse or quiet you. Furthermore, they want to continue to dominate and control.

- **Simply getting the right person to have a talk with your controlling husband is not likely to bring about major, long-lasting change.**

    Some abusers really will be upset that their *rav*, father, mother, grandfather, and so on has learned what's going on and has explained to them that they must change their behavior. And maybe it does give them pause. But as long as a more significant negative consequence does not occur, most abusers get over the sting of this "talking to" and keep behaving as they have up until that point. Your abusive spouse may also try to convince this person that you're overreacting, not well, making things up, and so on. Often, as soon as someone who seems close to an abuser tells him something he doesn't want to hear, the abuser quickly distances himself from that relationship.

    Consider carefully whether this "talking to" will have any real effect without additional longer lasting consequences. If you ultimately decide to use a confrontation as part of your plan for change, you also should think about what it will be like for you after your husband is confronted by this person.

- Doing something drastic may get the abuser's attention. But **trying to encourage change simply by doing something drastic almost never works: Empty threats don't motivate change.**

    Drastic alone is not a plan for change. Women may choose to do many drastic things. Having someone talk to your husband may seem drastic to you. Other possibilities are threatening to leave; some women actually get up and go. Both of these options have potential in a plan for change. But if the threat is empty, or if you leave without a plan and feel compelled to go back before seeing any change, you wind up in a worse position. Because you didn't have a larger plan surrounding your drastic action, you have now emboldened the abuser. He feels even more secure in his position of being in control, because he knows that you used whatever resource or leverage you had — and it didn't make any difference.

- **"Getting help" does not guarantee change.**

    Some women cling to the idea that if they can just get the abuser to therapy, they can relax. Often, however, the abuser is willing to start therapy simply to "calm things down," rather than because he is motivated to change. Typically in this type of scenario, the husband keeps going to therapy but doesn't get any "better." Or he throws the fact that he's going to therapy in her face: "I'm going for help, what more do you want? Why aren't you happy?" As a result, the woman often starts to feel as if *she's* going crazy. This is because therapy is not a car wash. Pushing someone through the process doesn't "get them better." Unless there is a consequence for not changing, he is unlikely to change.

- The abuser alone is responsible for his abuse and for changing his behavior. But **you will have to participate in the process as well.**

    Abused wives need to be involved in the process of promoting change in ways that may be difficult and draining. You will need to do more than simply disclose the abuse. Sometimes it will be up to you to keep up with the people in the process and the pressure that has motivated him to change. You will need to assess whether his efforts are genuine, and if not, you will need to be honest with the people involved — even when you just want to get back together, because you can't take the pressure.

- **Change will be very slow and difficult.**

    Even if the abuser does make an effort to change, be aware that this effort will run contrary to his natural inclinations. Expect him to resist change to whatever extent he feels he can get away with. Getting up the courage to demand change is just the beginning of a very long process that will require your careful attention and continued resolve.

As you can see from the above list, the process of compelling your abusive husband to change his behavior will be difficult. It will be easier for you to stick with this process if you understand how change comes about. Bear in mind, though, that even if you understand the situation perfectly, the effort to achieve change will not be easy.

Before You Begin to Plan

While the process of motivating your abusive husband to change his behavior is likely to be long and difficult, the likelihood of success can be increased dramatically by following a few relatively straightforward principles.

Understand the Abuser's Need for Control

To get your abusive husband to change, you must understand the motivation that drives all abusers to behave the way they do, as well as the key ingredients of change. Only then will you understand how to create a good plan that will compel him to stop abusing you.

Men who control and abuse their spouses typically *do not want to stop.* They have an expectation of power and control based on a belief system that says they are entitled to this in marriage.

To alter this behavior, an abuser needs to understand that continuing his abuse will result in negative consequences which outweigh his desire to keep things the same. The problem is that women who are being abused usually don't have an extensive arsenal of potential negative consequences that they can bring to bear to motivate this change. Consequently, the plan to bring about change will need to include the support and assistance of others, who may have some additional leverage that will compel the abuser's compliance.

It's important to avoid using the same person to motivate the abuser to change, and to address the restructuring of his belief system regarding marriage. For example, a *rav* may be asked to motivate change by letting the abuser know he is aware of the situation and will not tolerate it. This may provide the social sanction necessary to motivate change. The *rav* should not also be the one to address the abuser's belief system. When these roles are mixed, they invariably get confused and dilute the person's ability to be helpful.

NOTE: Some consequences may cause your husband to initially stop some of his abusive behavior. But there will not be long-term change if the consequences are perceived by him to be inappropriate or disproportionate to his actions. Change must go beyond the surface level for it to last. This includes accepting responsibility for his actions, acknowledging that you had no choice but to take action because of his behavior, and agreeing that he deserved the negative consequences. The process for maximizing the possibility of long-lasting change will be discussed in detail later in this chapter.

List the Abusive Behaviors That Must Be Eliminated

It is essential for you to have a specific list of abusive behaviors. This is because most people have a tendency to minimize the severity of abuse. No one wants to think of a family member, friend, or business associate as an abuser. The person you go to may try to put the best spin on what the abuser has done. The best way to defuse efforts to minimize abuse is to have a very specific list of abuses that you can recite or present to potential supporters. You must be able to clarify exactly what he has done that is so objectionable.

In addition, developing and writing down a list of the abuses will clarify your own thinking. It will help you articulate to your husband exactly what he has done that must stop. Working out this list will also help you develop an unambiguous set of goals for behavioral change, against which you can evaluate the success of your efforts.

Adequately Prepare for the Possible Fallout Avoid acting precipitously, because efforts to effect change in your husband's behavior that are not carefully thought through can easily backfire. When you finally decide that you want to do something, you are quite likely to experience an emotional upheaval that demands immediate action. At this point, many abused women feel an overwhelming need to *do something*. They want to confront their husbands, to enlist support, to demand change. And they want it to happen *now*. But acting without considering the abuser's possible reactions to your efforts can be extremely dangerous, as we see in the case of Miriam below.

> *Miriam had been married for eight years when she decided that she couldn't take her husband's abuse any longer. She went to speak to the* rav *of the shul where she and her husband* davened. *With the best of intentions, the* rav *immediately called Miriam's husband and read him the riot act.*
>
> *The aftermath of this confrontation was not what she or the* rav *had expected. Miriam's husband responded to the* rav's *intervention by threatening Miriam with immediate divorce. He threatened to go to* beis din *to write a* get *the very next day. Miriam was flustered, confused and completely horrified. She couldn't stand how things were — but she wasn't ready for this response.*
>
> *Her husband also threatened that he would hide all the money, and that he would get the children, because she was such a bad mother. He claimed he had documented countless examples of how unfit she was. Because she had not thought things through or gathered all of the necessary information documenting his abusive behavior, Miriam became extremely frightened.*
>
> *Her husband sensed her fear, and he told her that her only hope for making this all go away was to never have contact with that* rav *again. Because she was so scared and overwhelmed, Miriam reluctantly agreed to this demand.*

Miriam's unhappy outcome shows what can happen if someone acts without planning carefully and anticipating possible responses from the abuser. The *rav* in this case could have been a good resource. He was firm in his belief that abuse is unacceptable, and he believed Miriam when she told him about her situation. Unfortunately, Miriam wasn't prepared for her husband's response. Consequently, she was thrown completely off guard and was terrified into doing exactly what her husband told her to do. Instead of reducing his control over her, her actions cemented the control.

Before you confront your husband with a demand to cease his abusive behavior, you must evaluate your situation and make an appropriate plan.

Develop a Plan for Achieving Change

You need to make your specific plan for change *before* you confront your husband, and you need to consider your husband's possible responses when you make the demand for change. Even if you have already told your husband that you "can't take it anymore," which implies, "I'm thinking about doing something," it is not too late to make a good plan. After all, your husband is used to discounting the things you say. Just back off from whatever you have been saying until you have a chance to think things through and formulate a workable plan for change.

In preparing your plan for action, you need to address the following questions:

- Now that you understand that your husband will need to be motivated to change through consequences, can you think of any consequences that could potentially have this effect?
- Have you tried anything in the past to get your husband to end his abuse?
- Has anything that you already tried made a difference (either positive or negative)?
- If there was something that made a positive difference, what happened? Why did the positive effect of this effort stop working?
- If what you tried made things worse, what went wrong? Was it a miscalculation that could have worked if it had been planned

out more thoroughly, as in the case of Miriam? Or was it a plan with no merit?

- Has there been any police or court involvement? Was it helpful? If not, why not?

- Have you ever involved a *rav*? How did that work out? What was helpful and what wasn't?

- Do you have a specific idea of what you want your husband to change?

- Are you prepared for whatever response might come?

- Your husband might to some degree acknowledge a problem, but blame you or want you to look at yourself too, as we have discussed. Are you fully aware that his tactics of control and abuse are in his control, and that he has to give them up before anything else happens?

- Are you prepared for the possibility of extreme aggression and threats? Do you know your rights both halachically and legally, so he can't do that to make you back down?

- Have you gathered your thoughts and made a written accounting of which abusive behaviors have been going on in the marriage?

- Are you prepared, emotionally and practically, to stick to your resolve?

Once you have given thought to these questions, you will be in a much better position to know what you can demand and what resources you need to insure your request for change will have a possibility of working.

It can be difficult in times of extreme emotional distress to be composed and prepared. It will help to go through these tasks slowly, at a pace you can manage, as long as you aren't currently in crisis..

Always Consider Safety First

It cannot be stated often or strongly enough how important it is to carefully consider whether *you* think the plan being considered is safe. This is especially true if your support people are the ones suggesting or even pushing a particular idea. If something does not feel safe to you, pay attention! That doesn't mean the plan has to be completely discarded — you may just need to tweak it until you're able to make it feel safe. You may also want to check out a later chapter, where we discuss planning for safety in case your initial plan brings on a crisis.

Creating a Plan

There are three key elements when attempting to make a plan for change:

- A person, process or other fact that could be used as leverage to motivate the abuser to change.
- An appropriate person who will work with your husband in an ongoing relationship to address the change in his attitude about marriage, and his feeling that he is entitled to maintain power and control over you.
- Ideally, a professional who will help you determine whether real change is happening, or if it's just a change in tactics.

LEVERAGE AND SOURCES OF SUPPORT

The effectiveness of outside support people who may use social sanction and pressure to compel your husband to change will be directly proportional to the amount of leverage they have on your husband.

Leverage can take a variety of forms. Perhaps it is the threat of being embarrassed and losing his status within the family or his standing in the community. It may be the fear of losing his job. Regardless of the particular form of leverage employed, recognize that there must be a significant consequence to your spouse. If you are going to ask someone to intervene and tell your husband his behavior must stop, there has to be an answer to the question, "Or what?" That answer must be something that would make your husband sit up and take notice.

Before deciding whether to employ someone to pressure your

husband to stop his abusive behavior, you need to answer the following questions:

- Does this person's opinion really matter enough to be the long term motivation for change?
- Will this person deliver an unambiguous message, indicating that the problem is your husband's abusive behavior, and the behavior must change?
- Can this person really provide an "or else" that will work?
- Will this person continue to check in, stay involved, and monitor progress? Or will his interest and stamina for this problem wane? If your husband plays along briefly, will the "or else" of social stigma fade, along with the support person's involvement?

Let's consider some of your options regarding sources of support in terms of the pressure each can bring to bear on your abusive husband.

A Family Member *If your husband values the opinions of either*
or Friend a particular family member or a close friend in the community, that person's involvement and support for your demand for change could exert a positive influence.

There are times a family member or friend is a sufficiently prominent member of the community that he or she can provide adequate social sanction just by being informed of the problem and expressing disapproval for what's been going on. This is not, however, a typical scenario. More likely, the ability of a family member or community member to effect change in your husband's behavior will depend on his or her ability to enforce negative consequences that are sufficiently powerful to motivate the abuser to change. Social sanction can work, but demand for change tends to be most effective when it is backed up by more tangible consequences.

> *Shari had been suffering for all ten years of her marriage, and she felt that she needed to either do something or get out.*
>
> *I explained to Shari the concept of employing contingent consequences for abusive behavior to motivate her husband to change.*

Shari pointed out that her husband occupied a prominent position in their small community, and she suggested that if she went to the head rabbi of the community, or if she told her husband that she would go to the rabbi if he didn't stop certain abusive behaviors and begin therapy, it would have an impact.

Before she took either of these steps, I urged her to talk through the likely outcomes with me and give some additional thought to her ideas. The more she talked and thought, the more she realized that she didn't want to take these steps unless there was nothing else she could do. The community was small, and she didn't want to permanently sully their standing in the community by involving the chief rabbi.

In our next conversation, Shari suggested having her father talk to her husband. Her father was a big rav*, and her husband was actually a* talmid *of her father. Shari felt that her husband really did respect him. We worked with this idea for a while, considering what she should tell her father, how he would stay involved, who else would need to stay involved, and so on.*

Shari understood the importance of not rushing in, and decided to wait until we spoke again. By then, Shari had decided that involving her father might not be the best idea. She was concerned that when pressed, her husband would become defensive. Since it would be her father doing the pressing, she thought her husband might minimize what he was being told as being one-sided, because the message was coming from her father.

The next idea Shari came up with was to talk to the mashgiach *of her husband's yeshivah, with whom her father had a close relationship. In fact, Shari thought she could tell her father a bit of what was going on so he would make the initial contact with the* mashgiach.

Shari was nervous, but when she called the mashgiach, *he was wonderfully supportive. He was horrified by Shari's description of her marriage, and he was also able to help her with some details of her plan. He thought it would be best if he did not tell her husband that she had come to him. He suggested instead that he would tell her husband that Shari had called regarding a* she'eilah, *and he had started asking questions and discovered that there were unacceptable things happening in the marriage. This way her husband would consider her less responsible for revealing what had been going on.*

The mashgiach *also planned to tell Shari's husband that he thought he would need to talk with the chief rabbi of the community if things did not improve. Additionally, the* mashgiach *made sure that Shari felt safe being honest with him about what was going on in the home. When Shari said she did, he told her that as part of the plan her husband would know that he was going to be kept apprised about changes (or lack thereof), and be in touch with the therapist he was going to recommend in order to keep up the pressure.*

This version of the plan was one with which Shari felt completely comfortable. It had taken much back and forth and revision, but ultimately this course of action seemed to her to be the one that was both the most doable and the safest.

This case illustrates that sometimes ideas that seem good at first have flaws that may not be immediately apparent. Upon reflection, it becomes clear that the consequences to these actions would be problematic. Except in the case of crisis, it is important to plan, think through, and re-think before acting.

It also illustrates one of the most important points to keep in mind: The instincts of the woman in the situation regarding what will work and be safe *must* take the lead in shaping that plan. What others think "makes sense" cannot be more accurate than what the woman feels from her own experience.

Ultimately, Shari felt good about the plan not only because it felt safe, but because there were multiple consequences if her husband did not change. Her husband's motivation was not solely his concern over the *mashgiach's* opinion of him. He also knew that if he didn't change, the *mashgiach* would go to the chief rabbi of the city, and his *parnassah* and position in the community would be threatened. In fact, social sanction alone, even when provided by someone you think your husband really respects, usually is not enough. When he has to make a choice between this person and his own power, power and control often win out.

Whether the opinion of a friend, family member, or authority figure matters enough to your husband to motivate him to change depends on the value your husband places on the relationship, the degree of respect your husband has for the individual, and any history of a mentoring relationship that might exist. Another factor is the existence of economic ties that could be impacted if the relationship were to be adversely affected by your husband's failure to comply with these demands.

It may be reasonable to expect that an abuser's father or *rav* might be influential. But these individuals would be more important to some men than others. An individual in the community who is socially prominent and highly respected could be influential, assuming that your husband values his status in the community and feels that losing the respect of this person would adversely impact his own standing. A person who does business with your husband, or is in a position to recommend your husband's services to others, has clout based on economic motivation. Consider the situation of Tamar:

> *Tamar's husband Donny seemed to be a good guy until they had their first baby. While she was still in the hospital, he came in and told her, "Things are going to change around here. You're not going anywhere now."*
>
> *Tamar couldn't imagine what he meant by that. She actually started to wonder if she had imagined the whole thing. They moved into her parents' home for a while, and aside from the slight animosity that Donny always had toward her parents, he seemed fine. Then they moved back to their apartment.*
>
> *Soon Donny seemed impossible to please. He found fault in her mothering, her housekeeping, and particularly in the bedroom. He started going out a lot while refusing to tell Tamar where he was going or when he'd come home.*
>
> *During their first year of marriage, when Donny seemed negative*

about her parents, Tamar attributed this to the fact that he was in-
timidated by working in her father's business. It was his choice, and
he was enthusiastic about it, but also seemed to be somewhat re-
sentful.

After the baby was born, he used the fact that he spent so much
time with her father and brothers at work as an excuse to see them as
little as possible socially. He became more and more abusive, and she
became more and more isolated, choosing to keep what was going
on from her family for fear of ruining things for him in the business.

When her son was a year and a half old, she became pregnant
again. Thinking back to how horrible Donny had become after her
son was born, Tamar knew she had to get help to make a change.
Tamar decided to go to her parents.

Together with a professional, they planned a confrontation that
relied heavily on the fact that his economic well-being was inter-
twined with her family. In order to provide the consequences Donny
needed to motivate him to change his behavior, they clearly indicat-
ed what he had to lose if he didn't stop his controlling and abusive
behavior and go for help.

Only you can judge whether a particular person will be able to influence your husband to change. But avoid falling into the trap of choosing
according to what you would *like* to be true, and losing sight of what is
more probable. An individual on whose opinion your husband places
little or no value, or whose opinion he can easily shrug off, may still provide you with moral support, but is not likely to be of much real help in
the effort to get him to change.

The other important question to ask yourself is whether you can be
certain this individual will deliver an unambiguous message to your
husband that the problem is *his abusive behavior*. Supporters must be
clear that they are discussing the matter with the abuser specifically to
get him to stop being abusive. You need to be very careful that the potential ally whom you recruit to apply pressure on your husband does
not take it upon himself to engage in amateur marriage counseling. The

most effective supporter will do nothing more than deliver a simple, unambiguous message: that the abuse must stop — *or else.*

We will talk later about utilizing therapists and *middos* counselors in this process. But because they have no connection with your husband, such figures cannot provide the consequences necessary to motivate him to end his abuse. Likewise, the people who are capable of providing consequences are not usually professionals in the field of domestic violence. These are separate roles and should be divided accordingly. If you meet with a therapist who believes he or she can play both roles, beware!

When requesting that a family member, boss, community leader or friend delivers the message that your husband's abuse must stop, do not ask or imply that he or she should be doing anything beyond delivering the message, ensuring that professionals (or appropriate para-professionals) get involved, and following through on the consequences if change does not take place.

A Rav In some circumstances, a *rav* may be able to provide social sanctions that would motivate your husband to change. Often, however, a woman thinks her husband's *rav* has that type of influence, when in fact he does not. That is usually a function of her husband's assumption of power and control.

As close as your husband seems to his *rav*, if the *rav* told him his behavior was unacceptable and that he had to change, would he be ashamed and listen, simply to keep the respect of the *rav*? Can the *rav* provide an "or else" of sufficient magnitude to make an impression? The unfortunate fact is that many abusers would rather relinquish the relationship with the *rav* than relinquish control. Carefully evaluate the potential influence of the *rav* on your husband's behavior, just as you would evaluate that of a family member or friend.

You must also decide if the *rav* will deliver a clear, unambiguous demand for change. If the *rav* is going to cushion his comments regarding the problem to avoid alienating your husband, ultimately his intervention will not be helpful. This is particularly true if he's supposed to be providing the consequences for continued abuse in the form of social sanctions. The bottom line is that the decision to use a *rav* must be based on the same criteria as the decision to use a family member or a friend.

It is important for you to be clear about the role you want the *rav* to fulfill before asking him to talk to your husband. Are you asking him to counsel your husband on his distorted belief system? Or are you asking him to provide the consequence/social sanctions that would motivate your husband to change?

If you do use the *rav* for the motivating role, someone else needs to be providing counseling. Or, if he is providing the counseling, there should be a different motivating consequence in place.

You also must consider your ability to fully disclose the specifics of the abuse to the *rav*. After all, he is not a family member. He is an authority figure with whom you have a formal relationship. And he is a man. It may be quite difficult to bring yourself to disclose the particulars of the abuse to the *rav*, particularly if the abuse has a sexual component. It may also be difficult to be clear with the *rav* that you do not want him to intervene unless he is prepared to place the blame squarely on your husband, tell him in no uncertain terms that the abuse must stop, and clearly indicate the negative consequences of continuing the abuse.

You may feel that it would be impertinent for you to make such demands. You may even feel that you must defer to the *rav's* better judgment on how to handle the situation. Before taking this step, then, you need to carefully think through how you will be able to disclose all the aspects of the abuse (will you write it down? have someone tell him for you?) and how to clearly and respectfully ask of the *rav* what you need him to do.

You may decide that your *rav* is the right motivator, or can provide the counseling your husband needs to work on his belief system. Even if you do not, though, a *rav* can still be a very important part of your support system. It may make sense to meet with a *rav* you have a connection with and explain what you are trying to do, as well as your goal: to motivate change and keep your marriage intact. This way, if your husband tries to exert pressure on you to give up, you will have support.

The Police and the Courts — Women in the Orthodox community generally feel reluctant to resort to calling the authorities or using the court system. There are two primary reasons for this.

You may be concerned about issues of *mesirah*. If you think there might come a time when you will fear for your physical safety and have to call on the authorities, get halachic information beforehand. Speak to a *rav* about the possible implications of calling the police. When is it *mutar*? Under what *pikuach nefesh* considerations is that option available? Speak to a battered woman's advocate and their legal consultants. Does the law require that someone be arrested when you make a complaint? Is it possible to make a police report regarding abusive behavior after the fact? If your husband gets violent enough that you might need to call the authorities to get safe, being prepared with knowledge in advance is very important.

The same cautions apply when utilizing the court system. There are some *rabbanim* who will support your use of the court system when you feel that you need protection, while others may put pressure on you not to use the courts under any circumstances. Make certain that you speak to a *rav* who understands the safety issues.

The thought of police officers arriving at the house, with lights and sirens announcing that a crime has been committed, is incredibly painful for women. It is understandable that women hesitate. They may be horrified at the prospect of this kind of scene. Given these realities, you should try to have supports around you if at all possible.

For these reasons, a woman usually will not use the police or court system in her plan for change. A woman only calls the police or goes to court because she feels she *has* to. Once that step is taken, the involvement of law enforcement and the subsequent consequences to the abuser could motivate change. The police and the courts have clout; the police and the courts can make an unambiguous statement to your husband that he must cease his abusive behavior. They can also provide consequences to husbands who do not comply with their mandates.

The limitations on this is that it is only the case when physical harm has been done. The police have no authority over husbands who use demeaning language, ignore their wives' requests, or use the children in ways that are undesirable but not physically abusive.

Withholding Something He Values

Sometimes an abused wife has leverage that she can bring to bear on her abusive husband as a motivating force, because she has the ability to withhold or deny him something upon which he places great value.

Penina and Tully were married in July. The plan was for the new couple to spend Yom Tov with their parents, who both lived in the same general area, and then go to Eretz Yisrael, where Tully was going to learn for the year and Penina was planning to go to school. This was something she had hoped for years would be possible when she got married.

But as the days passed, Penina became very concerned about the plan to leave everyone and go off to Eretz Yisrael with Tully. He was bossy, insulting and talked more and more about "getting away from everyone" so they could be "focused on each other." Penina increasingly felt that Tully wanted her to focus only on him, to the exclusion of all other social contacts and activities. He tried to limit who she saw and where she went, telling her that she should be more focused on "them." Tully had even started to question her decision to go to school, wondering if it would take up too much of her time, and whether she would be better off forgoing her plans and instead concentrate on settling in, so they could spend as much time as possible together.

Penina tried to let Tully know that she thought they had issues to work out, and that they needed to deal with them before going to Eretz Yisrael. Tully response was to argue with her, then declare, "I can't believe I married someone so silly!"

It was clear that she couldn't communicate this on her own and she needed some backup. So Penina involved her family's rav. Although the rav might not have motivated Tully to change on his own, including him in the process gave Penina the support to tell Tully that unless he agreed to work on their marriage and he changed his attitude about her, she was not going to Eretz Yisrael.

Deferring something that was planned and even mutually agreed upon may be the only leverage a woman has to demand change. Seeking guidance and support in taking this step will be a vital part of this process.

Threatening to Leave or Seek a Divorce

No woman should ever use an empty threat of divorce or leaving as a tactic to try to get her husband to change. Women who threaten to leave if the abuse doesn't stop, but don't actually follow through because they weren't really prepared to do so, are left in a worse position because they have shown that they are powerless. If the abuser calls your bluff and wins, then it is twice as clear that he is in control.

It is also important to carefully investigate and speak with resources (a *rav*, an attorney) about the options and the realities of divorce before actually doing anything. This topic will be discussed in the next chapter.

However, if you have genuinely come to a point where you can no longer take what's going on, you can use this fact to give him a push to take a look at himself. Perhaps you actually left, or kicked him out, after many attempts at therapy or interventions. Now that you've actually separated, your husband suddenly seems to want to listen to you, to the *rav*, and to the therapist. Now there is a real consequence to his behavior, and this *may* change things.

In this scenario, you may decide to see if he is sincere this time and if he will actually consider changing himself. He may be genuinely frightened at the prospect of losing his family. He may also be very concerned about losing face within the community. He may feel having a failed marriage reflects poorly on him, and he will certainly fear losing face if it becomes widely known that the reason for the divorce was his abusive behavior. Those consequences may in fact present a motivation for change.

Ongoing Intervention

Once the initial plan is put in motion to provide the consequences for motivating change, there is still much work that needs to be done. The initial motivation is just that — a beginning. The second part of the plan involves having the abuser work with someone who will deal with his distorted belief system, and enable him to accept responsibility for his abuse.

There are a few different categories of people who may fit that role. Once again, remember that for this to be effective, the counselor cannot be the same person who provides the motivation for change.

A Therapist   A therapist who is appropriate for this work must have the correct perspective on abuse and his or her role. The correct perspective means:

- keeping the focus on the abuser's responsibility for his behavior
- not minimizing the abuse, or implying that it "takes two to tango"
- not co-opting you into the process by insinuating that his abuse is something you caused or can control
- does not expect you to be part of the process in a way that feels unsafe to you
- keeps the responsibility for participation in the process on your husband
- understands that if your husband refuses to acknowledge his behavior, he is not changing
- can maintain boundaries for outsiders who want to get involved in ways that will be unhelpful

You'll know if a therapist fits these criteria. You will not be pressured into working on yourself at the same time, or to shoulder some of the responsibility for how your husband has treated you. This does not mean that you will have to do nothing, but you should not feel pressured to work on yourself while not seeing any changes in him.

It is very helpful to have your own therapist during this process, preferably one who specializes in working with victims of abuse. These therapists will readily appreciate the gravity of the abuses that you report. They will understand that the dynamics of abuse lie in the abuser's need to control and dominate, and they will understand that the dynamics of change depend on negative consequences.

You and your therapist may discuss the possibility of her consulting with his therapist. (It is more appropriate for you not to have to have direct regular contact with his therapist.) She can also help you gauge whether you feel his process is putting undue pressure on you. She can help you formulate the aspects of his behavior that must change, if the relationship is to continue. She can be your sounding board to help you determine if he is really changing or just changing tactics. She can also help you address your feelings toward your husband's change, whatever they may be.

Middos *Counselor*　　In some communities, the family member or *rav* who provides the consequences to motivate change may prefer referring the husband to a lay person, rather than to a professional, for this ongoing work. He may be someone without a degree who provides counseling based on halachic and *hashkafic* perspectives. We'll refer to him as a *middos* counselor, although this is by no means an official term.

This counselor may be a better choice than a professional therapist in some cases. He may have clout based on his knowledge of halachah, and he may have further legitimacy because he has been recommended by the *rav*.

This was the case with Hindy:

> *Hindy had been putting up with her husband's abuse, including a few incidences of physical abuse, when a close family member let her know that he had proof that her husband was being unfaithful to her. This was the last straw for Hindy. She kicked her husband out and wanted a divorce.*
>
> *After they had separated, there was a lot of pressure on Hindy to see if this wakeup call would motivate her husband to change. She*

agreed to hold off on pursuing a divorce, but was not willing to let her husband back into the house until there was change.

Their rav *was part of the confrontation with her husband, and Hindy felt that he was very supportive. The* rav *wanted her husband to see a lay person who was very well known in the community, a respected* maggid shiur *whom the* rav *felt would be the most effective person to work with her husband. Hindy was skeptical, but the* rav *assured her that if things did not improve, he would support whatever decision she made. Hindy then met with the* middos *counselor. The result was that she felt he had the proper perspective on abuse, and she agreed to proceed with this plan.*

If you are concerned regarding the appropriateness of using a *middos* counselor, use the same criteria provided earlier to assess a therapist's ability to work with domestic abuse. Remember you need someone with the proper perspective to see through your husband's rationalizations, minimizations, and manipulations, to confront his distorted belief system. If this person has the right perspective, he does not necessarily have to be a mental health professional. Abuse, as it has been defined for these purposes, is not a mental health problem.

Dealing with Inappropriate Interventions

Sometimes women are pressured to do things that are contrary to the standards and suggestions in this book. If your situation becomes public, many people will appear to "try to help." Sometimes they will appear on their own, and sometimes they will approach you at the behest of your spouse. This can constitute a major struggle. You may feel that having more people involved will undermine you and the process you have developed, but you don't want to be cast in the role of uncooperative spouse, or perceived as not wanting to try.

In a different scenario, a support person may make his help dependent on trying the intervention *he* feels will work. A woman may feel uncomfortable with the suggestion, but may also feel trapped — concerned that if she ignores the suggestion she may lose that person's support. At other times, a woman may feel hopeful that the suggested intervention will work, while recognizing that it does run contrary to what has been suggested here.

Always remember that it is your choice. It may in fact be what you need to do. Just don't forget that it is important to keep safety firmly in mind.

Marital therapy is one of the most common interventions recommended by those who want to help, but don't understand domestic violence. It is also one of the interventions that women get hopeful about, because their husbands are actually willing to do this, though he completely resists going for help on his own. Again, recognize that in all likelihood the abusive husband does not want to take responsibility for his actions; he agrees to couple's counseling because he hopes to demonstrate what a problem *she* is.

There are two separate issues to consider if you are being pushed to try an intervention that doesn't fit with the model presented here. First, do you want to try it, and does it feel safe enough to try? Sometimes women want to try something to satisfy those around them, and sometimes they want to try to satisfy their own sense that they have tried everything. This can be an important process for women. No one should belittle your desire to try what you feel you need to do. In fact, when you are pushed not to try something you think might work, that often leaves you feeling lost in a confusion of "what if's."

Having said that, sometimes the people in a woman's life will *never* agree that she has tried enough. It is pointless to spend more time trying to satisfy these individuals.

> *Simmi stayed in her marriage for the sake of her children. When they were all grown and married, Simmi decided that she had sacrificed enough and was ready to get divorced.*
>
> *Her children were horrified. Yes, they were already married, but it would still be "embarrassing" for them if their parents got divorced. Simmi explained to her children that she just couldn't take*

it anymore. "You have until now," they countered. "Maybe it's not really so bad? Maybe you can get help?"

Simmi responded that it was actually worse now that she was all alone with their father. They had been to so many therapists and rabbanim for help over the years that she'd lost count. Their father did not seem to care about any consequences or any individuals who tried to intervene.

"You just haven't found the right shaliach *yet," her oldest child insisted.*

There is trying something that you don't think will work so you can gain someone's support, and then there is trying to satisfy someone who will never concede that you have tried enough, no matter what you do. Try to find the balance and the ability to say no, when you recognize that you have reached that limit.

If, however, you decide the intervention being proposed is safe, what can you get in return for agreeing to try this intervention? You may be offered a variety of deals: "Just try couple's counseling for three months" or, "Don't go for a separation just yet" or, "Don't tell your parents for a while." Consider asking, "If I go with your plan and it doesn't work, then what?"

Perhaps the person suggesting the "deal" has the potential to offer you powerful support, and this may be a way to get that support. Before agreeing to an uncomfortable intervention, explore if there is something you can get for cooperating which may make it worthwhile — even if it makes you uncomfortable.

Perry had separated from her abusive husband. She spoke to her rav, *in whom she had confided over the years, about getting a divorce.*

There was another rav *in the community who had not been involved in the situation. Her husband went to that second* rav *to ask for his intervention in pressuring Perry to come back. The second* rav *was very powerful in the community, and both Perry and her* rav *were feeling pressured. Perry worried that if her husband's* rav *wanted to help him fight the divorce, she'd have a very hard time.*

The second rav *asked Perry to give couple's counseling three months. If she didn't feel that things had changed and still wanted a divorce after that point, he would support her fully.*

Perry was extremely uncomfortable with the idea of couple's counseling. Her husband was so manipulative! But she realized that if she stayed separated while this went on, she would still feel safe, and then if things didn't change, she'd have the support she needed for her own plan. Perry decided that despite her discomfort with the whole process of couple's counseling, it was worth the benefit.

One last point to remember: If you participate in a plan for change that doesn't seem to make sense, but has the possibility to gain you support, make sure you are not compromising your physical or emotional safety. Compromising your safety isn't worth anyone's support.

Chapter Five

Evaluating Change

You've made a decision to disclose the abuse, and you have a support network in place — friends, parents, a *rav*, a therapist for yourself. The necessary elements for change are in place — someone who will motivate your husband, and a therapist/*middos* counselor for him.

How will you know that your plan is working and that real change is taking place?

Drawing a Roadmap

Before starting on a trip, it's a good idea to map it out. Knowing what signs you need to look for in advance, so you don't have to try to figure it out along the way, is very helpful in making sure you're on the right road. If you know you are supposed to see the exits going up in number, for example, and you do, you can have more confidence that you're on the right road. Trying to determine whether you're going in the right direction when you're already feeling lost does not work very well!

Creating a roadmap for your personal journey will likewise help you see if progress is being made. It's important to know in advance what to look for and what indicates real change, as opposed to a change of tactics (which will be discussed later in the chapter). Once the process has started, there will be a lot of pressure and a lot of opinions, solicited and unsolicited. It is better to have a clear sense at the outset of what you need to see change and what will constitute change.

You may find the following table to be helpful to you as you begin to create the roadmap for your own personal journey. The table consists of a checklist that you can personalize to your own situation. It also contains what I refer to as the *signs on your roadmap*. These are the signs you would see if the abuser is on the road to actual change.

The table has a checklist of controlling tactics on the left hand side. The signs on the roadmap, which tell you in which direction things are headed, are on the right hand side. I've included the most commonly reported control tactics and forms of abuse. Use this checklist as a *starting point* in identifying the specific abuses that you have experienced. This list may not have everything you have experienced, or may have items that do not fit your situation. Feel free to adapt the checklist so it fits your personal situation.

BEHAVIORS THAT NEED TO CHANGE	SIGNS OF REAL CHANGE
Punishes you for disagreeing with him, having a different opinion, or wanting something different from what he wants by withholding privileges, name calling, silent treatment, or physical violence.	Listens and will compromise (a process you feel you have a say in) when the two of you can't agree. Note: A compromise takes both sides into account, where *each* gives a little. It is not a solution that is *dictated* by one party.
Prevents you (or tries to prevent you) from seeing family or friends by: (1) overtly telling you that you are not allowed to do so, (2) manipulating you with lectures about why they are bad for you, don't treat you well, or are beneath you; and/or (3) making a scene so unpleasant when you want to see someone that you choose to avoid seeing people yourself.	Whether he participates or not, does not make it uncomfortable for you to have and maintain the important relationships in your life by being either aggressive or manipulative.
Expects you to account to him regarding where you go, who you see, and what you talk about.	Casually sharing about your day feels just that: casual. It no longer feels like you are being interrogated.
Checks up on you several times a day. This may lead to embarrassing scenes with friends or family, who wonder why he calls so often; or may lead to problems at work where his excessive calls disrupt the work environment.	Checking in, which a lot of couples like to do (when both do like it), feels very different from being checked up on. *Checking in* is not disruptive, and can be cut short if one or the other is busy, without repercussions.

BEHAVIORS THAT NEED TO CHANGE	SIGNS OF REAL CHANGE
Maintains unilateral control of the family finances by: (1) making all of the decisions himself; (2) keeping you on a strict budget while having no restrictions on his own spending; (3) making you account for every penny that you spend; (4) looking over your purchases and deciding what you can and cannot spend money on; and/or (5) expecting you to give any money that you earn or get from your parents to him.	He no longer hounds you over how every penny is spent. You feel you have some discretion on finances, as does he, although you each discuss any major purchase. You no longer feel that you have no access and he has total control. There may be some variations in what you specifically are comfortable with and what would make you feel that you are no longer being controlled in this area. Different couples negotiate this area differently, and therefore this category is subject to many different interpretations.
Threatens you with: (1) divorce; or (2) physical harm to you, your children, or your family, or (3) with suicide.	Does not use threats to try to get his way.
Tells people false things about you, your mental health, your fidelity, or the way you mistreat him in an effort to make you believe that you will have no support if you seek help or want to leave him.	No longer uses the threat or the actual use of demeaning tactics in an attempt to undermine you or your confidence or your sanity — either overtly or by pretending to be "only trying to help."
Intimidates you by (1) menacing, throwing things, destroying your personal possessions; (2) not allowing you to leave your room; or (3) using his anger and displeasure to get you to back down from something that you really want.	Gives up all tactics of physical intimidation. And gives up all attempts to intimidate you by intimating negative consequences for disagreeing with what he wants.

BEHAVIORS THAT NEED TO CHANGE	SIGNS OF REAL CHANGE
Tries to control how you look and what you wear by: (1) hounding you if you do not meet his standards — asking you about it relentlessly; (2) telling you how much it is hurting him or how much he needs you to change; or (3) putting you down for not doing "what your husband asks." His ideas of how you look or dress may or may not conflict with your own religious standards. (While compromise in many areas are a part of marriage, compromise is different from dictating: it goes both ways, and the process doesn't pressure you to give up your standards.)	He accepts that you can make decisions for yourself about how you look. Sometimes this gets murky when the abuser uses religion: "I'm only trying to help you work on yourself. You know that it would be better if you didn't go out like that" or, "You need to look a little nicer so I don't look at other women. You need to help me with my *yetzer hara*, by attracting me so I'm not attracted by others." Has he stopped this and other attempts at trying to control how you look?
Demeans you by: (1) calling you names; (2) throwing money on the floor and telling you to pick it up if you want it; (3) messing up a clean room and then telling you to clean it up; and/or (4) talking to you about former girlfriends and telling you how much better they were than you.	Treats you with respect: respects your opinions, understands that your ideas and how you feel about things are valid, doesn't try to make you feel bad about yourself.

BEHAVIORS THAT NEED TO CHANGE	SIGNS OF REAL CHANGE
• Uses the children by: (1) putting them in the middle; (2) taking it out on them if he is upset with you; (3) telling them things to turn them against you • Uses the children to make you feel guilty by: (1) threatening to take them away from you; or (if you are separated) (2) playing games with visitation.	Leaves the children out of your arguments and doesn't use them either to hurt you or to get you to drop your demands for change. This includes telling them, "I would come home but Mommy doesn't let me" or, "Why don't you ask Mommy to stop being so mean, she got me in trouble with..."
Minimizes his abusive behavior by telling you that you have misperceived, misunderstood, or simply overreacted to his behaviors.	Acknowledges and takes responsibility for his abuse without downplaying it.
Tries to convince you that you are responsible for any abuse because you: (1) provoked him or "pushed his buttons"; (2) have some flaw that causes him to behave this way; or (3) should have stopped him sooner.	Accepts responsibility for his actions. Responsibility sounds like this: "I'm sorry. I know I was wrong and that I hurt you. I need to listen to you to understand what I need to do differently." There is no "but..." and there isn't any continued sense of bargaining. He doesn't acknowledge only some things and tell you what he will change without acknowledging all of the things he has done to hurt you (especially the things he doesn't like to admit), then telling *you* what he'll be doing to make up for it, without actually listening to you.

BEHAVIORS THAT NEED TO CHANGE	SIGNS OF REAL CHANGE
Tries to get you to compromise your religious, ethical, or moral standards by pressuring you relentlessly.	Respects your standards in different areas and doesn't use pressure to get you to back down from them or from your plan for change.
Abuses you sexually by (1) insisting on sexual acts that you find demeaning or painful; (2) forcing you to be intimate against your will; (3) forcing you to have physical contact or intimacy when you are in *niddah*; or (4) puts you down for your sexual inadequacy.	Respects you sexually by: respecting your decision if there is something you aren't comfortable with; respecting you if you want to keep the laws of *taharas hamishpachah* strictly; respecting you if you're uncomfortable with intimate acts that *he* likes; and tries to make sure you are happy.

Remember, this checklist is meant as a general guide. It may not articulate your specific experience, nor is it meant to be inclusive. Rather, it can help you understand how to articulate the abusive behaviors that you see which need to change. It can also serve as a guide to help you articulate what would constitute real change and point to your signposts along the way.

This list is meant for your frame of reference. Sharing it with someone else should be carefully considered. Sharing could result in it being used by the abuser to check off behaviors that he has stopped for a while, or to argue over the specifics of what he thinks he has done or needs to change. Giving your input about what needs to happen should be done thoughtfully, not in a way that puts you under scrutiny.

Also, keep in mind that your expectations for change are not about trying to reverse your roles — as in, now *you're* going to be the one in control. This shouldn't be your goal, nor should you feel intimidated if you are accused of this. The demand for change is meant to establish *balance* in the relationship. A healthy relationship is one where both are giving respect. The abuser, who is not used to giving respect, will perceive — or pretend to feel — that having to give it is being controlled. It is not uncommon for abusers to try to get you to back down by accusing *you* of being controlling now. On the contrary — the intention is for you to keep giving respect, but to expect respect in return.

Tactics for Avoiding Real Change

Let us suppose that your plan for change is met by your husband with a promise to change. The next question you must answer is whether he is *really* changing, or if he is just saying what he must until the consequences and the attention on his abusive behavior has waned. The checklist and roadmap can help you anticipate what you need to see as proof that change is actually occurring. In addition to that, however, there are a few common roadblocks you need to be aware of regarding this process.

Appearing Remorseful to Others

In answering the question, "Is he really changing?" it is critical that you keep in mind that only *you* can answer this question. When he was abusive, he was abusive toward you and with you. You are the only one who knows if this has changed or not.

An abuser typically presents himself entirely differently to those outside the home. Some are considerate to friends, family, business associates, and the *rav*. He might be regarded as a model of virtuous behavior by everyone in the community. Other abusive husbands might be viewed as average. Still others might not be particularly impressive to anyone. Rarely, however, does a woman say that everyone thinks of her husband as an abuser, because he reserves these behaviors for her. People don't really understand how he treated you when he was abusive, and they will not know now whether his behavior toward you has changed. After all, he never treated them the way he treated you, and they can't know if he has changed how he treats you.

Therapists who are inexperienced in working with domestic abuse cases can be fooled into believing that a husband is changing, when in fact he is simply putting on a good show to make everyone believe that he is acting differently. The abuser may talk movingly and remorsefully about his past behavior. He may make sure his *rav* sees him at *minyan* on time, and at the *daf* regularly. To his parents or yours, he may cry about how sorry he is. This may all be genuine, but it has nothing to do with what kind of husband he was, and it cannot be used as a measure of whether anything in that arena has changed.

Although others may be involved in your process, you are the only one subject to the abuser's use of tactics that are aimed at circumventing the promised change while avoiding the negative consequences. Others may try to convince you that *they* see a change, and therefore he must be changing. If you feel differently, remind yourself that you're not crazy. Even smart, important people may forget that what they see has no bearing on how he treats you as his wife. Only you can evaluate this.

Changing the Packaging for the Tactic

Not all change-avoiding tactics are obvious. Some abusive husbands will make small changes, perhaps eliminating the most obvious forms of abuse that are unmistakable to the victim and easily documented for outsiders, while maintaining their control through more subtle tactics.

> *During the course of their marriage, Sammy had managed to isolate Shira from friends and family members. Sammy would tell her that this one was not* frum *enough, the next one had a low-class job, the third was too materialistic, and so on. He told her that a good wife listened to her husband and that she shouldn't be spending time with people he didn't approve of or feel comfortable with.*
>
> *In time, the abuse escalated, involving so many aspects of her life that Shira couldn't take it anymore. Shira enlisted support in a plan for change. Sammy professed his intention to stop this abusive behavior to the professional therapist who became involved, as well as*

to the rabbi who provided the motivation to change. And in fact, he did stop forbidding her to see friends.

In spite of this change, Shira found that she was still feeling iso-lated and discontented. When she discussed her situation with her therapist, she realized that Sammy had simply switched the tactics he used to keep her home. Now, instead of forbidding her to go out or telling her that she had to clean, he asked her to stay home with him so they could work on their relationship. "How can we focus on changing our relationship if you're wrapped up in all these outside relationships?" He would make her feel guilty by asking her, "What's really important now?"

In short, there was still a great deal of pressure on Shira to stay away from her friends and even family. Yes, the orders were gone, and the tantrums had ended. However, the isolation remained. Sammy worked very hard to subtly make Shira feel that if there was any problem in their relationship, it was now due to her.

What Sammy did to Shira is representative of a whole category of tac-tics that abusers use to maintain their control after they have agreed to change. The abuser does make changes, but the change is *how* he con-trols; he has not stopped trying to control.

In fifteen years of marriage, Linda never had access to the couple's financial resources, nor did she have any idea of the family income or her husband's expenditures. Larry gave Linda money whenever he saw fit. He expected her to manage on whatever he gave her, and to give him an accounting of every penny she spent.

The amounts she received were not consistent, and there were times when Larry simply did not give her enough to cover all the household expenses. Sometimes he gave her as little as $40 to feed their family of eight for an entire week. If she told him that this was simply not possible, he would berate her for being incompetent, call-ing her an "idiot." At the same time, he often made extravagant pur-chases for himself.

When Linda's plan for change elicited a promise to change, he complied by giving her a credit card. He made sure everyone involved knew about the credit card he had given her. He told her that she should be happy now, since she could make purchases without worrying about how much money he gave her. He added that it would still be necessary for them to go over the bill together, so he would know what went into the household budget. But, he said, this would take only a few minutes each month.

In fact, though, Larry quizzed her each month on every expenditure she made, and he frequently complained that she had made unnecessary purchases. It became clear to Linda that Larry had given her the credit card to demonstrate to everyone that he was being reasonable, but he still maintained the level of control — only its shape had changed.

Furthermore, Linda's request for details about the family's income and savings continued to be met with passive resistance. Larry insisted that explaining the family finances to her would be too confusing, and giving her access to bank accounts could possibly lead to miscommunications and overdrafts. Larry rationalized his resistance by explaining that he was not being financially controlling — he just wanted to keep their lives simple.

Larry was not about to give up his control. Giving Linda the credit card may have had some positive impact on her plight — she didn't need to worry about having enough money in a given week to buy groceries. But Larry still wanted to know where all the money was going, and he was in a position to cut Linda off if she spent money in a way that he deemed frivolous, or if their "reconciliation" did not proceed as he liked. He still kept her completely in the dark about the overall financial picture. The small concession of the credit card was directed more toward appearances than any real change.

There are times when there is just enough change to be confusing, and perhaps to convince others who became involved that it's okay to back off. Your roadmap will help you recognize what *real* change looks like for each situation, and help you find the discrepancy if you feel that change isn't really happening.

If you're worried that you might miss a cue and not realize what he's doing, ask yourself on a regular basis: "Am I feeling better about how things are going?" The next section will explore ways to monitor change, to make certain things are moving in the right direction.

Change —
With a Catch
Abusive husbands who promise to change frequently cloak their continued attempt to exert control in an argument that stresses the need for the couple to be free from outside influences, so they can work together to restore their relationship. The abuser might say, "Now that I'm aware of the problem, there is no need to continue to report to your therapist (the *rav*, your friend, your sister, the court, and so on). They will only interfere in our efforts to get close to each other again." Or, "Things are looking much better now, but it's hard for me to feel close to you and trust you if there are people looking over my shoulder."

There are many different permutations on this theme. Be wary of any suggestion on the abuser's part that in order for the relationship to continue to improve, you must isolate yourself from your supporters.

Recognizing Real, Long-Lasting Change

It can be difficult for a woman to determine whether her abusive husband is truly trying to change, or merely changing the packaging. It's important to carefully monitor your feelings as time goes by. *Ask yourself continuously whether you feel less controlled.* If the answer is no, then consider how and why you still feel controlled. It is beneficial to have a domestic violence counselor help you with this, but the following section should help you regardless.

In making this assessment, I advise women to return to the Abuse Checklist. For each and every item included in this checklist, you can indicate at regular intervals what changes have occurred and how satisfied you are with the progress that has been made. Ask yourself if you are seeing elements of the signs that you determined would indicate change — or are you seeing control with a new twist?

Regularly revisit what is going on between the two of you and determine whether you see change. This should enable you to have a clear picture of what positive changes may have occurred, and what still needs to change.

A crucial part of the process comes when you need to tell your husband that he is continuing to engage in controlling or abusive behaviors. The very act of telling how you feel, having it taken into account and accepted, and seeing your husband make a change, will tell you if the promises of change are being kept. Does he respect your opinion and input, or does he try to tell you that you're wrong, blame you for nitpicking on irrelevancies, and pressure you to back down?

It's an understandable tendency, if things start to seem better, to start letting the smaller things go to avoid "rocking the boat." The memories of past abuse may also cause you to hesitate from having any confrontation. Do not give in to those instincts! If you never raise these issues, there is no way to tell whether his attitude toward you has changed.

The task of sharing your assessment of change with your husband may feel less frightening if one of the people involved in the process (for example, his therapist or a support person) does it with you. Bear in mind, however, that if you really are unable to give feedback safely to your husband alone, if you know he will resort to either old tactics or new tactics to get you to back down, it's a clear indication that things have not changed.

Part of seeing change is being able to tell him what is bothering you without fear of consequences. This will be difficult and anxiety provoking even if he has changed, because you have been afraid for so long. But unless you push yourself to give your honest feedback and see what happens, you won't know if his change is real. Of course, be careful if it feels unsafe to do so.

This monitoring process will also help you better understand your own responses to the changes that your husband is making. Your emotional response to his efforts and to changes in his behavior can be confusing and difficult to understand. When you aren't closely looking at the process, it can be easy to question yourself and get bogged down with self-doubt.

Ilana's husband Eitan had promised to change his abusive behavior. Ilana had been seeing a therapist, and her husband had begun counseling with a separate therapist after being confronted by his rav as part of Ilana's plan for change. After some weeks in counseling, Ilana acknowledged that her husband had in fact made changes. However, Ilana still felt miserable in the relationship.

Eitan was righteously indignant with Ilana's continued misery. He told both Ilana and his therapist that it was clear that the real issue in the relationship was Ilana's depression, not his abusive behavior. He had been claiming that this was the problem all along, minimizing his abuse with statements like, "Maybe I've made some mistakes, but I'm not a bad husband — there's just no pleasing Ilana." He used her continued negative attitude to reassert his contention that Ilana needed to be on medication.

Ilana acknowledged that she was still unhappy even though there were changes that Eitan had made. She didn't think that she was depressed or needed medication, but she was starting to wonder whether she just wasn't going to be able to forgive the past abuse, enjoy the changes that Eitan was making, and move on to a new phase of their relationship. When talking about a specific example, Ilana related the following:

Ilana was bedridden with a terrible case of the flu. She knew she needed to see a doctor, but she couldn't go by herself. Eitan was attentive to her needs during her illness and offered to take her, a definite change for him.

This particular incident was one Eitan cited as proof that despite his changes, Ilana didn't seem to have any appreciation for his efforts. Ilana acknowledged that she had remained unhappy after this incident, despite the help her husband had given her. But there was a reason for that.

After returning home from the doctor, Eitan expected her to show her appreciation for his changed behavior by being intimate with him. When Ilana told him that she did not feel up to it, he accused her of not being appreciative and being unable to forgive. Ilana acknowledged that after Eitan's inconsiderate request for intimacy and his insensitive response to her refusal, she ceased to feel much appreciation for his having taken her to the doctor.

Differentiating real change from a change in tactics is confusing, so keep using your checklist and roadmap throughout the process. Continue to fill in your need for change, and keep in mind that *you* are the one with the ability to detect change.

Beyond the Checklist:
Other Questions to Ask Yourself

Your checklist looks at the specific behaviors that you want changed. The following questions help you examine the *process* of change, and some of the tactics of coercion or minimization that an abusive spouse may use if he wants to *look* like he is changing, while actually trying to get his spouse to give up this process.

- When you try to tell your spouse that what he is saying is harmful or disrespectful, does he accuse you of being overly negative, never having anything good to say, insinuating or actually saying that *that's* what the problem is?

- After years of mistreating you, when he is finally forced to change by someone stepping in, does he expect you to be back to normal and get over it on *his* timetable?

- Does he expect you to give him respect and trust when he feels you've had enough time to "get over it," instead of recognizing that it will take time, and *you* get to decide when you trust him again?

- Is he pressuring you to focus on the positive, rather than validating what you've gone through?

- Is he demanding that you act as if none of this has happened?

- Does he pressure you to stop going to counseling?

- Does he pressure you to go to the people who you have gotten involved and get them to stop being involved, to tell them he's changed and let him off the hook, even if the changes haven't been significant?

- Does he minimize with statements such as, "I said I'll change, what else do you want?"

- Does he say he can change only if you change?

- Does he focus on what *you* need to change, instead of what he's done and what he needs to change?

- Is he more focused on *you* — when you'll forgive him, stop going to counseling, say things are fine — rather than focus on *himself* and acknowledge his responsibility and the work he needs to do?

- If you have moved out, or made him move out, does he pressure you to come back/let him come back by sending people to talk to you, such as friends, family, *rabbanim*?

- Overall, have the areas in which you were being controlled changed? Socially, financially, emotionally, in terms of decision making, and so on?

- In terms of what has changed in those areas, does he still try to control you in some way, perhaps using milder forms of control?

- Are you still nervous about sharing your opinion, wanting something different, or making a decision you know he wouldn't agree with? Why? Have you tried?

- Are you afraid *because* he is still doing something that makes it frightening to change the way you act? If so, what is he doing? Or, because it was so frightening for so long, are you now afraid to try, even if things might be different? What can you do about that?

Responding to Change

You've made a plan for change, and elicited help in demanding that your husband cease his abusive behavior. Your husband not only promised change — he is actually changing his behavior. He may change significantly, or he may change superficially. He may be acting less controlling, or he may eliminate only the most blatant abuses to put on a good front, while trying to maintain as much of his control as possible. As you monitor the extent to which he has changed or not changed, you may experience a great range of emotional responses.

Some women fear that they will be "fooled again." Women often express their belief that because they were fooled into marrying him the first time, he will fool them into believing he has changed — perhaps by changing temporarily, or changing just enough to look as if he is sincere.

As long as you go slowly, have a clear understanding of what needs to be changed, and don't rush the process due to pressure from your husband or outside sources — you will see what you need to see. You won't un-learn what you have learned the hard way. Keep in mind, too, that a man who has no intention of relinquishing his control gets frustrated by this process very quickly. It's not long before the abuser who isn't really interested in changing shows his true intentions.

Some women fear that they will not be able to forgive and move on, even if he makes real change. The reality is that most women who have had strong feelings of love and respect for their husbands, even though there was also abuse, are able to forgive in the face of real change. These women welcome change, because they hope for better times and some form of close relationship.

Ask yourself, "If my husband stops abusing me, could I be happy married to him?" When asked this question, many women respond, "Yes. It's all I've wanted." While their husbands will almost certainly never measure up to the ideal they had before they were married, they genuinely believe that some form of positive relationship is possible. Many women are happy to stay married, as long as they can simply live peacefully.

There are times, however, that a woman finds that the feelings of love and respect she once had for her husband are gone. No matter what changes he might make in his behavior, it's impossible for her to develop a warm, loving relationship with someone who hurt her so badly. This is usually the case when a woman was severely abused, or where there was a very quick courtship and the abuse started right after the wedding. The fact that there was hardly anything positive to begin with, coupled with so many negative experiences, make it nearly impossible for her to develop any positive feelings toward him.

Some women become confused and disillusioned. They had assumed if the abuse stops, he will automatically become loving and respectful. They expect him to become an ideal husband, capable and interested in a loving, giving relationship. They find it less than satisfying when their husbands have stopped being abusive, but are still not capable of sharing a mutually loving, respectful, and emotionally satisfying relationship.

It is important for you to recognize your feelings, regardless of whether you come to feel warmly toward him again, or simply accept the changes as making an unsatisfactory relationship more bearable. Many women whose controlling husbands stop their most flagrant forms of abuse do choose to remain in the relationship, even if they don't feel very loving toward him. Remember, it's nearly impossible to know how you're going to feel in the future!

Should I Go Back?

After a woman has taken the step of separating from her abusive spouse, she may want to give him a chance to change before making a final decision about the relationship. Although this section can provide everyone with a deeper understanding of change which may be helpful in each process, it is directed toward those whose plan for change will not be happening under the same roof.

In a separation, the abuser is confronted unambiguously with the possibility of the loss of the marriage, and this eventuality carries with it both social stigma and the loss of normal family life. Under these circumstances he may very well promise to stop his abusive behavior. He may promise you, his *rav*, and all those who support you that he will change.

But the abuser's need to control is strong. Even when threatened with these highly adverse consequences, he may attempt to employ a variety of tactics to get you to return home, while still seeking to control your behavior.

The threat of leaving should not be used idly, as mentioned before. It takes a lot of wherewithal to persist in this decision with all of the pressure that comes from outside sources. Having support for your decision or plan will be key. Even with that support, however, do not be surprised if you are pressured to reverse your course of action.

Women who are contemplating making a demand for change in their husband's abusive behavior must make a realistic assessment of the difficulties inherent in this process, so they will not be derailed from the course they have set when the going becomes difficult.

> *After many years of abuse, which included attempts at getting help from rabbis and professionals, Chumi packed a few bags, picked her children up from school and went to her parents' house. The morning that she did this followed an incident in which her husband Shimmy, finding that she had not yet made all the beds, felt the need to impress upon her the importance of having the beds made by nine o'clock in the morning. He told her that only a fat, lazy, stupid and disorganized cow could fail to accomplish this simple task. He also smacked her for emphasis as he left for work.*
>
> *After Chumi had moved out, she started to see a therapist who had a specific expertise in domestic violence. Chumi began treatment with the hope that therapy might help her figure out the possibilities for change. The therapist explained to Chumi that the only real possibility for motivating change was if her husband really felt he had to change.*
>
> *In the past, both professional mental health workers and religious leaders had talked to Shimmy about the need to desist in his abusive behaviors toward Chumi. Shimmy would promise to change, but*

would instead continue his abuse. If the authority figure confronted him on his failure to live up to his promises, Shimmy would simply stop talking to that person. Dropping out of therapy was certainly easy. Finding somewhere else to daven *after the* rav *of the shul confronted him was not difficult either.*

Chumi's therapist pointed out that her husband simply didn't feel compelled to change. Shimmy was not about to give up his abusive controlling behaviors toward Chumi simply because a therapist or even a rav *told him to. Unfortunately, he just wasn't connected enough to his* rav *for this to have an impact. But when Chumi moved out, her husband's life was affected negatively by her departure. He did not want to be divorced.*

Based on the advice of her therapist, Chumi made it clear to Shimmy that she had no intention of returning to their home until she was quite certain that he had really changed. He was unhappy living alone, and he promised once again that he would stop his abuse. But at the same time, he sought to continue his control by pressuring her to return to their home immediately. He clearly had no intention of allowing her to continue to live with her parents while he went through the lengthy process of convincing her that he had changed.

Shimmy told Chumi that without her and the kids at home to motivate him, he didn't see how he could invest his best effort to become a more considerate husband. Shimmy also asked his rav *to call her on his behalf.*

Shimmy's mother also called Chumi to ask her to return. Chumi had a close relationship with her mother-in-law, and she had come to depend on her in certain ways. But while Shimmy's mother did want things to be better, she didn't recognize that Shimmy needed the proper motivation for change. She sought to convince Chumi to return home on the grounds that separation always leads to divorce. She told Chumi that if she really wanted to make the marriage work, she should come back home so the marriage could have a chance.

It became increasingly difficult for Chumi to stick to the plan of seeing change first before resuming marriage as usual. She was tempted to give in to the pressure and accept the idea that if she would just return home, things would really change. Deep down, Chumi wanted to believe that she could go home and that things would get better. It would be so much easier not to have to be strong and stand up to everybody. Chumi was also concerned that the longer she stayed with her parents, the more likely it was that people in the community would find out about her difficulties.

With all this pressure — from others, from her own needs, and from her unrealistic wishes for things to be better — Chumi moved back home. She hoped things would be different, even though she hadn't stuck to her original plan for change and did not see any evidence of change.

Predictably, things quickly went back to exactly where they had been before. Chumi realized that she had found it too difficult to resist all these pressures; she just wanted what everyone told her to be true. But now things were as bad as ever, if not worse, because she felt she had missed an opportunity.

If you get separated and that becomes part of the motivation for change, understand what usually comes along with this. Initially, at least, the abuser's focus will be on getting his control back, by getting you back under the same roof. He may pressure you himself, or he may enlist the support of others to convince you to return home, to "give the relationship a chance of succeeding." He and others may contend that you cannot work on the relationship if you are not under the same roof. People may pressure you to return, rather than pressure him to make changes, because the separation makes them nervous. They fear that separation leads to divorce. In their minds, if you are under the same roof, you are going in the right direction. They don't recognize that too often, the separation was a big, last-ditch effort to make things work. When a woman comes back and is simply abused again, she'll feel that she's had enough and will not be willing to try again. So if the reunion is pushed too quickly, without allowing time for real change, the reunion itself often ends up sabotaging the marriage.

So what process *should* a woman should go through if she has separated and now wants to give her husband and her marriage the best chance for health? Remember that an effective plan has three key elements: motivation for change, someone who will work with your husband to change his perspective on marriage, and preferably, someone you can work with to help you determine whether there has been real change. The separation is now acting as motivation. Is he working with someone? Are you? Now you are ready for the process of slowly determining, with distance, if your husband is changing.

To determine whether change has taken place, the best indication will be your interactions with him. That doesn't mean you need to live under the same roof, however. It's a step-by-step process that you build up gradually, assessing his changes along the way and determining with each step whether there has been sufficient change to warrant progressing to the next level.

Below is a list of steps for the process of assessing change and rebuilding trust.

Talking   Start by talking!

It is helpful to enter into this low level of contact with a clear plan and boundaries. His willingness to keep the boundaries will demonstrate if he has changed his ability to respect you, your requests or your opinions. It also gives you time to build up your strength, your fear of the past, and your ability to interact with him differently.

If he accepts what you've asked (for example, to talk on Mondays and Wednesdays for half an hour), he is possibly learning to respect you. If he wants to have just a little extra time, or a short call in between scheduled calls, or complains that you're being too rigid, or that now you're the controlling one — it's an indication that there hasn't been real change in his perspective on respect in marriage.

What should you talk about? Whatever you want. But as you proceed, consider two different aspects of the interaction between you.

First, evaluate how it feels to interact with him on everyday issues. Then, when you are ready, check if his perspective on his behavior has changed. To accomplish this, find out how he now feels about his past behavior, the events that led to your leaving, and your need for change. Is he still minimizing or denying his behavior? See what he thinks about those who support you and their role in monitoring the changes. Ask him directly whether he understands the problem, and if so, what does he understand it to be?

If he is apologizing and saying he's changed, ask him to get specific. What exactly is he apologizing for, and how will things be different between the two of you in the future? Don't be afraid to ask specific questions about how you will be able to regain control of your life and pursue your interests. See if he talks mostly about himself, or he is concerned about you and how you are doing.

Of course, what he *says* will only tell you so much. He may promise to make all the changes you have asked for, but not plan on delivering. However, talking with him will at least show you if he has *not* changed. Someone who cannot bring himself to even *say* the right things has certainly not changed.

If he does say the right things, you now have a valid reason to continue the process of attempting to rebuild trust. It is up to you to determine whether his actions are in accordance with his words. As you begin to interact more, your checklist will come in handy.

Be aware that your abusive husband may say that he has changed, but at the same time pressure you to return sooner than you want. He may try to use guilt tactics or use others to pressure you to come back. He may tell you that he cannot live without you, that the kids need a full-time father, or that his therapist thinks he would be able to change more easily if you were back together again.

Also be aware of your own contribution in keeping the process confusing. Consider a situation in which your needs and his wishes are in conflict:

> *Your husband wants to speak with you on Tuesday. You recently started a class on Tuesdays and you want to speak on Wednesday, as was originally planned. He tells you, "That's a whole week away!*

I really want to share my progress with you, to keep up the momentum and stay connected. Don't you want that too?"

Well, yes, you do want that. So you ask yourself, "Am I really going to be so stubborn about it?"

If you do give in at this point and change your plans, you are contributing to keeping the process confusing. You're not being stubborn or difficult if you insist on keeping the standards you have established. This was the plan. Sticking to your plan and seeing how well your husband respects that tells you a lot about his actual change.

Remember, an abuser feels entitled to power and control. He can ask you for something, but you'll know he still feels this entitlement by how he reacts when you inform him of your needs. His request can be nice and reasonable, causing you to think, "It's been so good so far. Why not just give this up? It's really not such a big deal to me." But you're not just giving up a class you had planned to go to. You're giving up the clarity you can achieve regarding whether his belief has shifted.

When you are wooed into changing your plans or feel too intimidated to stick with your plans, you are keeping yourself from vital information. What would happen if you stuck to your decision, even if he disagrees with it or wants to do otherwise?

His request and attempt to convince you to change your plans isn't evidence of controlling behavior on its own. His reaction to your refusal, however, will tell you a lot about him. So don't short circuit the process. Don't respond by quickly adjusting your plans. Stick with your plan and see what his reaction is.

Does he pout, have people call you to tell you how unreasonable you're acting, or tell you that himself? Or perhaps he says he understands, and he respects your decision? Now you have some information.

If he does pressure you, point out that he is once again trying to control you, and it is precisely this attitude that must change if you are ever to get back together. Use the talking process to reinforce the message that things have changed on your end and must change on his end if there is to be any chance for reconciliation. Make it work for you by making it a litmus test for change.

If you are still too afraid to point out the things that are bothering you, you will not be able to find out if he has really changed.

Dating   If you are satisfied that your conversations feel different, if you get the definite sense that he has given up his assumption of control, the next stage is to actually get together. Your goal is to see if it feels different when you're with him over a longer period of time.

Dating will widen your personal impression of his behavior, enabling you to see his reaction when he is in situations that might anger or frustrate him. The talking phase allowed only limited interactions, limiting the situations which might have led to abuse. Now you have a better opportunity to determine whether real change has occurred. As you have more complicated interactions, use your checklist to monitor the occurrence of the old behaviors in various situations.

> _Tova had separated from her husband and started divorce proceedings, but decided to see if Jonathan's promises to change were really true before ending the relationship. For some time, they just had talks on the phone, and Tova felt that she saw some changes. It seemed that he was more responsive toward her opinions. So she agreed to arrange some dates._
>
> _The first few dates were good. She enjoyed herself, and she remembered what had made her marry Jonathan in the first place. She was really excited about where they were headed. On the third date, however, Jonathon started in on an old theme: how she dressed. He had always pushed her to look more attractive by wearing a longer sheitel, more makeup, tighter clothing, and so on. He had always been very forceful about it. Now, although he remained calm, he told her that he needed his wife to look a certain way. If he was willing to make changes for her, then she should make certain changes for him, and then their life together would be beautiful!_

This made Tova realize that she still had a lot to explore before she could go to the next level by getting back together with Jonathon. Was this really about "you do a little something for me and I do a little something for you"? Or was this sliding back into Jonathan's assumptions of control over many aspects of Tova's life?

Tova appropriately slowed things down and began a discussion of her reactions to his request. This way she allowed herself further opportunity to determine Jonathan's progress, as well as his intention and ability to establish a give-and-take relationship.

Spending More Time Together

Assuming that the steps up to this point have gone well, you may feel comfortable spending some time together with your husband in a more private setting. Begin slowly. You might consider having Shabbos meals together. This would give you a further opportunity to experience your spouse's responses and interactions. Ask yourself if he has changed.

Next, ask yourself if you would feel safe, *physically and emotionally*, spending a night under the same roof. If you do feel it would be safe, then continue to proceed slowly. Spend an entire Shabbos together — without committing to doing this every week, or every other week. After each time, consider what happened and how you felt. Ask yourself — did his behavior seem genuine, or did it feel manipulative?

If you begin to feel some trust and comfort, consider spending a whole weekend together. Once again, proceed slowly and give yourself a chance to digest the events of each occasion that you spend together. Continue to resist any pressure that he may be placing on you to return home before you feel ready to do so. If he does pressure you, continue to remind him that he is being controlling, and that he will have to recognize that this is unacceptable. Re-examine what happens when you do this.

Children

One of the pressures you'll have to withstand is concern for the children's well-being. Obviously, if your husband attempts to use the children to get you to short circuit your process, it's a sign that he is trying to get back in control. Even without that, however, there is a certain social pressure women feel when they separate, including the pressure from her own children who ask her to make things normal again. Alternatively, they may be pressuring her to stay away, out of fear of what they've witnessed or experienced in the past.

You will need to find a way to go through your process while taking care of your children's needs. Seeking professional guidance on how to best help them through this process is really your best option. If this is not possible for you, think about what each of your children might be struggling with. Ask them what their questions are. Try to be honest with them, on their level, and only to the extent that would be appropriate. While you should not over share, gauging their possible fears or concerns and addressing them will make sticking with your plan a bit easier.

Intimacy This is a very sensitive subject with a number of considerations: safety, halachic, and personal willingness. Think through this issue with the same attention to detail you used for other aspects of coming together. In regard to halachic queries, take the time to compose your question, determine the best person to ask, and how you will include all necessary information, even if it's a bit embarrassing.

Seeing a Professional If everything has gone well so far — talking, dating, the initial Shabbos, perhaps spending some weekends together — you may want to consider seeing a professional as a couple before moving back completely. By now you have hopefully found a therapist to help you evaluate change along the way. For this, the final stage of coming back together with your husband, seeing a professional can be especially helpful. In the office of a professional, you can safely and comfortably express any remaining reservations and identify specific aspects of his behavior that continue to raise issues in your mind.

You will need to make a conscious effort not to avoid touching on sensitive issues. This is a time of testing the limits of his capacity to change. You cannot pull back from discussing contentious issues for fear of angering him. The idea here is to see if the two of you can discuss such issues. Can he tolerate this type of discussion? If not, you have to wonder what living with him full time will be like — probably no different than it was before. This process will also give you practice in being assertive, a skill that may have atrophied during the period that you were being controlled, dominated, and abused.

Move at Your Own Pace

It is important throughout the process of rebuilding trust to move at your own pace. You do not have to make a quick choice between returning home immediately or getting a divorce. Take the time you need.

This may be difficult, given all the pressures that women go through in these circumstances. Still, make sure you are comfortable with each of the steps above before proceeding. Taking the time you need will not only benefit your mental health, but will also become a sign of that health. Most important, if you do things slowly and allow the proper time for real change, you have the potential for building something much sturdier. As mentioned before, rushing the reunion before everyone is ready can sometimes unnecessarily result in the *end* of the marriage, when perhaps it didn't need to.

After a particularly nasty incident when he cursed at her and broke her phone in front of the children, Ruchama told Motti to leave or she was going to go to the rav. Motti left, moving in with his parents. He insisted that he was horrified with himself and that he was committed to change. Ruchama was skeptical. She had been trying to get him to go for help for years. In fact, they had gone to a few therapists, but every time they went Motti would hear something he didn't like, and he would leave. Now, though, he said he had gotten a wake-up call, and that he was ready to listen.

Ruchama really wanted to work things out with Motti, since they had two children, but she felt that doing this while separated for a while was the best way to keep things on track. Everyone else, however, was very nervous about the situation with Motti out of the

house. His parents, their rav, and even some of his siblings kept tell-
ing her that "separation means divorce."

Motti had started seeing a therapist. He sounded so committed
and despondent. And there was all the pressure. So Ruchama let
Motti move back three weeks later.

Things were good for a couple of weeks. Motti was respectful, at-
tentive, and responsive. He continued going to his therapist and Ru-
chama was so excited that things were getting better.

But then the setbacks started. The crisis seemed to wane, and with
it, Motti's attention to the process. He started to miss sessions with
his counselor, and eventually began to revert back to his controlling
and abusive behaviors.

Ruchama decided that she was done. She wanted to end the mar-
riage. She didn't believe Motti was interested in change, and didn't
want to live this way for the rest of her life.

Short circuiting the process of change doesn't do anyone a favor: not you, not your husband, and not the marriage. Don't think that it is an act of kindness to allow yourself to be pressured into moving too quickly.

The same caution applies to consequences. Sometimes women are tempted — either themselves, or via pressure from others — to go easy on the abuser, minimizing the consequences. But it is the consequences that have the ability to motivate change. Yes, in the short run, lessening or eliminating consequences allows everyone to breathe a sigh of relief. But it doesn't help give the marriage a chance for real change. The abuser needs the extended period of motivation that it takes for real change to happen.

Remain committed to keeping up the pressure of the crisis and the consequences so the abuser's motivation for change remains strong. If the abuser never progresses beyond the initial appeasing stage to accepting responsibility for what's happened, he is not likely to make long-lasting change. The longer he has pressure to work on himself, the more likely he will come to understand it on the deeper level necessary for there to be real change.

Chapter Six

❧

For Those
Who Are Staying

This chapter will address strategies on how to cope when married to an abuser. Whether you have decided to stay for now while exploring the possibility for change, or you have chosen to stay even if no change takes place, this chapter will guide you through issues you may want to consider while living and raising a family in the context of domestic abuse.

Another area to explore is whether there are pockets of opportunity for you to change things for yourself within the relationship, even if your husband does not change, or if your plan for change does not result in a complete end to the control and abuse. Here we will encounter the greatest variability from one situation to another. Some women will find a pocket of opportunity in the area of employment. Some will be able to broaden their social network or activities. And there are those who will not find any opportunities except in activities that are permitted by the abuser — and he permits almost none. Regardless of which of these categories describes you best, you should be able to use the information in this chapter to guide you in surviving and strategizing while staying in your marriage, if that's the choice you've made.

As we discussed earlier in this book, women who live with abusive husbands frequently vacillate between denial, with the hope that her husband will simply wake up one day and spontaneously be different; and despair — the realization that he won't just spontaneously be different. While you may understand that your husband has an expectation of control, you still periodically allow yourself to believe that things will improve on their own. You may seize upon the smallest sign of affection as an indication that he has started along a positive path, leading to the end of abuse and a new relationship characterized by mutual love and respect.

Women allow themselves to indulge in this hope because it seems to help. It gives them something positive to hold on to.

The strategies presented in this chapter accept the reality of the situation. Yes, that may cause you to feel despair. But it also opens up new possibilities.

Why Women Stay

Women decide to stay married to an abusive spouse for a variety of reasons. For some, the decision is based on emotional and religious factors. For others, the decision is a more practical one. Often the decision is complex, involving a combination of reasons to stay. Some women have it clear in their minds why they want to stay; others don't, but they simply know that they are not going to leave.

Being able to articulate why you are making this choice can be helpful when you reach out for support, something that is crucial when staying with an abuser. Some people wouldn't question why you are staying — their belief is that a woman remains in her marriage, no matter what. Others have a different attitude. The person you reach out to may fit into that second category. If you are aware of your reasons for staying and can articulate them, it might make your relationship with that support person more satisfying for you.

This can mean different things to different women. Consider Millie:

"This was Meant to Be" *Millie and her husband had ten children. Millie's husband Sonny was always overbearing and controlling, financially and emotionally. While Millie acknowledged that things were very difficult, she felt that this was her husband, they had a family together, and that was that. She put up with his control and abuse with the assumption that if this is the way things are, that must be how it was "meant to be."*

As her children grew older, they begged their mother to leave their father. Several were married already and were concerned about their younger siblings who lived at home, who were suffering along with their mother. Others were unable to get married because their father would interfere and sabotage anything that came up.

But even with all the suffering, and even with the children begging for change, Millie still felt that this was her husband, no matter what.

Many women grapple with the idea of *bashert*. Others might think, "This must be my *nisayon*." Often these are conclusions that a woman comes to based on lessons she's learned about these concepts.

These are serious *hashkafic* questions. You may be satisfied that these concepts are reason enough to stay in your abusive marriage. If you find yourself grappling with these questions in connection with being abused by your spouse, you may want to seek out a competent halachic authority who understands abuse to discuss your theories of *hashkafa*, as it applies to your situation.

A Strong Connection It is difficult to explain the strength of the bond you feel with your husband, despite everything. This bond causes many women to feel love, care, commitment, and a desire to keep trying. It's not surprising that women who feel this close connection, yet are regularly hurt by their husbands, feel very confused and have an extremely difficult time trying to explain this to others.

> *Faigy's grown children went to the family's* rav *after a particularly violent outburst by their father led to their mother running out of the house with the two children living at home to the home of one of her married children. They all agreed that their father had a terrible temper. Over the years, he had really worn their mother down, making her doubt herself and sometimes even her sanity. The* rav *suggested that the couple stay separated for a while so Faigy could regain her strength, and possibly her husband would be motivated to change.*
>
> *But after just a few days with a lot of promises and apologies — which Faigy admitted she had heard before, without any real results — Faigy couldn't continue. She felt that being separated was too difficult. She missed having a husband, she felt bad for him, and yes, she still loved him — so she went back home.*

For some women, it is an actual feeling of love that keeps them in the relationship. For others there is a fear of being alone. The thought of being alone is too terrifying to contemplate, even if the alternative means living with the abuser.

Hope for Change Often women stay because they are *hoping* for change, even though they are unable to engage in any real action to achieve it. They stay hopeful because the alternative seems more painful. Rationally, you may come to understand that hoping for change and making an active plan to try to achieve change are two different things.

He's Changed "Enough" As long as some change has taken place, many women feel that this is enough to make life manageable. Even if attempts at intervention didn't have the full desired effect, the process did accomplish something. More people are involved in your life and keeping tabs on your situation. That seems to be enough motivation to make the abuser keep the abuse to a minimum. Perhaps you can even put your foot down sometimes and stand up for yourself without fear of unbearable consequences. It might not be great, but for some, living with him the way he is now seems better than getting divorced.

Be aware, however, that if you stay with someone who demonstrates this partial change, it's important not to allow the situation to return to its former severity. In the absence of deep, meaningful change, an abuser may try to regain the control he lost by telling you that things would be even better if you stopped talking to this person, stopped being so hard on him, and so on. It's tempting to believe that he'll change even more if you capitulate.

Be very careful. Most of the time, the only reason you are getting partial change is because your husband has people looking over his shoulder. If you let go of that support, he will likely head straight back to the place you were in before. If he gets you to back off, he will see that as a sign of renewed weakness and signal to him that he doesn't have to worry about what he does to you, because you aren't going to do anything or go to anyone about it.

In short, if you are staying because he has changed "enough," keep doing whatever you did to make that change happen. Usually this means keeping in touch with the people who have at least helped you get to where you are now.

It's for the Children

Why do women believe it is best for the children to stay in an abusive relationship? There are a number of reasons.

You may feel that the children love their father, and you don't want to disrupt their relationship with him. And in fact, he actually seems to be a good father to the children in many ways.

You may fear that a separation or divorce could result in the loss of the children's affection for you, or even the loss of custody of the children. You may fear that a divorce will result in unsupervised visitation of the children with their father, and that something dangerous might occur if you are not available to protect them. This fear may be based on the fact that he has already been abusive or inappropriate toward or in front of the children, or it may be because he has threatened that he would harm them if you left.

Finally, some women stay because they believe it is better for children to grow up in an intact family than one in which the parents have divorced. You may worry about your children's *shidduchim*. You may worry about who will play the father's role in your children's lives if he is not around. You may simply worry about your children's general adjustment. Perhaps your parents got divorced, and you always promised yourself that you wouldn't do that to your children.

Is it better to leave for the sake of the children, or is it better to stay for the sake of the children? There is no one right answer to this question. Even within the same household, there may be some children who would do better if there was a divorce, and others who would gain from retaining the status quo. In some cases, a divorce brings the children relief from stresses associated with marital abuse and conflict, while in others a divorce can create stress of a different kind.

The nature of the conflicts in the household is an especially important factor. It is very detrimental for a child to observe physical violence. On the other hand, divorce can be particularly difficult for children if they become an instrument through which the abusive husband exerts control over his ex-wife.

Although there are those who think divorce is the worst choice for children, no matter what, you may also come across those who don't understand why you don't get out for the sake of the children. This is not a simple determination to make, particularly since some of the factors that must be considered involve hypothetical judgments regarding what might occur in the future. But as difficult as it might be to anticipate likely outcomes, and as confused as you might feel about the question, you are still the best person to make this decision.

If you are seriously grappling with this question, don't do it alone. Seek guidance, based on what is best for your children.

If you have considered carefully the pros and cons of staying, and you have decided to stay, then *no one* can tell you that your assessment is objectively wrong. The only possible exception to this is if your husband is abusing the children as well abusing you, or if the children are exposed to physical violence.

The Stigma of Divorce

Divorce affects many people: the woman herself, her children, her family. A woman may worry about disappointing her parents. This might reflect a general attitude about marriage and divorce in her family, or it may reflect things that are *going on* in her family. Some women are miserable and want to leave the marriage, but won't because of the effect it might have on their siblings' *shidduchim*. Others have a divorced sibling; they have seen the toll it has had on their parents, and can't imagine doubling that pain.

Some women feel that they would be unable to face the community, or particular people in the community, following a divorce. Women who are prominent leaders in the community might be particularly uncomfortable with the idea of getting a (possibly messy or public) divorce. This is especially true of women who are married to a prominent man. There is a fear that no one would ever believe that there is something wrong with their husbands, which naturally makes them fear that people will think there must be something wrong with them.

Women sometimes hesitate to divorce because of social responsibilities in their own family, such as a son's impending *bar mitzvah*, or the need to maintain a good public image for the sake of a daughter who is dating.

Fear of What He'll Do

A woman might stay because she fears her husband will commit suicide if she tries to leave, and she doesn't want to feel responsible for that. Perhaps the husband has even threatened to do so. Other women fear that they themselves will be harmed if they try to leave. Women who have been physically assaulted by their spouses in the past may fear that he will become even more violent if they try to leave. Some women worry that their decision to divorce will drive their husbands to harm the children or perhaps other family members. He may in fact have threatened as much.

In the situation where a woman is being assaulted, many people cannot understand why she wouldn't be more afraid to stay than to go. Remember, they don't know what you know. He will be his angriest, and potentially the most violent, when you challenge his control, and this is what leaving does. Your recognition of this reality is implicit in your thinking when you feel *afraid to leave*.

Leaving is Too Difficult

Many women decide not to leave their abusive marriage because they can't imagine how they will manage the divorce or living on their own. They are paralyzed by questions: Where will I live? Will I be able to stay in the house? How will I manage to pay a lawyer or *beis din*? How will I manage financially after the divorce? Who will support me emotionally? Where will the Yamim Tovim or Shabbos be spent, with and without the children?

If you are concerned that your family will shun you for your decision to divorce, you may worry about sources of emotional and financial support. This worry will be intensified if your husband has isolated you to such an extent that you feel as if you have no one you can rely on. It may be exacerbated as well if your husband has been able to cause a rift between you and your family or friends. Often, it is the most isolated and controlled women who feel they have no other option but to stay.

This list makes it clear that while the decision to stay may be a choice for some women, for others it is because they feel they have no choice. Whatever your own reason for staying, the rest of this chapter will offer some perspectives and suggestions that may help you cope if you have decided to stay even though the abuse has not ended.

Developing a Support Network

If you have chosen to remain in your marriage with your husband, it is highly desirable for you to maintain relationships with trusted friends or family members in whom you can confide. Women who remain in marriages with abusive partners often feel that having people in their lives who understand their situation helps sustain them. Having confidants who recognize what you are going through makes life more bearable, because you don't feel so alone.

Confidants can also validate your perception of what is happening, providing you with a sounding board against which you can measure your sense of reality. Women are often conflicted and ambivalent about their perception that they are being abused. In addition, a controlling and abusive husband may seek to convince his wife that he has done nothing really bad, and that she is overreacting. Having people with whom you can share your experiences can go a long way toward reassuring you that you are not losing your mind.

This does not include your children. Every now and then, a woman who has a need for support but a desire to keep things quiet uses a child as a confidant. This is never in the best interests of the children. It can cause them further emotional and psychological distress.

Choosing Your Confidants In the short term, the same criteria and considerations used for confiding in someone initially apply here. However, there are additional factors to consider when building a network of support for the long term. Some of those in whom you confide may have their own agendas that they seek to implement. Confidants who push their own agendas will end up being an emotional drain on you, rather than a source of strength.

One possibility is that a confidant will have a strong interest in keeping your marriage intact. While this might seem helpful if you have decided to stay, it is not always helpful. Some confidants will seek to minimize the severity of the difficulties you are experiencing, believing that if they fully sympathize with the abuses you describe, they will be encouraging you to end the relationship. They may act this way even though you have already made it clear that you have decided to stay. In this case, the confidant may hesitate to validate your experience, and instead give you speeches, *mussar*, and rationalizations that make you feel as if you are exaggerating the problems. Once you have decided to stay, it is *not* helpful to have a confidant tell you or imply indirectly that the abuse isn't that bad. This can really make you feel crazy.

On the other end of the spectrum, there may be a confidant who will fail to respect your decision to keep the marriage intact. She may respond to your complaints of your husband's abuses by constantly suggesting that the only solution is to get out. Some confidants in this frame of mind will even go so far as to ask you not to tell them your problems if you are not willing to take real action to help yourself. Even if this confidant does not directly recommend that you leave, she may communicate to you in a myriad of ways that she simply cannot understand how you can stay with this man.

Such a confidant is not helpful, because she is only adding to your distress by not respecting your decision. You already have a husband who is not respectful of your wishes. You will probably feel better if you have confidants who are. Give some thought to the likelihood that a potential confidant will be able to accept your decisions with respect to leaving the relationship or sticking it out.

Many people will find it difficult not to pressure you to do what they think is best for you, even if their idea of what should be done is very different from your own. And the more they care for you and your welfare, the more difficult it will be for them to be told, "Just watch and listen, but don't do anything."

> *Dini and Shani had been close friends for many years. Shani had always been a good listener when Dini told her what was going on in her marriage. Shani was honest about how she felt regarding Dini's situation and what she thought of Dini's husband. She thought the abuse Dini described was intolerable, that Dini needed to get out of the relationship, and that Dini's husband was an insufferable brute and control freak who was not likely to ever change.*

For a number of years, while Dini resisted Shani's suggestions that she leave her husband, Shani still continued to listen emphatically to the litany of abuses that Dini shared with her. Eventually, however, Shani became impatient with Dini for "not doing anything to help herself," and more insistent in her exhortations to "leave the relationship."

One day, following Dini's disclosure of a particularly offensive and demeaning instance of sexual abuse, Shani clearly felt that she could no longer tolerate hearing about the abuse if nothing was done to stop it. She told Dini, "If you're not going to do something about this, then you need to stop telling me about it. It is too painful and frustrating for me. So please don't talk to me about your marriage anymore."

Dini was stunned by Shani's reaction. Over time she had come to rely heavily on Shani's support. Now it felt as if her friend had pulled the rug out from under her. She felt betrayed, almost as if Shani had joined up with her abusive husband to hurt her even more.

When you are experiencing abuse, it is only natural for you to focus your attention on your own problems and lose sight of the emotional responses of others. When Dini was dumping her complaints on her friend, she saw Shani as a support she could lean on. She failed to consider Shani's emotional response to the disclosure and to Dini's choice to stay in the marriage.

If a confidant is really empathic toward your plight, she is vicariously experiencing some of the pain you are disclosing. You may need to give some consideration to the impact of your disclosures on her emotional health over a long period of time. If that confidant's natural response to such distress would be to act decisively by leaving the abusive relationship, your decision to remain in the relationship can be both intellectually frustrating and emotionally distressing.

While Dini had difficulty understanding Shani's reaction, it really isn't so surprising. Shani didn't understand that talking about what was going on is what Dini had chosen to "do about the situation." To her, that wasn't taking action. To Dini, it was.

Be aware that different confidants can have different reactions to the abuses that you disclose and to your responses to the abuse. Some confidants will be more alarmed than others by the abuse you report. Some will tend to agree with the decision that you have made to remain in the relationship, while others will strongly disagree with this response. And among those who would do something different, some will be better and some will be worse at tolerating the frustration associated with you pursuing your chosen course of action.

The confidant who does think you should stay, but is starting to feel overwhelmed at hearing about the abuse, might show her burnout in another form. She might start suggesting that there are things you can do to stop the abuse, or make him be less abusive. She might even suggest that you could be contributing to the problem: "Maybe you could be less negative, that might help." Although you might appreciate being supported in your decision to stay, this type of support will likely not feel very supportive.

As a result, you need to recognize the possibility that some confidants will burn out with respect to their empathic response. Some will simply not be able to remain supportive for extended periods of time. A confidant is, by definition, someone who cares for you. It is difficult for someone who cares about you to act as if she doesn't care that you are being hurt.

This is why a network is so important, instead of relying on a single confidant. When one source of support is lost, it is good to have other supports available. Having multiple confidants will also provide you with different perspectives on the abuse you are experiencing. This will help you make better judgments regarding the severity of the abuse, the danger to which you may be exposed, and the response options that are available to you.

If you become aware that a confidant seems to be getting impatient with your complaints, perhaps it is time to take a little break from talking with this person and reach out to another. Of course, this may be difficult, since one of the hallmarks of an abusive relationship is the isolation the abuser imposes. Nevertheless, to the extent that it is possible, try to develop multiple sources of support.

In an effort to facilitate this process, here are some suggestions regarding what to look for when you are seeking support.

Trust and
Respect Before you disclose your marital difficulties to someone, ask yourself, "Is this a person I can trust? Is he or she someone whose judgment I value with respect to other issues? When I have discussed other significant matters with this person, such as schools, parenting, and religion, have I valued his or her perspective and input?"

Go Slowly Try to "test the waters" to a degree before you reveal too much. Your potential confidant may have reservations about discussing subjects that she regards as "personal," or she may feel that it is not her place to get involved in the relationship between a husband and wife. She also may be the type to become overwhelmed by unpleasant accounts of abuse. Even though she is sympathetic, she simply can't process unpleasant details.

When you broach the subject of abuse, begin by simply mentioning that you have been having some trouble with your husband. This allows you to determine if your potential confidant is comfortable discussing such matters. As you disclose the nature of the difficulties, you might want to begin by describing the abuse in only the most general terms, to ascertain whether she can handle knowing the details.

Beware of
Minimizers Some people tend to minimize reported abuse. They may feel more comfortable if they deny how horribly your husband has treated you, or they don't want to fully comprehend the extent of the problem, since that would compel them to recommend that you take some action, which they are hesitant to do. Such people are simply not open to hearing the most negative aspects of your situation.

You might find that your confidant responds to your disclosures with comments such as, "Are you sure you're not misreading the situation?" or, "He must have had a stressful day and he just lost it. I'm sure he feels bad and it won't happen again," or, "You guys always seem so great to-gether. I can see that he loves you and I'm sure this will pass."

Regardless of why a given confidant would tend to minimize the problems you report, the effect is potentially quite harmful. His or her refusal to see the reality of the situation may be confusing for you, causing you to doubt your own sense of reality.

Beware of Pushers

Guard against confidants who push you toward a particular course of action, rather than allow you to make your own decisions. Such confidants may push you to leave the relationship, or they may push you to go to certain people or to undertake specific actions. You may hear something like, "You really need to tell your brother (or some other particular individual) about this situation," or, "Why don't you (do the following...)?" or, "I would never let my husband do that to me. You just tell him ..." or, "What you have to do is..."

Not only is this invalidating, it is also potentially dangerous. You may feel pushed to do something to please this person that you rely on so heavily, feeling that you owe something to him or her, while the course of action recommended is actually detrimental or even unsafe for you.

Educate Your Confidant

Of course, you have respect for your confidant, or it wouldn't mean anything to have her support. But this does not mean she has the necessary understanding of the dynamics of domestic abuse or issues of safety. If you have chosen to disclose the abuse you have been experiencing to a professional, that individual may have such knowledge, though as we mentioned before, it does need to be ascertained. If you are disclosing to a friend or a family member, there is an even greater chance that he or she won't have adequate understanding.

Give your confidant some information on the nature of domestic abuse. It is also important to make it clear why you have chosen to remain in the relationship. Finally, tell your confidant directly and clearly what it is that you want from her. Some confidants will automatically assume that you wouldn't be telling them this stuff unless you wanted them to *do* something. This may be the last thing that you want. Most likely, at least initially, you are only seeking validation and emotional support.

If you let a confidant know up front that you are seeking support rather than tangible action, it will go a long way toward avoiding the possibility that she will try to push you into a certain course of action.

Look Beyond His Family Members

Many women consider disclosing to one of their husband's family members. At least initially, this may be an attempt to get help for dealing with the husband's abusive behavior. Women hope that his mother, father, sister or brother can talk to him and get him to stop treating her inappropriately. If this person is sympathetic, even if he can't get the abuser to stop, he will often become the support person you lean on, because he already knows what's going on.

This connects to a related reason a woman might reach out to her husband's family — she doesn't want it getting out that her husband is abusive. His own family members are the least likely to "spill the beans." The woman assumes that she can tell them everything, since his family will be as invested as she is in keeping it quiet. And she is usually right.

So while it might make sense to have a member of his family as your confidant (as long as that family member does not divulge this, which could create an unsafe situation), this support can be limited in scope. It is not unusual for an abused wife to get sympathy and support from the husband's family, *as long as it appears that the relationship will continue.* If, however, you eventually decide to obtain outside help or to separate, do not be surprised if this sympathy and support disappear. This is why it will be to your benefit to have some support that is not related to your spouse in any way.

A Professional

Some women think that if they are not leaving the marriage, there is no role for a professional to play. You may even be convinced that a professional will tell you to leave the marriage. In fact, however, the ongoing, understanding and unconditional support that a domestic violence expert can provide can be a tremendous source of strength for women who live with abuse. A competent professional will understand everything you are experiencing and what goes into your decision making, and can respect your decision-making process without getting in its way or asserting an agenda of her own.

If you follow these guidelines in selecting and working with confidants, you'll find that you will have the best chance of getting the support that you need without undue pressure in any direction — without being told that there is really nothing wrong, and without being told that you must leave.

Adjusting for Childrearing Difficulties

Women who decide to remain in an abusive relationship often feel that keeping the marriage intact will benefit the children. But there are also significant difficulties in raising children when you are married to an abuser. Fortunately, there are ways to maximize your ability to provide your children with the best possible environment.

Once you understand the challenges and difficulties that your children face living in this situation, you will be able to make certain shifts in the way you parent your children that take your unique situation into account. This may mean giving up parental guidelines that would apply in a healthier, non-abusive situation.

Here are some of the problems that mothers in abusive relationships frequently experience with regard to the children, and some ideas for addressing those problems in your home.

Lack of Support Some abusive husbands consider raising the children to be the sole responsibility of the mother. You may find that he expects you to handle anything that comes up in regard to the children, without bothering him with it or asking him for anything.

You may feel it is important for your husband to help the children with their homework, positively interact with them on Shabbos, intervene with a *rebbi*, participate in a school activity, and so on. But your husband may feel that this is beneath him or "not his job." He may expect when he comes home each day to find the children all fed, bathed, and asleep. He may consider the children to be a disturbance and interference in his access to you.

> *Tikva relates: "If I go out to run an errand, no matter how I rush, as far as my husband is concerned I always take too long. If something happens in the house that is beyond his control — a pipe bursts, a child is crying, a Shabbos meal goes longer than expected — he explodes and blames me. He needs an inordinate amount of control and attention or he becomes angry and volatile.*
>
> *"On the one hand, I feel that my husband is a good person, a respected member of the community. His need for precision makes him very helpful around the house, although he also expects that everything be done his way, and will tolerate no input from me on almost anything. On the other hand, there is no end to his needs — and his needs must always come first.*
>
> *"I am embarrassed to say this, but I really think he is jealous of his own children. They have to be fed dinner, helped with homework, bathed and upstairs when he comes home from work. Even if it's not their bedtime, they know that they must stay upstairs for at least forty-five minutes after he comes home. Not only does he expect to have nothing asked of him for the children, I better not have to put something off, or put him off, because of the needs of the children!"*

Despite this, the abusive husband will often criticize you if the children fail to live up to whatever standards of behavior and achievement he wants. He may refuse to help a son with his math homework, yet criticize you if the boy does not do well in this subject. It is impossible to point out how unfair this criticism is, because the abuser holds himself above criticism and expects you to conform to his notion of how things should be.

Possible solutions:

It can be very overwhelming, especially in a large family, to have the entire responsibility of the household and the children on your shoulders. Explore possibilities for help that may be available to assist you in your various roles. Some schools have homework help programs, or after school programs. Does your husband allow you to have domestic help? If so, maybe you need more hours. If he keeps this very restricted, perhaps there's a way to keep him from knowing if you ask your help to stay a few extra hours. This obviously depends on your financial situation and how much time your husband spends at home.

Even if your options in alleviating this stress on the practical level are limited, you can control your own expectations. As difficult as it is keep up with the abuser's demands, your distress may be exacerbated by your unfulfilled hopes and dreams. Perhaps you imagined doing bedtime with your husband, or having him help the children with homework. Maybe you dreamed of a quiet scene, your husband learning with your son — instead of the yelling and belittling that actually takes place. You might have imagined a beautiful Shabbos table, where your husband asked the *parshah* questions and helped the children relate the *d'var Torah* they learned in school. Instead of these dreams, you have disinterest, harshness, and anger.

As painful as it might be to let go of these dreams, if you've made the decision to stay — and you know he's not changing — it's time to move on. Stop imagining the ideal father and mother who provide stability and nurture together. Find a time when he is not around to provide what you wish to provide for your children, but don't beat yourself up for what you had hoped he would provide. See if there is a way to supplement what they are lacking. Recognize, too, that under these circumstances, *not* having him around the children when he chooses not to participate in their lives in a positive way is probably better for them anyway.

Opposing Views

An abuser assumes that everything should be as he wishes. He will typically inform you of how things are to be handled, rather than discuss options. Whether or not your husband's expectations leave him with the belief that he has the right to dictate *all* of the smaller day-to-day decisions, he will almost certainly assume that he is in charge of making any *important* decisions regarding the children. This is usually manifested in decisions regarding the children's education, whether and where they should go to camp, if they should be permitted to pursue extracurricular interests, certain friendships, other outside activities/relationships, and so on.

This places you in a situation where you are expected to perform all the daily tasks of childcare, yet can give virtually no input regarding important decisions. This is particularly difficult when your closer involvement in routine care places you in a better position to make judgments about options that might be best for a child. Perhaps you have read more about parenting, know more about resources in the community, or have a clearer picture of any difficulties or weaknesses your child may have. Yet your husband is not interested in a suggestion that comes from you, which may be contrary to what he has already decided.

Possible solutions:

You can employ a number of different strategies to secure what is best for your children. Try to make it appear as if the preferred choices are recommended or endorsed by sources the husband respects or admires. These might include teachers, counselors, or your *rav*. There is a delicate balance here — the controlling husband can be sensitive to anything he perceives as an effort to manipulate him, or to get him to do anything that he has not decided for himself.

If being indirect does not seem to be working, consider if it would be safe to approach the person whose approval you were hoping to use, and ask him or her to approach your husband directly. "Safe" here means if you ask the person to approach your husband, but not let your husband know that you spoke to him or her, would that person keep your confidence?

For example, suppose you feel your child should have tutoring, or be involved in an after-school activity, or go to a particular program that your husband has said he doesn't want. Can you approach the school principal or counselor, let him or her know that your husband doesn't like this idea, and ask that the person call a meeting to encourage this idea with your husband directly — without letting on that you are behind the request?

If this sounds like it could work, but you are concerned about disclosing your situation to school personnel, keep in mind that you don't have to. It's not necessarily unusual for a woman to tell someone at school that it would be good for her husband to hear a suggestion directly from the principal. You don't need to mention abuse to ask for help in this way.

Once you're thinking in these terms — getting support from others *without* disclosing the abuse — you might come up with solutions to other issues.

He may not allow the children to spend Shabbos at a friend's home, participate in school activities, or have an outside activity or hobby, even when it's age appropriate. It could be, though, that if the suggestion does not come from you, and if you do not seem to have a vested interest in it, he will no longer feel a need to forbid the children from doing these things. The key is to recognize that it is all part of his desire to control you. If you can find ways to remove yourself from direct involvement, you may be able to expand your children's horizons.

Using the Children to Control You

This is often done subtly. It's a pattern you observe over time. You notice that when things displease him in some way, he takes it out on the children. Perhaps he is harsher or stricter with them, refuses to provide them with things they need, even blaming your incompetence for his bad mood and the need to teach everyone a lesson. Alternatively, you may notice that when you work hard to make your husband happy and do things exactly as he wants, he lightens up on the children in various ways.

Possible solutions:

Unfortunately, there are very few options here. It may help if you *stop* trying to talk the abuser out of this behavior. When you try to reason with him and beg him for better treatment of the children, he recognizes that he can hurt and control you by hurting the children. If instead you make it seem as if you are focused on keeping *him* happy, instead of making the children happy, it may appease his feelings of entitlement to control.

The more you talk about and focus on the children, the less he feels that his concerns are primary. Keep your priorities to yourself; give him the impression that he is always the priority. This might keep your children out of the line of fire.

Poor Role Modeling

Your husband models abusive, controlling behavior, and your children may start to follow his lead. They hear your husband criticize you, call you names, put you down, telling them that they need not pay attention to what you say. You may find that some of your children begin to behave toward you in this same way. They may also model this behavior toward their siblings; they may become bullies at school, as they imitate their father's behavior with their peers. Regrettably, it is also common for the male children of abusive fathers to become abusive husbands themselves.

Sometimes an abusive husband specifically tells the children to disregard their mother. At other times, he allows a child to do something which is in direct conflict with one of her standards. For example, the implied standard at the children's school doesn't allow going to movies — but your husband takes them anyway. Perhaps he knows you think the children aren't old enough to cross the street or walk to a friend on their own — but he lets them do it anyway. Perhaps you have specific bedtimes for the children, but when they beg to stay up later, he gives permission — even though he knows how hard you work to establish consistent routines.

The message here is, *"I'm* the boss. Not you, not the school, not anyone else."

Possible solutions:

Decide on a parenting philosophy and follow through. Do not be afraid to provide your children with structure and boundaries. Establishing appropriate expectations for behavior, setting limits, and enforcing rules help your children grow and blossom.

How do you do this? Start by looking for sources of parenting guidance that makes sense to you. There are numerous parenting books and resources readily available in bookstores, online, in public and private Jewish libraries (some women will have to hide any reading material from their husbands). Look some over, but don't try to use them all. Pick out one with which you feel comfortable.

Perhaps you have been inconsistent in your parenting and discipline because you are afraid of replicating the roughness and harshness they experience from their father. This is confusing discipline with abuse. It's important to differentiate between the healthy boundaries and limit setting of positive parenting, and the harsh, demeaning behavior of abuse.

What happens when women try to compensate for their husband's behavior by not setting any real limits? Can a woman assume that if she loves her children and is good to them, they'll turn out to be loving and good?

> *Kayla writes: "I don't understand it. When is all the good stuff that I showed them going to kick in? I mean, yes, they've seen how their father is. But I stayed so they would have a stable environment, and I treated them with love and care. Now I see them behaving like their father. When will they behave with the* middos tovos *that they should have learned from me?"*

Why doesn't this work? When a child sees one parent behaving badly and the other parent behaving positively, if there isn't any commentary or talk about these behaviors, the child understands that these are two different ways of behaving — *and both are acceptable.* If, when the child behaves badly, the mother resists disciplining in an attempt to compensate for her spouse's behavior, the child receives the message that his inappropriate behavior is also acceptable.

Women who think that their children somehow *know* that behaving as their father does is wrong should ask themselves, *"How* do they know that? And do they know of another way to act?"

You *can* provide your child with an alternative education about healthy and appropriate behavior. Begin by implementing appropriate discipline so they engage in appropriate behavior themselves. Do not shy away from discipline in an effort to make up for their father's harshness — it does not serve them well in the long run.

If your husband deliberately tries to undermine your attempts to provide structure and boundaries, try not to draw attention to what you are doing. Decide to discipline on your own so your husband has less opportunity to sabotage your efforts at asserting control in the parenting arena.

You can also address the poor role modeling directly with two methodologies: relationship skills training and cultivating positive role models.

RELATIONSHIP SKILLS TRAINING

If it's safe to do so, point out to your child (in private, if necessary) some of ways that his father behaves that are not appropriate. Then give your child suggestions regarding appropriate ways the situation could be handled. Pointing out the inappropriate behavior isn't enough. You also need to teach your child the proper attitude about marriage and how to treat one's spouse, as well as the right ways to handle conflict and relationships in general, so he will have the tools he needs to do it right.

- **Only briefly mention their father before moving on to the lesson.**

  "Remember when your father was calling me names? I need you to know that in a marriage both people should be respectful to each other, no matter what."

  "It is never all right to treat someone badly because we are frustrated. It's really important to always be a *mentsch*."

- **Engage your child in the process of thinking of alternative behaviors.**

  "What do you think you could do if you found yourself angry or frustrated with someone? What are different ways to handle that situation?"

- **Try to relate the skills you discuss to their real lives.**

  Have them practice with you or their siblings. "That was not a *mentschlich* way of speaking to me, your sister, your brother. You need to try that again."

All of this could become very dicey if your child then turns around and tells his father what you said. You must make some judgments regarding what you can say and when you can say it. The payoff is that your child will learn that your silence does not mean you have accepted abuse as appropriate behavior. He or she gets a clear message that it is not correct to act that way, along with lessons on appropriate ways to handle these situations. You are also sharing the appropriate perspective on marriage.

In this process, **you should not:**

- **Denigrate your husband.**

  "Your father's such a lowlife. You don't want to grow up to be like that, do you?"

- **Unburden yourself to your child.**

  "I can't take it when your father does this; he makes me so miserable. I don't understand what I did to deserve this; I don't know what to do anymore. Don't you ever treat your wife like this. You see what it's doing to me!"

There is a very difficult balance between naming the bad behaviors and avoiding name calling. Often, because this is so difficult, women just leave the whole thing alone and hope for the best. Unfortunately, without the training only you can provide, the abuser's attitudes and behaviors have a good chance of being repeated in the next generation.

CULTIVATE POSITIVE ROLE MODELS

You may be able to provide your child with appropriate adult role models by cultivating relationships with outside mentors such as a *rebbi*, counselor, recreation leader, coach, teacher, or instructors in music or martial arts. Perhaps there is a mentor program in your community.

You do need to be careful about the person with whom your child forms such a relationship. People with predatory tendencies look for vulnerable children to prey on. Monitor these relationships carefully by being involved and asking your children what happens each time they engage in such outside activities.

A controlling husband may resist the formation of such relationships, due to his basic insecurity and his need to be in complete control. It is possible to diffuse this resistance if the activities are popular ones in which many of your child's peers participate. Activities sponsored by youth programs in the shul are relatively difficult for a controlling father to resist and still maintain his standing in the community. The degree to which it will be possible for you to facilitate your child's getting involved with positive role models will depend on how controlling your husband is in this area.

The same strategies apply when you facilitate this for your child: Try to make it happen in a non-confrontational way, perhaps having it come as a suggestion from somewhere else; and keep your interest and investment hidden. As hard as it is to live with secrets, your best chance of getting your child's needs met may require living with that discomfort.

Here are some ideas you might consider in helping your children cultivate healthy role model relationships:

- Does your community have a big brother/big sister program?

- Does your child have an outside interest in sports, drama, music or art, and could the person running the program or the instructor be someone he or she looks to for guidance? These programs may have great value even if no mentoring relationship develops, simply because participation usually gives children a boost in self-esteem, which is especially good for children with a negative home environment.

- Is there a special friend or relative whom your child likes to spend time with? Do you have the sense that the friend's family is a good place for your child to be? If so, don't discourage your child from spending time there. You might encourage your child to accept invitations to spend weekends or vacations with the friend and his or her family. This will give your child an opportunity to see how the parents in other families relate to each other and to their children.

- Is there a teacher or counselor with whom you feel you may speak in confidence? If so, you might ask that person to take a special interest in your child, to facilitate his or her getting involved in school activities. This request might involve some disclosure of your husband's nature, as you see fit — depending on the particular circumstances. Having the school personnel actively seeking to involve your child might work, where your own suggestions would not.

PARENTING AROUND YOUR HUSBAND

All these solutions echo one common idea: the need to parent around your husband, so he does not sabotage your parenting efforts. Parenting around your husband is a fairly simple concept. If you wish to implement a particular parenting strategy, *avoid discussing it with your husband*. If he knows about it, he is likely to forbid you from following this strategy, or will otherwise undermine your efforts to implement it. Working to keep him out of your process of parenting may open up possibilities.

Consider the following questions:

- Which parts of your parenting perspective can you implement only if your husband doesn't know about it?
- If you are careful implementing those strategies, what would he notice, and what wouldn't he notice?

Susan's girls were doing okay socially and academically, but she saw a real downward spiral with her son Shaya. Shaya was very aggressive with his sisters. While he got along with his friends at school, his grades were seriously slipping.

Ronen, Susan's husband, would berate Shaya for his poor academics, but any attempt on Susan's part to intervene were thwarted or forbidden by Ronen. Susan spent a lot of time trying to convince Ronen to allow various strategies to address the problem, to no avail.

After struggling with this for a couple of years, Susan came to terms with the fact that the only way to do anything was to work around Ronen. The idea terrified her at first. But she thought if she

was careful about it, she might be able to accomplish something re-
ally positive for her son. So she decided to try it.

She began by speaking with the principal at school to see if it was
possible to have Shaya tested for learning issues, without her hus-
band being told about it. She explained a little bit about what was
going on, and the principal assured her that her husband did not
need to be informed. Susan next had to decide whether she felt safe if
Shaya happened to tell his father about "this woman Mommy took
me to talk to." She decided she would chance it and deal with the
consequences if she had to.

It emerged as a result of the testing that Shaya had no learning
issues. Instead, the school suggested a behavior modification system
at home, together with counseling. The school was able to provide
counseling on the premises during school hours, something Ronen
never knew about. In addition, Susan implemented a chart system
that centered around school performance and behavior with his
sisters. She worked on this with Shaya when her husband was not
home. This led to a dramatic improvement in her son.

Originally, Susan had felt that she had no options because her husband wouldn't allow her to do anything constructive. Contributing to
this problem was her conviction that everything had to be *shared* with
her husband. Once she was willing to work around him, she was able to
come up with a good solution and really help her son.

There was a degree of risk here for Susan. You might find yourself in
the same position, but with a more significant degree of risk — to the
extent that you are not willing to put yourself in that much danger. If,
on the other hand, you don't feel it would be too unsafe to try parenting
around your husband, perhaps you should consider it.

The natural question most women struggle with is, "Isn't that dishonest?
And isn't that wrong?" When this worry creeps up on you, ask yourself,
"Why am I being dishonest? What is my goal?" Are you doing this to help
your child have the healthiest possible upbringing? Are you lying by omis-
sion to get the help of a professional or an educator to further this goal?

There's no question that this is uncomfortable. In fact, in a regular parenting situation, withholding information would be considered highly inappropriate. One of the most basic rules of good parenting is that both parents need to work *together*: don't contradict each other, don't undermine each other, be consistent with your rules, and so on.

The problem arises when you try playing by the regular rules when you're in an irregular situation. *It doesn't work.* When your spouse is not interested in being on the same page because *he* wants control; when he *won't* work with you, purposely undermines you, uses the children to abuse you, or is even abusive to them directly; you simply can't use the same approaches that apply to a healthy, positive marital relationship. You do not have the foundation for these normal guidelines to be beneficial. It would be analogous to trying to use basketball rules to play football, rationalizing that "a sport is a sport is a sport."

You need to adjust your perspective on parenting. There is a significant difference between a marital relationship where these guidelines can work, and the reality of your own relationship. While in a healthy relationship, the guiding principle is for both parents to work together, in your relationship you will need to work alone and around your husband, to give your children the healthiest environment possible.

Creating Opportunities for Change for You

It's a natural expectation and desire for you to want to share your life with your spouse. You got married hoping for that connection. But your husband has a very different idea of marriage. Therefore, the first thing you need to do is shift your expectation regarding how marriage should be. If you want to make some changes for yourself to make life somewhat more bearable, you are going to have to look for other opportunities.

Again, the degree to which you will be able to do this is dependent on what is safe with your husband.

Friendships   Stop focusing on failed efforts to connect with or get support from your spouse. Think in a different direction: consider sharing with a friend or family member.

Your support people aren't just there to talk about the abuse. There may be things that you wish you could share with your husband — a child's issue or accomplishment, your own personal accomplishments, challenges with an ailing parent. These can be shared with those support people instead. And remember, you can be there for them too!

Sometimes it is hard to develop this "other" contact with friends because the abuse is so all consuming. You may also have to steal what time you do have, which does not allow you to have fun friend time. Still, when you contact your friends, make an effort to talk about other things in your life. Ask about what is going on with *their* lives, with their children and interests, even if you have to do so in secret because your husband would not allow this.

Activities   Consider if there is any outside activity, job, or volunteer work which you would find rewarding and that your husband would allow. What were your interests before you got married? What did you enjoy doing, or hope to do in your future? Then think about the best strategies for being "allowed" to pursue an interest. Ask yourself:

- Is there any way to present an interest so he will *want* you to do it? Perhaps you can make him feel that it reflects well on him.

- Consider asking someone who he respects to "ask you" to help with a shul or school project.

- Can you present it as something that you are not particularly excited about?

- Can you think of something you'd like to do that he would not feel threatened by?

- Is there something you could be involved in, or even a friendship that you could pursue, that he does not have to know about?

You may uncover possibilities you never considered before when you adopt this approach. Once you come to terms with what your marriage is really like, the shift in perspective can allow you to see different options. These might not be your first or second choices of options, but they are your options for making changes nonetheless.

Unfortunately, some women do not have these alternative options available to them, since the abuse is so extreme.

Preparing for a Possible Crisis

Some women stay in an abusive relationship despite knowing that there could be physical violence. Others feel secure that even though there is abuse and control, there hasn't been physical violence. *In either case,* it is important to make a plan in the event of a crisis. Being prepared for this possibility is important for you and your family.

When you plan in advance what you should do in an emergency, you won't end up in a panic, scrambling to figure out what to do, and likely winding up doing nothing because it's almost impossible to think and plan in the middle of a crisis. In addition, if you do not plan ahead, your options may be quite limited.

Develop a plan that provides you with guidelines regarding exactly what to do if violence appears imminent, or if your husband becomes violent and you feel you need to leave to thwart further escalation. Consider these questions carefully:

- What have you done before when you felt threatened? Have you ever left the house? If so, what happened then? What signs made you feel that you needed to get out? What was going on?

- Would you call the police if you were in danger? Do you know what their response might be and what your rights are in such a situation?

- Do you understand the need to speak to a *rav* about leaving — if not before you leave, then after you have left?

- What is the probability that violence will escalate if your husband catches you leaving or finds you after you have left?

- Do you have a safe place to go to in the event that you have to leave? A safe place means someplace where, if necessary, your husband will not be able to find you. Many abused women choose to go to a relative's home. Think through whether this is actually a safe choice. Will your husband be able to track you down there? If he does find you there, will you be protected?

- Do you have the number of an abused women's shelter where you could go in the event that you need to leave and have no other place to go?

- Do you know what an order of protection is? Do you think an order of protection would be helpful? Would you be willing to enforce such an order if that became necessary? Is there a *rav* you can talk this over with?

- Do you have important documents put away in a safe place, preferably somewhere outside of your home, such as with a friend, family member or in a safe deposit box? These should include: (1) birth certificates for you and your children; (2) immigration papers or passports; (3) your children's medical records and their school/vaccination records; (4) a list of important phone numbers (domestic abuse hotline, Rabbi, battered women's shelter, lawyer, hospital, counselor); (5) social security numbers (important for shelter placement); (6) *Kesubah*; (7) marriage license; (8) public assistance ID/Medicaid cards; (9) lease, rental agreement, or house deed; (10) insurance policies or information; (10) documents for any savings you have; and (11) documentation of the abuse you have endured. Might you need to consider keeping such documents in a safe place outside the home?

- Do you have an emergency cash reserve?

- Do you have access to a car? Do you have a set of keys hidden so they cannot be taken away from you?

- Do you have the number of a *rav*, therapist or abuse hotline that you could call to talk things over if you need to leave?

After considering the above questions, review the following emergency plan checklist. Make sure you have made provisions for each of the items on the list.

EMERGENCY SAFETY PLAN CHECKLIST

_____ 1. I know the fastest route out of the house.

_____ 2. I have important documents and items in a safe place.

_____ 3. I know where I can go if I need to leave home in a hurry.

_____ 4. I have all the important telephone numbers I need written down and in a safe place.

_____ 5. I have a signal or code word worked out with a friend that will alert her to call a previously designated individual or the authorities for help.

_____ 6. I let a neighbor know that she should call a previously designated person or the authorities if she should hear screams or any other alarming sounds.

_____ 7. I have instructed the children on how to get out of the house quickly and which neighbor they should go to.

_____ 8. I have taught the children how to call 911.

_____ 9. I have informed a rabbi of my situation, should I need to call the authorities.

_____ 10. I have set aside in a safe place enough money to take a taxi to safety, or I have secure and immediate access to a car.

_____ 11. I have developed strategies to calm my husband down long enough to get out of the house, if he should become violent.

_____ 12. I understand that the kitchen and bathroom are dangerous rooms to be in should my husband become violent. I will get to a safer place in or out of the house.

Finally, should you need to leave or go to the authorities because of your husband's abuse, you should have as much documentation as possible of what has transpired. These documents could include:

- copies of police reports
- hospital records or doctor's notes attesting to injuries you may have received

- a diary of incidents of abuse, including dates and descriptions of what happened
- a record of discussions you have had with different individuals regarding the abuse, including dates
- a record of any witnesses to the abuse that you know of
- pictures of the injuries, if available
- any relevant tape recordings (these may or may not be usable in civil courts in your area, but are admissible in *beis din*)

The decision to remain in an abusive relationship is complex and difficult. There could be many good reasons why you choose to stay, and you may be convinced that the potential risks are manageable. Even so, it is better to be prepared for a crisis and not to ever have to put your plan into effect, than to find yourself in crisis and not know what to do.

Summary

In some ways, all women choose to stay. In a sense, anyone who doesn't leave at the first incident of abuse — and almost no one does — has, in some way, decided to stay. As time passes, some choose to stay for a while; some stay forever.

There are strategies that can help you with the relationship if you decide to stay. All should be considered carefully to determine that they meet your needs and will be safe for you and your children. For the most part, they will be more easily accomplished if you shift your perspective on what is appropriate for you to do in order to make the situation work.

Many of the strategies are easier to achieve when you do not continue to try to create a loving, mutually respectful relationship with your husband (assuming that he shows no interest in doing so). As long as you keep up that hope, you will share plans and concerns as would be expected in a normal, hopeful relationship. But when you share your plans or hopes with an abuser, it usually results in his having a better understanding of the areas in which he can control you. In your situation, this sharing will only undermine your efforts to get yourself and your children what you need.

Chapter Seven

Leaving Your Abusive Marriage

The decision to leave an abusive marriage may come after two months, two years, two decades or more. Some women never come to make this choice. So what pushes a woman to take this ultimate step?

For some, the cumulative effect of abuse has finally gone beyond a certain point. For others, it is a particularly nasty or violent incident. Yet another might have tried for change — without success.

Whatever your reason, in a domestic abuse situation, this decision must include attention to psychological and physical safety. It is important to get guidance from people who know about domestic abuse, a *rav* knowledgeable in the halachic and *hashkafic* issues associated with divorce who understands domestic violence, and a knowledgeable lawyer, in case your husband pushes you into court.

There are several issues that typically arise throughout the course of the divorce process, and many will be discussed in this chapter. Life, however, is not a recipe, and it's not possible to write a cookbook that lists the precise steps and the order in which to take them to achieve a particular outcome. Different issues will arise in each situation; women will deal with these issues at different times in the process. When taken as a whole, however, this section will provide you with important guidelines for each stage of your personal process.

Prepare for Stress

You will be experiencing certain stresses that are associated with getting divorced. If you haven't already established a network of people to help you, now is a good time to seek out those who can support you through this process. If you have been completely isolated until now, and fear for your safety has propelled you to consider divorce, you may not have the leisure of discussing your situation with someone before making a move away from the marriage. Being aware and prepared for the issues you might have to confront will be critically important.

Pressure to Change Your Mind

Almost all women will face this — perhaps from the abuser, from individuals, or from the community at large: pressure to change your mind. Getting divorced is never a quick process, which gives the abuser (and anyone else who disagrees with your decision) time to try to pressure you or talk you out of your choice.

Sometimes the abuser will use aggression and threats to try to dissuade you. His attempt to halt the process may also come in the form of protestations of love and promises to change — if only you give him one more chance!

And in fact, this may be an option. If this is the most drastic step you've ever taken, and if you've never tried for true change, as described earlier, perhaps this is your chance to see if change can really happen. Just remember — promising is easy. Change is hard. If you've reached the point of making a decision, it's probably in your best interests not to reverse it without seeing evidence of that change.

Your past experiences may have taught you that you can't take his promises seriously. Perhaps you've already tried for change and he hasn't changed. And perhaps the abuse has been so extreme that you're not willing to reconsider under any circumstances. In cases where the abuser recognizes that *you* can't be fooled any longer, he may try to get *other* people — who typically don't have the complete picture — to convince you to give him another chance. These may be people you are reluctant to refuse. Or he may speak generally to random people, in the hope that one of them will decide to help by talking to you.

Abusers can be very successful at getting people to believe that this divorce is without cause, a tragedy they should try to stop. These emissaries may tell you that this is a terrible, misguided decision — how could you do this to your family? It's likely they have good intentions. But they don't understand an abuser's ability to be manipulative, and they only have *his* perspective on his behavior, remorse, or promises for change. When he talks about vague difficulties, cries, and professes his regret and his love for you and the children, a divorce will indeed seem like a tragedy.

These emissaries have no information on the extent of your suffering. They might cast you in a terrible light, making you sound frivolous, flighty, and coldhearted with regard to marriage and your family. You may get lectures in the street from neighbors, letters from elderly relatives questioning your judgment or *frumkeit*, some intimating that you probably made this decision without thinking it through from every angle. People may be sent to pressure you, your parents, your *rav* or your therapist.

In actuality, of course, most women have tried many different strategies before coming to this decision. Along the way, you have hopefully cultivated a network of people, including a *rav*, therapist, friend or family member, whom you can speak to when you are feeling frustrated with these comments and assumptions. It may not keep those who think they know better from approaching you, but this support will help you feel more confident.

Unwanted Advice

You may find that casual friends, distant family members or members of the community whom you barely know take it upon themselves to offer you advice. They may urge you directly to reconsider your decision, either for the sake of your grieving husband or for the sake of the children. They may warn you that the world can be difficult for a "divorced woman." They may tell you that you won't be able to find a new spouse. They may tell you that you will have difficulties with your children. They may make it clear to you that they will not be welcoming or accepting toward you if you follow through with these plans. In short, there may be any number of different approaches that they might bring to bear on you to shift your thinking.

Many women feel trapped in this situation. Saying nothing in response to these accusations feels like you're agreeing with Aunt Tilly, Mrs. Schwartz, Mr. Berger or Rabbi Miller when they disparage you, your decision, or your attempts for change. Explaining yourself, on the other hand, is tremendously invasive. You've already had to share the lurid, demeaning details with enough people. Just sharing with the people you need to in the divorce process is more than enough.

In general, most women try to minimize what the community knows, partially for their own dignity, but especially for their children. So while letting the intrusive do-gooder know that you were beaten, called names, forced to be intimate, or never allowed to speak with your friends might get him to keep his assumptions or suggestions to himself, you probably would prefer not to give any more people this level of detail.

The best strategy to employ is to thank the person for her concern, but tell her firmly that she does not have all the facts, you do not think it is appropriate to frivolously relate personal details, and you have sought responsible guidance for everything you are doing.

> *Tzipora was thirty-five years old with four children when she discovered her husband Yaacov was being unfaithful to her. She told him to leave the house, but although her family thought she should immediately ask for a get, Tzipora decided to give him a chance to change. They each went into counseling.*
>
> *During therapy, Tzipora realized that her husband's unfaithfulness was not the real issue in her marriage. There had been a*

prolonged pattern of abuse and control throughout the marriage, including a few occasions of physical violence. Tzipora had suffered the abuse because she told herself that Yaacov really loved her, in his own way, and that it wasn't enough reason to break up a family. His unfaithful behavior shattered the illusion of the deal she had made in her mind: "I put up with Yaacov's control and abuse, and in turn, I have his total love and dedication." When Yaacov's devotion turned out to be a mirage, Tzipora took a fresh look at everything that went on in her marriage. She realized that she had to confront and demand change not only in terms of his adulterous behavior, but also for his abusive behavior.

While Tziporah did try to work with Yaacov for change, she ultimately decided she could not stay in the marriage. Yaacov did profess regret for his unfaithful behavior and expressed his willingness to re-dedicate himself to her and to their marriage, but he refused to validate or move toward changing the abusive behavior. When she tried to address the control and abuse, Yaacov would accuse her of trying to make things worse, or he would change the subject, letting her know all the things he was going to do to regain her trust: let her have access to his texts, e-mails, phone log, and so on — while never addressing or acknowledging the other issues.

To most of those involved in the situation, the focus was solely on Yaacov's infidelity. Tzipora only wanted to share the issue of abuse with the most significant people. She felt humiliated and worried about how people would view her boys if they knew their father was abusive. As a result, there was an entire group of people who knew about the separation, knew it was because of infidelity, knew Yaacov was in treatment, remorseful, and desperate to do whatever it would take to regain her trust — because that had been the public reason for the separation.

Tzipora was dismayed when these people came over to her, and while acknowledging that what Yaacov did was wrong, would implore her to see how sorry he was and all the changes he had set in motion to regain her trust. They would say things like, "He's so sorry, how can you throw your family away? Don't let your pride get in the way of reconciling. Think about your children!"

In her distress, Tzipora wasn't focused on the fact that these comments were coming from people who only had half the picture. She became highly disturbed by what she perceived as insensitivity and lack of support.

While you may not want to disclose the entire truth of your situation, if you are planning to bring in someone as support or to seek advice, it is important that you give him or her the whole picture.

AN EXTREME RESPONSE

The decision to leave the marriage is likely to bring about an extreme response. Abuse is about power and control, and the decision to divorce represents the ultimate threat to this control. The response is his attempt to get back in control. It may be immediate, or it may occur after applying pressure has been unsuccessful.

Threats   When pleas and pressure from others doesn't work, the abuser may attempt to use threats to intimidate you. He may try to dissuade you from your plans to divorce, or he may try to weaken you for the court or *beis din* process. He may blame the failure of the marriage on you. You may start hearing rumors about yourself: that you have always been a bad wife, that you are insane, that you have been unfaithful, or that you are too attached to your mother.

He may threaten suicide. He may threaten to take the kids away. He may threaten to never give you a *get*. He may attempt to make life difficult for your family. He may refuse to give you an equitable financial settlement, or even threaten to withhold financial support for the children. He may drag out the divorce process to wear you down financially or emotionally so you will give up. He may threaten physical harm to you and your children.

When the threats start, stay strong. Keep your record of events close by and your support network closer, so you are in close proximity both to your emotional protection and the physical proofs you have gathered for protection from his threats.

As frightening as these threats can be, for many women they are oddly comforting. They confirm her choice to continue with the divorce process. They are proof that despite those people who kept pressuring her to relent and convince her that he's changed, in fact she was right: He hasn't changed at all.

Violence   One of the most dangerous times for an abused woman is during or after a separation. This act is a challenge to the authority your husband feels he is entitled to have over you. He may respond with the strongest possible attempt to regain control: violence.

A woman who has endured physical abuse will be aware that her decision to divorce may result in a violent response. But even a wife who has never been physically assaulted should recognize that the announcement of her intention to seek a divorce may be viewed as an inexcusable insult and defiance of her husband's previously unquestioned authority. It is potentially a dangerous time, and one that you should plan for accordingly.

Planning for your physical safety means thinking through your plan for announcing your intentions to divorce, using the guidelines mentioned earlier in planning for a crisis. In addition, consider the following scenarios and possibilities:

Some women will feel safer asking for a divorce *after* removing herself and her children from the marital residence. Think about what you know of your husband and what you have seen him do, and be aware that this will make him angrier than he has ever been. Then seek appropriate guidance and decide your best course of action.

If you can't or don't want to leave your residence, but you need to let your husband know that you want a divorce, think of ways you can keep yourself safe during this time. Sometimes having a parent or other family member move in will keep the tensions under control. But this can also escalate tension and the potential for violence. Some women have told their husbands this decision in the presence of their *rav* or a therapist, so the abusive husband knows that there are other people involved who are aware of what is going on. Again, you have to think carefully about your husband and your situation and what will be safe for *you.*

In making this plan, it's important to take halachic and legal issues into account. Can you leave with the children before informing him? Is there a place you can stay during this period? What about allowing him to see the children? How might this work, and what are your options if you are fearful about this? If you are not fearful, what are the arrangements? Consult with someone about these details. Make sure you have the answers so you can proceed with the likelihood of the safest possible outcome.

WHOSE DECISION IS IT?

If you find yourself nagged by recurring doubts about leaving your marriage, ask yourself: "Am I hesitating because this is big and scary — but I know it's the right decision? Or am I hesitating because I'm not sure if it's the right decision?"

Most women who decide to divorce have had a great deal of advice and counsel from friends, family, counselors, and/or religious advisers. The opinions obtained from these different sources often contradict each other, and this can be very confusing. Remember that no matter how much they care about you or how well meaning their input may be, these advisers have not experienced what you have experienced. They have not felt what you have felt. And they do not have to live with what comes after the decision to leave.

If you are feeling pushed or pulled, take some time to focus on your feelings regarding your decision. If you feel hesitant, but recognize that this is solely because of how frightening divorce seems, let your support people know that. If they sense hesitation, some people will assume you are questioning your decision, so they may push you to keep trying to save the marriage — when what you really want is that they should hold your hand through the process.

Alternatively, you may be hesitating because you need more time for processing the decision, but the support people in your life can't understand what you're waiting for. The people you turn to for support may not have the stamina to see you all the way through the process at *your* pace. They just want to see the issue come to a conclusion, and they start to push you. As painful as it is to live in an abusive marriage, living forever in the realm of "what if" can be a different kind of torture.

> *Malka was quite young when she got married, and she was still young a year later when she went to discuss her marital situation with her parents. She wanted to solicit their help and support in confronting her husband. After a year of controlling her in most areas of her life, that night for the first time he had hit her.*
>
> *Her parents were horrified. After hearing all that had gone on in the past year — how the abuse had started right away, extended into almost all areas of their life together, and now escalated into violence — they told her she was coming back home. Malka's parents used their position in the community, their connections, and the threat of police action to move the process along and push for her get.*
>
> *Malka ended up in counseling afterward because she could not make peace with the fact that she had not given her husband any opportunity to change. Intellectually, Malka believed that her parents were probably right, and that it was best for her to get out while she had the leverage to do so quickly. But emotionally, she couldn't help regretting that she hadn't even tried. For years, she wondered, "What if?"*

It can be unsettling to have regrets that you can't do anything about. This affects your peace of mind. Very few women — even those in extremely abusive relationships — are happy to leave their marriages, especially if there are children. No one dreams of growing up and getting divorced. But you are likely to feel better about it if you can leave with the certainty that you have done everything you reasonably could to work things out and effect some change in your husband's behavior.

Even if your efforts were completely futile, you will have peace of mind with the knowledge that you tried your best.

Don't allow anyone to rush you out of the marriage so quickly that you wonder whether it could have worked. On the other hand, if you know this is the decision you need to make, resist allowing outsiders to keep throwing new ideas into the mix to try to help your marriage. They do not live and understand the context of an abusive marriage, and they cannot appreciate the finality and difficulty of your decision.

QUESTIONS ABOUT THE FUTURE

Once a woman starts to move toward divorce, she may allow herself to begin thinking about the future. Until now, many women have only been able to focus on getting away from the abuser. Now a woman may start worrying about being alone, wondering whether she will ever get a chance to establish a loving and satisfying marriage. Of course, there is no way to answer this question. Some divorced women do remarry, and remarriages, like first marriages, are variably rewarding and satisfying.

Do your concerns about the future indicate whether you are ready for this decision? While almost no one wants to be alone, divorcing in order to find someone else to marry is not a good decision. No one knows what the future holds. Certainly, you can hope to have a good marriage with a kind man in the future. But divorce is for when you can say to yourself that at this point, you would rather be alone indefinitely than stay married to this man. Divorce is for when staying with your husband is more unbearable than living alone.

Financial Support Anticipating how you will manage financially during and after a divorce is a serious issue. You will need to have sufficient financial resources to support yourself and your children. Many women who divorce expect that their husbands will provide these resources, or at the very least a substantial proportion of the necessary resources. Even when a woman realizes that the abusive husband may fight providing support in an effort to exert control, she may not recognize how far things can go.

The reality is that even if your husband is mandated to provide support by *beis din*, court, or through mediation, and even if he is good about paying the support (rather than playing games by not paying or paying late), there are still two issues that commonly cause problems. First, there is the length of time it takes to reach an agreement or mandate of support. From the time you request a divorce until you actually have a divorce and support, you may not be getting much from your husband financially. Second, even after things are settled, you are likely to receive substantially less than what you and your children need to live.

It is therefore best to consider various options in advance: how you will support yourself during the in-between period, and how you will supplement the support for the long term.

If you have personal financial resources, make sure these are under your control and easily accessible. If you will be relying on your family for support, sit down with them and find out what they can and can't do. This may mean asking your family to prepare their home for you and the children to move in, or it may mean setting up a residence of your own to which you can move directly upon leaving your husband. Sometimes families pitch in for legal or *beis din* fees, and daily living expenses.

If you have no personal resources and no family or other sources of support on which you can rely, you will need extensive planning and action well in advance of informing your husband that you will be seeking a divorce. You may want to get a job, or obtain training or education that will enable you to become self-sufficient. You may decide to delay telling your husband that you want a divorce to give yourself time to prepare.

Be cautious during this period, and don't be surprised if your husband undermines your plans — even though he doesn't actually know about them!

> *Lori made the decision to leave her marriage. But she had no resources: She had no access to the family finances, she was not working, and her parents lived out of the country and were without financial means.*

Lori therefore decided to get a job. Although she knew she could go on public assistance, she was nervous about the idea of leaving without so much as fifty dollars in her pocket.

Lori started working and to her astonishment was even able to start putting away some money. Her husband didn't demand that she turn her salary over to him. She couldn't believe it.

And then the other shoe dropped. Her husband came home one day and announced that he had been let go. He would be getting unemployment benefits, but he let her know that if she didn't pitch in her salary for rent, they wouldn't make it.

Lori wasn't ready to leave her marriage yet. But with her salary being used for rent, she wouldn't be able to accumulate as much money as she had originally hoped.

You may need to look into public assistance as a resource. There are many government subsidy services for people in need, up to and including shelters. Women sometimes don't consider this option because they feel the stigma of utilizing these services. But if you have no other options, that's what these programs are for. A domestic violence program will be able to direct you and possibly help you navigate the programs and services that exist in your area.

Your plans for financial support will vary, depending on your access to personal and family resources, your education and employment skills, and any special expenses that you may need to meet. From the moment you decide that divorce is the only option, plan to aim for self-sufficiency. Be prepared with your family's financial information as you go into this process. Even if you do not have access to the finances, if you can find documentation of your husband's assets (and it's safe to do so) make copies of bank statements, bonds, CD's, investments or properties. If you do have access to money, find a way to secure it in preparation for leaving — and so your husband can't seize it when you tell him you want a divorce.

Before you take any action, keep your safety foremost in mind. You will also want to make sure that everything you do is halachically and legally permissible.

What comes as an extremely unpleasant reality is a situation where everything has finally been settled, your husband has started paying what he will be required to pay, and you realize that you will not be fully covered financially. Even if your husband was financially controlling, if you haven't had to worry about rent, tuition, utilities, and other household expenses, getting divorced will probably be something of a shock. Though you might have had to beg for money in the past, at least it happened within the privacy of your marriage. For a lot of women, it is particularly demeaning when they have to rely on others, or go on public assistance: now their neediness is more public. With time you will likely get your feet back under you, but it will be a struggle that may go on for a while.

What About the Kids?

Many women endure an abusive relationship out of a belief that their sacrifice will benefit the children. Perhaps your husband abuses you, but you think he is still a good father. Perhaps you believe your children deserve to have a father; perhaps you don't want them to endure the stigma of divorce (and perhaps they are almost in *shidduchim*).

Some women will stay indefinitely; some until after the children have grown up and are married or living on their own. Sometimes, however, something happens to tip the scale, and a woman decides to leave *because* she believes it will be best for her children.

Informing the Children   Given the importance of the children's welfare in your decision about divorce, their reaction to your decision and to the ensuing transition will be a matter of great concern. In some cases, the children have been anticipating the possibility of divorce for some time. In other situations, they will be surprised that you are taking this step. If the situation was very bad and they were quite aware of it, they may even have been looking forward to your taking action. Needless to say, if your husband was abusive to the children as well as to you, the children may be relieved. On the other hand, if they were not exposed to your husband's abusive side, they may have a good relationship with him, and they may be frightened or upset at the thought of losing him. In any case, children are often very frightened by the uncertainty that divorce generates, and they are quite likely to be apprehensive regarding the stigma they associate with being a child of divorced parents.

The way you inform them about your decision will affect the way the children react. Research supports a set of principles regarding how children should be told:

- Don't inform them until the decision is final
- Wait until immediately before something is actually going to happen before telling them
- Tell your children together
- Reassure them that the divorce is not their fault
- Be specific — let them know exactly what is going to happen
- Describe how their lives will change

While this is ideal, recognize that in your case, you almost certainly will not be able to follow all these guidelines. If you are divorcing because of abuse, it is highly unlikely that you will be able to sit down and negotiate with your spouse so you can present the details to the children calmly, with a unified front. Abused women often must leave suddenly, or the abusing husband is removed in the midst of a crisis. He may use the children to hurt you (as described earlier) or blame you for the breakup of the family. The reality is that you don't know exactly what is going to happen, or how their lives are going to be affected. You may find yourself simply reacting to what your husband does at any point in the process.

Despite these likely uncertainties, there is one thing you can control: *how* you communicate with your children. Communicate honestly and appropriately, and keep the lines of communication open. This enhances your ability to help them through the process.

Libby began experiencing recurring nightmares which caused her to lose so much sleep that she literally could not function during the day. In her dream, Libby was eight years old — the same age as her daughter. She was wandering down a long hallway. At the end of the hallway was a door with a big bolt and lock. Just as she tried to push open the lock, she woke up in a panic. This happened night after night, and once she woke up from the dream, Libby was unable to fall back asleep.

Why was this dream so frightening? And why was she experiencing it now? Libby didn't know, and she decided to get professional counseling to see if she could resolve it.

Libby's therapist told her that immediately after awakening, she should write down all the feelings she remembered having in the dream. At her next session, Libby described feeling lost as she walked down the hall — with no awareness of where she was coming from or where she was going. When she first looked at the door, she knew there was something important behind it, something that she was supposed to get to. But she could never get through the door because the panic would set in and wake her up.

Eventually, Libby and her therapist concluded that the dreams and her feelings were connected with her parents' divorce when she was eight years old — the same age her daughter was now. Libby remembered knowing that her mother wasn't happy, but she also remembers thinking that the divorce was an abrupt surprise. One day her mother picked her and her sister up from school, drove to a new apartment and announced that this was her new home.

At some point, they started having infrequent visits with their father. Libby always wondered when their father was going to start staying with them in their new apartment, and she remembers being confused as to why he wasn't staying there already. It wasn't until Libby was in high school that she found out that her parents had actually been divorced for years. She felt foolish for her lack of awareness.

The feelings came back now, when her daughter turned eight, and the adult Libby recognized that she had been very much affected by this lack of information and understanding about her own parents. Libby realized that her fearfulness and extreme shyness were borne out of this experience of knowing that there was more to know — but not knowing what it was. Years later, Libby felt terribly resentful of how this had been handled.

There is no formula that will tell you exactly what to say. Take the time to think about how to explain the situation to your children in the most reassuring manner possible, taking into consideration your children's personalities and what they are capable of understanding. There are books specifically on this subject that can help you think through this process. If you find that your situation does not perfectly fit the recommendations, think of the suggestions as loose guidelines for you to follow where possible.

Deciding *when* to talk to the children is also a key consideration. Telling them before you tell your husband means possibly exposing your plans before you're ready, or before it is safe to do so. Telling them after you tell your husband might mean telling them in the midst of a crisis, rather than being able to calmly prepare them — but this might be the safest thing for you. Thinking this through before you reach a state where you *have* to tell the children will make the task much easier. Getting professional guidance and intervention is ideal.

It's usually when there is an extreme — too much or too little communication — that issues tend to arise.

During Naomi's first kallah *class, the teacher mentioned that sometimes difficult or inappropriate things can happen to girls in their homes or in another setting. She encouraged them to work these issues out before getting married.*

Immediately after class, Naomi approached her teacher to describe what she was coping with at home. Naomi's father, a well-respected member of the community, had been emotionally, physically, economically, and sexually abusing her mother for years. Naomi's mother needed support, but was terrified of having people find out what was happening in her home, so she refused to speak to anyone about the situation — not a friend, a family member, or a professional.

Instead, Naomi's mother turned to her daughter for support. She would place Naomi right in the middle of the disputes — by encouraging her to get things from her father, or hide things from her father. The worst part, Naomi felt, was her mother's emotional dependence. She would cry to her daughter, describing her distress as she tearfully told her all the things her father did to humiliate her. More recently, since Naomi had become a kallah, *her mother had also begun to confide her pain at the demeaning things her father did to her in the bedroom.*

Naomi now realized how much this was affecting her outlook on marriage and her ability to look forward to her own relationships. She was concerned about how this would impact her upcoming marriage — that she would be unable to fully connect and open up to her future husband.

This is an extreme example of the inappropriateness of discussing the details of abuse with a child. Triangulating a child into the relationship between the parents is never healthy. Not only did Naomi fear marriage as a result, but since her mother had made her a confidant, Naomi felt guilty each time she left her mother at home. This compromised Naomi's ability to become an independent adult.

What to Share   While gratuitous sharing of information about the abuse in your marriage is a bad idea, there is a circumstance under which carefully and appropriately sharing some facts is necessary. This is the situation if your husband attempts to alienate your children from you.

Parental alienation is commonly observed when one spouse wants to divorce but the other does not. If you are divorcing an abusive husband, it is possible that he will express his fury with attempts to alienate the children. Many abused wives attempt to do the "right thing" by refusing to say negative things about the father of their children. They may even hesitate to defend themselves from the negative things he is saying about them. While ordinarily it is inappropriate for one parent to contradict or speak badly about the other parent to the children, there are times when this can backfire. These are the times when it may be crucial for you to stand up for yourself and tell your side of the story.

In addition to the abuse that Bracha suffered, her husband also began to lessen his religious observance. Although Bracha managed to maintain her religious standards, her husband would berate her, ridicule her and demean her for continuing their "old way of life."

Eventually — after trying for intervention and seeking help, to no avail — Bracha decided to leave. While she might have continued to suffer the abuse for the "sake of the children," her husband started being mechalel Shabbos *openly; he also told the children that certain* aveiros *weren't "so bad" and that other* halachos *could be ignored.*

During the separation and divorce process, Bracha tried to keep the children out of the nastiness and controversy. Still, they seemed angry and withdrawn from her. When she finally asked one daughter why she was so upset, she responded, "All Tatty wanted was for you to be with him in life. You chose to throw him out rather than make some compromises!"

Bracha realized that while she was trying to preserve her children's relationship with their father and spare them the difficulties of the divorce process, this clearly was not her husband's agenda. Instead, her husband encouraged the children to believe that their mother "threw him away" and split up the family over "nothing."

When you find yourself following the rule of "don't talk badly about your spouse to your children" but your spouse refuses to play that game, you may want to consider an alternative. If you don't explain yourself, or correct an "explanation" of your husband's, your children will be left to conclude that you agree with *his* version of events, and your husband's distorted perspective will become fact.

This does not compromise the general principle of not talking negatively about your spouse. In a divorce situation, it is best not to talk about your spouse to your children unless you are giving a general explanation about the divorce, *or* to respond to a question from a child about the divorce. When children make statements such as those of Bracha's children in the above case — statements which are usually provoked by something their father said — they are actually asking a question. They are asking you if what he said is true.

Inquiries from children often come in the form of a statement, and these statements are often made in an aggressive, assured way. This often leaves the mother speechless, because she doesn't want to speak negatively about their father. But these children are actually confused and need you to respond. They are really saying, "Daddy said XXX, is that true?"

It is important to clarify the situation, rather than saying a general, "That's not true." Until you offer a concrete alternative explanation to what their father has proposed, they will be left with the impression that what their father said, often extremely strongly, is the real truth. This leaves children bewildered, because while they instinctively know that something is wrong, when their father justifies it and their mother doesn't respond they are left with a confused sense of reality: They know something is wrong, but no one is naming it. This can lead to distress and anger.

The following section has general guidelines to help you prepare for your discussions with your children. Further research from books or professional help will be even more beneficial in guiding you through this process.

GENERAL GUIDELINES FOR TALKING
TO CHILDREN ABOUT DIVORCE

- **Take into consideration the children's ages.** If there is a great disparity in age, you might want to have separate conversations. This will make it easier to adequately explain and address the situation appropriately to children of different ages.

- **Draw on what you think your children already know.** Many women avoid talking to their children because they are worried about saying the wrong thing. This often stems from a mother's concern that she'll somehow make things worse, fearful that she will bring more pain to her children by exposing them to information they are not prepared to understand.

  Start by thinking back to comments your children have made. You will probably be able to identify times when your children said something to you about your husband's abuse. Perhaps it was about the way he treated them, how he treated you, or about his behavior in general. Use the same language your child used at that time to describe the abuse. This should help you feel confident that you are not exposing them to information they can't handle.

- **Do not tell the children that you are divorcing to protect them.** While it is useful to use a child's own words to explain why you need to get a divorce, it is not healthy for children to think that you are getting divorced *because* of them. Too much guilt and emotional conflict is created for children when they are under this assumption. To avoid this, when you use their language, rephrase what they told you in such a way that it becomes *your* reason.

  For example, suppose your child once told you that he hates it when his father hurts you. You can change that to: "It's wrong for a Daddy to hurt a Mommy and I couldn't take it anymore." There should be no suggestion that you are divorcing because of how their father treats *them*, or because of something they said, or because of a feeling they expressed.

- **Be prepared and calm when answering their questions.** Think in advance about the questions your children may have and how you would like to answer them. There may be technical questions about what is going to happen, and there may be emotional questions about your feelings toward their father and the feelings of his family members towards them or you. If you think about or talk with someone in advance about possible responses, you will handle the questions a lot better.

You can stay calm by remembering that you don't have to have all the answers on the spot. This will help you avoid blurting out something that you will later regret, or become nervous and agitated because you are feeling pressured. If you feel unsure of your answer, let your children know this and reassure them that you are going to think about it and get back to them. Make sure you follow through and actually do get back to them. If they ask about what is going to happen, let them know what you know now, and commit to letting them know about new information or changes when you find out yourself.

- **Be prepared for a difficult reaction.** There are a number of reasons children react badly to divorce. Some are concerned about the stigma of divorce. Others are scared about what will happen. Some fear what their father will do. Some are more afraid of your leaving the marriage than your staying. Still others might be so distressed by the lack of action until now, that they don't feel secure with you as a parent.

  If a child starts yelling at you or blaming you or saying that she wants to be with her father, it will hurt. It can be very traumatizing, because *you* have the responsibility for deciding to take this drastic step, and you have probably done so only after much contemplation, consultation with professionals and/or trusted confidants, and diligent efforts to preserve the marriage. This decision reflects your considered belief that *both you and your children* will be better off if there is a divorce. To have the children blaming you or fighting the decision can be most disheartening.

  Know that it is natural for children to be afraid for the future when the issue of divorce comes up. Try to speak about some of the fears they might be having. Ask what they fear about divorce. Even if they don't answer the question, talk about some of the typical things children fear, and try to reassure them regarding concerns such as safety, getting through the initial stages when the news first gets out, where they will be living, what will change, and what will remain the same.

- **Have a support system in place for your children *before* letting them know about the divorce.** Having supports in place may mitigate a bad reaction from a child. This may also alleviate some of your own anxieties during this very difficult, unpredictable and often turbulent time.

The potential importance to your children of having mentors or other positive adult role models in their lives as a way of coping with the abuse in the home was previously discussed. If you have already facilitated the development of such relationships, then you already have a resource for your children. If not, now is a good time to think about any individuals they may have in their lives who could serve as an extra support. This should be someone with whom you can safely communicate, and who can look out for your child — perhaps a school counselor or a favorite teacher, a *rebbi*, a principal, the parent of one of your child's friends, or someone from shul, an after-school program or activity.

Such an individual can be helpful for many reasons. Children will naturally lean on their mother for support, but you may have several children who need support, and you may be drained from the turmoil of the divorce. You may not have sufficient emotional energy left to satisfy everyone during this process. The children may also be too angry or hurt to turn to you. Or they may be of an age when they can't allow their parent to be their support. Finally, some children are aware of the toll the divorce has on their mother, and they don't want to add to her burden. Making sure your children's needs are met, whether it's by you, a professional, or a concerned community member, is crucial to determining how they will get through this upheaval.

As mentioned previously, you do need to be careful about those with whom your child forms such relationships. Do not relinquish too much oversight. Keep open communication with your children about these relationships, and make sure your child knows what is appropriate and inappropriate in a relationship between a child and an adult.

Resources for the Divorce Process

By now it should be clear that your decision to divorce is likely to result in the appearance of one or more significant issues that you must consider and plan for in advance. In negotiating this stressful process you will need help, both emotionally and for the practical aspects of getting divorced. Knowing where to turn and which resources are available to you can help you navigate through this process.

Recognize, however, that you cannot necessarily depend on others to take care of things for you. The divorce process can be grueling, and you may hope that there is someone who can work it out for you. Unfortunately, while there are those who certainly can help you and be your advocate for certain parts of the process, getting divorced is a lot of work — and that work belongs to *you*.

Your Process Will Be Unique   Wouldn't it be helpful to have a section called, "What you can expect the process of divorce to look like?" Unfortunately, there are too many variables to make this possible. Consider the *beis din*, for example: Different *batei din* can have different procedures for starting and continuing the process. For women whose husbands bring them to court, there are different laws from state to state regarding certain issues which will affect the process. In fact, many women report that, according to their lawyers, there can be differences based on the judge who is assigned to the case.

On the other hand, there are certain uniform standards, whether in *beis din* or in court, regarding what is considered usual and customary in determining custody and financial agreements. And it is always a good idea to remain composed, organized, and clearheaded when you present your case for custody and financial issues.

Since there are so many variables in your particular circumstances which will make your case unique, a specific, step-by-step plan is not practical. Instead, this section presents a guide to recognizing possible resources to help you through your process. These resources encompass the emotional, legal, and spiritual spheres and custody settlement, whether it is through *beis din*, court or mediation.

A good support network can be immensely helpful in coping with the stresses of the divorce process. Those in your support network can provide a sounding board for your planning and decisions, a source of ideas for new approaches to problems that arise, and a source of validation. Your support network may include informal supports such as family, friends, your *rav*, and perhaps members of abused women support groups. You will also have formal supports, those who will help you with the practical matters of your divorce, such as a *rav* for *she'eilahs*, a *toan*, and possibly legal counsel.

Your therapist or counselor may be a hybrid of these two categories. While she is there for emotional support, she may also be able to provide you with resources for your practical needs and guidance for additional sources of support. With her past experience, she may be in a good position to help you understand what you are likely to be facing in the divorce process.

Informal Supports

The most important function of informal supports is emotional support and validation. Hopefully, you have built up some relationships which have sustained you until now. To provide support at this stage, friends and family members should be willing to listen to you, understand your feelings, and respect your judgment. They should be capable of resisting the temptation of telling you what to do, and they must be willing to defer to your needs and judgment.

The friends and family members who fit this requirement are more than just helpful — they give you strength and energy, because while they might make suggestions, they do not fight your ultimate decision. Expending energy on resisting unhelpful suggestions, attempting to convince others that your decisions are appropriate, and fighting to be heard about your life will deplete you. You have a limited amount of energy, and you must be careful to use it wisely: for yourself, your children, and your goals.

If you find that you are exhausted arguing with a friend or family member about your interpretation of events or your plans to proceed, it's a strong indication that this may not be the right person to see you through this part of the process. This can be confusing or disturbing, especially if this was someone you had been leaning on, or who you had assumed would be there for you when you made this decision. Although it may add to your distress to have to make changes in your support network, it will probably be less stressful in the long run. This does not necessarily mean dropping that person from your life, but you may want to avoid discussions involving the particulars of your plan or decisions.

Sometimes friends or family members expect you to fight for things that would be important to them, but are not necessarily important to you. Supporters may want you to push harder in a way that makes you uncomfortable, or to avoid bringing up issues that you believe are a safety concern. When they are encouraging bolder steps or softer tactics, remember that they are giving advice based on what they *think* they would do in *your* situation. But they *aren't* in it, and after you have considered all of the possibilities, you will be happiest with *your* decision.

There is a particular issue that needs to be addressed with respect to your parents being your primary support in your divorce process. When there is a close family relationship, and the abuser has no other defense for his behavior, he will claim that your desire for a divorce is the result of parental meddling. He may say, "If her parents weren't so involved with us, she would be perfectly happy with me," or, "She was happy until her parents started pointing things out to her and she decided not to be."

The unfortunate fact is that many people are susceptible to believing his claims, since these cases do occur, and many would prefer believing this than accepting that there is abuse in the community. If you have any concern that this *does* describe your situation, you should seek counsel and guidance from other sources in addition to the parental support you value so much. Even if you know this not to be the case, it is still helpful to get that outside validation, so you have ammunition against his assertion that the problems are all in your parents' heads.

The Rav   Before going to a *rav* to discuss your desire for a divorce, consider what role you want the *rav* to fill. Are you going for additional support and validation? Are you seeking a *psak* about whether you should get a divorce? Do you want the *rav* to educate you and help you navigate the *beis din* process, to pursue the outcome you have *already* decided you want?

Let's examine the different potential roles of a *rav* in your process, as well as the problems that arise when you are not clear yourself — and therefore not clear in your request.

If you are seeking the type of support and validation that you might want from a friend or family member, ask yourself, "Do I have that type of relationship with this *rav*?" If the *rav* is not a family friend, but is instead the *rav* of your *kehillah*, he might see his role differently. You might view him as someone you can turn to who will completely accept what you tell him and act on your behalf. However, the *rav* might see his role as mediator or impartial judge. This can mean listening to both parties and then weighing what he hears. If this scares you because of your husband's power of manipulation or persuasion, you might want to ask yourself whether what you're looking for is realistic.

Sometimes a woman makes erroneous assumptions about what a *rav* can and is willing to do. Even if you think the *rav* is an appropriate choice for support, recognize that in his position as a *rav*, he usually expects to help someone *fix* the problems in his or her marriage — not to actively help the process of divorce. Even if you are very specific at the outset about what you are looking for, remember that you have chosen to go to him because you respect his authority, leadership and *daas Torah*. The *rav* may not feel comfortable in the role you have chosen for him, either because he doesn't see his role in the same way, or because he thinks your request is not appropriate for him.

Sometimes women have so much faith and respect for a *rav's* leadership and Torah learning that they expect the *rav* to read their minds. A lack of proper and careful communication with the *rav* can lead to disappointment.

> *After multiple interventions had failed to change her abusive husband's behavior, Batya decided that she needed to end her marriage.*

Batya had primarily discussed this with her therapist and a friend. Now she decided that she was ready to tell Rabbi Goldberg that she wanted to get divorced.

Batya was a baalas teshuvah, and the Goldbergs were essentially her adopted family. She had been a bas bayis at their house for several years before meeting and marrying her husband. She was grateful to have someone of Rabbi Goldberg's stature in her corner, and she knew he would understand her decision, since in the past he had expressed his concern over some of the things he noticed when she and her husband would visit them for a Shabbos or Yom Tov.

Batya was understandably distraught when her meeting with Rabbi Goldberg did not have the intended result. Instead of accepting her decision to leave her husband, he started questioning her: "Is it really so bad? Is there anything else you can do?" He also spent some time pointing out her husband's positive traits. Batya walked out in despair, not understanding why he hadn't been more supportive of her need to leave the marriage — just as a father would be.

Eventually, Batya realized that Rabbi Goldberg's response was natural, since she had never told him how significant the problems were, and to what lengths she had gone to try to get help. While he had seen things that disturbed him, in her desire to keep peace between the Goldbergs and her husband, she had downplayed the problems. Now, when she had told Rabbi Goldberg of her decision to divorce, she had expected him to fill in all the blanks, without taking the time to give him the complete history of her process. Without taking that step, most people — parents included — would naturally begin questioning and trying to help.

Batya went back to the Goldbergs and clearly laid out the history of her marriage and attempted interventions. She was also very clear about what she wanted from Rabbi Goldberg — support and information about how to go about the divorce process. This time she was not disappointed.

As you think through the process of going to a *rav* or *beis din*, prepare yourself for a lot of questioning about your decision. It is a tremendous responsibility to end a marriage and for a *beis din* to give a *get*. For this reason, a *rav* and the *beis din* will leave no stone unturned and no question unasked about whether this really has to happen, especially if your husband is saying that a divorce doesn't have to happen and he doesn't want it to happen. Don't take the questioning personally — if you sound defensive or angry, this will not serve you well in getting support or empathy in *beis din*. You may think that the truth is on your side, but you have to be able to clearly and coherently present it. Don't get ruffled by the questions: Keep presenting the facts, with the understanding that this process is taken very seriously and will be examined very carefully. It's not about you, it's just how the process works.

Even a *rav* who has been supportive of you and validated your right to not be mistreated in marriage might have a hard time transitioning from that role to actively helping you get divorced. After all, a *rav* usually sees his role primarily as building marriages and the community — particularly if the *rav* you have sought out is the leader of a *kehillah*. If you are firm in your decision to divorce, and you are looking for guidance and help with navigating the process of receiving your *get*, you might want to reach out to a different type of *rav*: one whose role is to navigate and advocate for you in your divorce process and in *beis din*. That *rav* is called a *toan*.

The Toan

A *toan* is a halachic authority who can serve as your advocate in a *beis din* proceeding, similar to the way an attorney represents someone in court. The *toan* can also advise you before a *beis din* proceeding has commenced regarding how you should proceed and what you should do to prepare. The *toan* is typically a *rav* himself, a person who has great knowledge in this area of halachah. However, in his capacity as *toan*, he is your paid advocate. He is not a *rav* from whom you would seek advice about whether you should get divorced. A *toan* is a rabbinic authority who you go to after you've decided to get divorced, who represents your best interests in the *beis din* proceedings.

You are not required to bring a *toan* to *beis din*. In fact, some *batei din* and communal rabbis will actively discourage the use of a *toan*, on the theory that the presence of this type of advocate tends to make the proceedings unnecessarily aggressive, contentious, complicated, and drawn out. Nevertheless, for an abused woman, a *toan* can be an excellent resource.

An abused woman is understandably frightened by the prospect of negotiating the process of *beis din* on her own. Knowing her husband as she does, she is certain that he will behave aggressively, and she feels out of her depth as she contemplates facing her spouse in a system she doesn't understand and where she feels unprotected. This is why some women try to avoid *beis din* altogether, and go straight to court where they know they will be represented by a lawyer. This is unfortunate, because if she was not given permission to do so by a *rav*, a woman who does this could find herself in trouble when she does go to *beis din* for the *get*.

For women who are frightened, the *possible* fallout from exacerbating hostilities in *beis din* by using a *toan* is far outweighed by the confidence and security they feel when they have that official advocate. This feeling of security can help women be more comfortable with the *beis din*, lessening the likelihood that they will inappropriately use other avenues.

A *toan* plays the role of advocate — period. Unlike the community *rav*, who may pull back at the suggestion of divorce because of his primary role in building the community, the *toan* has no role confusion or ambivalence to get in the way. This is why many women find it more reassuring to have a *rav* who is clearly in the role of advocate to help them through the *beis din* system.

Finding a Toan

Finding a *toan* is usually done through word of mouth. You may know someone who has been through the divorce process and used a *toan* in the proceedings. Alternatively, your *rav*, rabbi or someone well connected in the community might know of a *toan*. In a smaller community, it may not be a common practice to use a *toan,* and you may want to seek advice from other women who have gone through the *beis din* process about whether they were okay without one, or wished they had known about using one. If you cannot find representation where you live, it may be possible to consult with a *toan* from another city on the phone so you can understand how events should proceed, what you should expect, and how to best navigate the process.

Preparing to Consult a Toan *(or Attorney)*

Whether you have already decided to consult a *toan* or you are still not sure, it is important to prepare for this meeting and for the divorce itself, if you are close to that decision. There are a number of documents that you should bring with you when you meet the *toan*. In addition to the following list, ask the *toan* if there are any specific documents he would like to see.

- Copies of all bank statements and financial records
- Copies of any medical records that document injuries you may have sustained
- Any proof of abuse (or any other offenses in the marriage) in the form of pictures, recordings, or statements from friends or associates
- Your journal in which you have recorded instances of abuse.
- Of course, you may not have all these items. Your husband may have hidden all financial documents from you. Even if you know where these documents are, you might be afraid to remove them. Try to make a copy and put the originals back at a time when your husband will not notice.
- All of your documentation should be kept in a safe place that your husband cannot access, such as a trusted friend or safe deposit box. Consider carefully whether the place you have for these items is truly safe.

Rena had recently started secretly taping the tirades to which her husband had been subjecting her for almost her entire ten-year-marriage.

(NOTE: In some states such taping is legal, while in others it is not.)
Sometimes his vulgarity was in the form of demeaning speeches about
her incompetence and her stupidity. Sometimes he would subject her
to vulgarly explicit speeches about her body and her self-worth.

Her husband had started intimating that if she ever tried to tell
people what was going on and leave, he would convince them that
she was crazy. Rena is a pretty quiet, "to herself" type of person, and
she knew that her husband had a very good name out in the com-
munity: He was generous, successful, well-liked and respected. She
was worried that if he really did launch a smear campaign, it would
work, so she started taping him secretly as proof. Rena knew she
couldn't keep these tapes in her apartment. Since they lived upstairs
from her sister, she thought it would be safe to keep the tapes there.

One day, however, Rena's husband caught her taping him. Rena
tried to get downstairs to her sister's apartment to give her the tape,
but this led her husband to understand that there was a whole stash
there. He barged in, ran to the closet that Rena's sister was guarding,
shoved her aside, and got the whole collection.

Soon after this incident, Rena discovered that her husband had
started to drop words to their rav that Rena "wasn't herself lately."
She believed that now that her husband realized she had a plan, he
was trying to insure that when she went for a divorce he could con-
vince people that it wasn't what she really wanted.

This situation is a good illustration of the importance of exercising
great care in obtaining, copying, and storing confirmation of the abuse
that has been going on in your marriage. This is true of all necessary
documentation, including hospital reports, police reports, school records, birth certificates, your *kesubah*, and any financial documentation
you can find. While documentation of the abuse will be significant in
varying degrees in divorce proceedings, it can often be important simply so the abuser can't claim, as many do, that this whole effort to leave
him is frivolous, baseless, and over nothing.

Meeting a Toan

If you choose to employ a *toan*, you should have a preliminary meeting with him to ascertain how he works and prepare for the process. Here are some questions you might consider asking:

- What course of action would you recommend for me?
- What information do you need from me?
- How do things proceed and what can I expect from the process?
- My husband's name is X and my in-laws are Mr. and Mrs. X from Y, do you have any conflicts of interest?
- What are your expectations with respect to custody and visitation?
- What are your expectations regarding financial awards and/or settlement? What is customary and what special circumstances do you see in my case that might impact the final decision?
- What can I expect from you through this process? How do you see your role?
- What are my rights and responsibilities in this process?

You need to feel comfortable with the *toan's* commitment to you and his lack of connection with your husband. You need to feel certain that he will represent *your* best interests, and you need to feel confident that he is capable of doing so effectively. Your *toan* can also give you an idea of the typical outcome in these types of proceedings.

Some women have a particular outcome in mind, based on what they have been through and feel they deserve. In fact, however, there is often a typical custody and financial award that is rarely deviated from except in the most extreme situations. This is true in both *beis din* and secular court. Your *toan*, if you are in *beis din*, and your lawyer, if you are in secular court, should be able to prepare you for likely outcomes so you don't waste time and money fighting improbabilities.

On the other hand, you don't want to be pushed to accept something that will be part of your permanent settlement simply because your *toan* wants to be finished with it already, or because the *toan* isn't on top of things. If you are wondering if you are getting the best advice, you have a couple of options. You could seek a second opinion. You can also discuss it with your therapist, counselor or domestic violence advocate, who might have some ideas about whether what is being proposed is in the realm of "usual and customary."

If you find yourself holding out for more than what is recommended, these resources can help you as well. Working with a mental health professional can help you unravel the emotional piece that may be standing in your way. Getting a second opinion might also help you come to terms with the reality of how cases of divorce are usually settled — with the recognition that these settlements often do seem unfair to a woman who has lived through such an atypical marriage.

A Mediator   Mediation may be suggested by community members, the *beis din*, or court. Coming to an agreement using professional mediation is an attempt to avoid a potentially protracted, expensive, and acrimonious process. Before considering mediation, it's important to understand what it is, how it works, and its benefits and pitfalls.

Mediation is a process in which an impartial professional mediator helps divorcing couples come to a mutually acceptable agreement regarding one or more issues that must be resolved in order to reach a divorce agreement. In some cases, the entire agreement is worked out through mediation. This procedure has the advantage of saving the considerable time and expense involved in litigating these issues, either in *beis din* or in court. Professional mediators will charge a fee for their services, but their fee is lower and they generally require less time to arrive at an agreement.

Women who are getting divorced from an abusive husband need to exercise caution in considering the mediation process. Unlike in *beis din* or court, there are generally no formal advocates representing your interests at the negotiations. This leaves many women concerned about how they are going to be able to articulate their position and fight for what they believe they are entitled to.

Mediation is also predicated on the premise that there is an equal balance of power. This may not be the case for some abused women. Furthermore, an underlying presumption in mediation is that the two parties are both interested and willing to compromise, engage in joint decision making, and desire to settle the issues equitably. Women who are separating from an abusive husband don't see him fitting that description. Additionally, they worry that after so many years of feeling fear, being manipulated, and needing to accommodate their husband's demands or suffer the consequences, the possibility of being in a room with his overwhelming personality while remaining clear and strong seems quite improbable.

Although the mediator has guidelines and is supposed to be impartial, a woman who has seen how manipulative her husband can be and how well he is able to positively represent himself is justifiably fearful that without someone there to help her, she will be unable to get the mediator to see her husband for the man he is. Some mediators will allow you to bring along someone for support, whether that is a family member or close (hopefully savvy) friend. It would be helpful to determine a mediator's policy regarding this before agreeing to a particular one.

Some women choose to try to reach an agreement through mediation without signing a binding arbitration agreement. Once a binding arbitration agreement is signed, the woman is bound to the arbitration process with *that* mediator. This has been problematic for some women, who have found that when the mediation is not working because the husband is not interested in compromise, the mediator will attempt to get the wife to accept unfair terms in order to push through an agreement. If the woman feels she is being unfairly pushed, or senses that the mediator is biased toward, intimidated by, or swayed by her husband, there is little she can do if she has signed a binding arbitration agreement. It will be difficult to move her process to another venue.

Sometimes a friend or family member may offer to serve as an unofficial mediator. Alternatively, a professional mediator in the community might approach you to let you know that he can help you mediate your divorce process. This has at least one potential downside for the abused woman: A mediator who is not an expert in divorce law may not know what the woman is halachically or legally entitled to. Even in the case of a professional mediator who is *frum*, if *he* has approached *you,* rather than the other way around, it is important to have your eyes open and be cautious before proceeding.

Before you agree to enter the mediation process, ask yourself, "What are we mediating?" You may be planning to mediate terms of a divorce settlement. Your husband, on the other hand, might only be interested in "mediating" your return to the marriage.

Temimah was separated from her husband Baruch, and had start-ed the beis din *process. Baruch wasn't making it easy for her — in fact, he made it quite clear that he was going to fight her every step of the way.*

Temimah was approached by Doniel, a man from her parents' community, who told her he could help. He explained that he was a mediator who had experience dealing with divorces and received many referrals from batei din *and lawyers. He told Temimah that he had a lot of experience mediating in difficult situations like this. He asked Temimah to tell him what had been going on, why she wanted to get divorced, and what she wanted in a settlement.*

Temimah told him the whole history of the relationship. Doniel indicated that he understood why she could no longer be married to her husband, and would speak to Baruch about mediating a settle-ment so the process did not drag on any longer.

Temimah was so excited. Here was someone who wanted to help, was willing to get his hands dirty, was trying to get things settled — and was confident that he would be successful.

A short time later, Doniel called Temimah back with an update. He was pleased to report that he had made progress: Her husband had agreed to give a get *if she would first commit to six months of couples counseling.*

Temimah was devastated. For all of Doniel's claims of being there to mediate, he was clearly not mediating a divorce settlement.

Instead, he was proposing a plan of manipulation. Doniel wanted her to play along with the couples counseling so she would be "guaranteed" a get in six months. Otherwise, he argued, her husband could drag things on much longer. Frustrated and confused, Temimah instinctively knew that this was not the result she had hoped for from the mediation process.

Why was Temimah's experience so problematic? The term "mediation" was used, but it wasn't an accurate term in this case. Mediation is when both parties enter into it willingly and with the objective of achieving a settlement that is fair. In a professional mediation situation, both parties agree to engage in the process to mediate a divorce settlement. They approach the mediator — not the other way around. The process is explained. The terms are agreed upon. Questions are answered. Only then does the process of mediation begin.

When family members or community members offer unsolicited help, the initiative is only coming from one side of the relationship. As a result, the agenda for the mediation is not a mutually agreed upon goal. The abuser may instead have the goal of getting you back into the relationship.

This is not to say that an informal person in the community cannot intervene and be helpful in doing so. However, prior to allowing a non-professional to become involved, or a professional who has sought you out as opposed to the other way around, you need to be clear about what you want, and you need to be extra cautious about trying to work out your divorce settlement through a process in which you are not protected by an advocate.

In Temimah's case, perhaps Doniel's plan could have worked. But if the process is not official or straightforward, there is no guarantee that it will be viable. Without a legal way to enforce the terms of the arrangement, Temimah could have waited six months — only to find her husband refusing to cooperate yet again.

If you choose to try a similar process, make sure you are protected. Do not simply accept the volunteer's assurance that the plan will work.

Consult with a *toan* or lawyer so you know you will not be in a worse place at the end of this process, or waste time on something that has no real potential for success.

An Attorney   Many Orthodox women question the need for an attorney. "Why do I need a lawyer? I'm a *frum* woman. Won't everything be decided in *beis din*?"

Even if you do plan on using a *beis din*, you don't know what your husband will do. Although a *beis din* can send an *hazmanah* summoning your husband, and serve a *seruv* if he does not respond after three times, this is only meaningful if he cares about the repercussions.[8] If you have tried to call him to *beis din* but he does not care what his reputation is in the *frum* community, or if he is willing to leave the community, it may be difficult to get him to respond. On the other hand, refusing to go to court could land him in very big trouble.

In some circumstances, a *rav* might recommend the court system if the abuse is so severe that he fears the *beis din* with not be able to protect you or keep you safe. Another possible scenario is that your husband summons you to court to decide matters of custody, because he suspects you have proof that would be extremely damaging in *beis din* but less important to the courts in deciding matters of custody. Examples would be infidelity or extensive use of pornography.

This is why it's a good idea for *every* woman to have some thoughts about finding and at least consulting with an attorney.

Finding an Attorney

There are two different forms of legal services. There is a private attorney, who is paid for out of pocket. There are also legal services for battered women and other free legal services that you may apply for. Some women are under the impression that if you don't want to press criminal charges against the abuser, you will not be able to use the services of specific

---

8.   There are also different opinions about whether you should be calling your husband to *beis din*, or should wait for him to call you to *beis din*. This is something that should be discussed with your *toan*.

domestic violence legal services. This is almost never the case. If you are still concerned — ask!

If you have the funds to hire an attorney, or if you have someone who is willing to supply you with the funds, you will need a referral. You may ask your local domestic violence service for a referral. You may check with the local woman's bar association to see if they have they have referrals for attorneys whose expertise is in divorce and custody proceedings. You might also approach someone you know who has been divorced. You can ask her if she used an attorney and if she was happy with the results. You can ask your therapist or domestic abuse counselor, who may be familiar with attorneys who have expertise in divorce cases and have good reputations. If you are a member of a support group, you might also raise the question there.

Choosing the Right Attorney

The attorney you choose should not only be knowledgeable about divorce, but also be respectful and sensitive to the fact that you are an Orthodox woman with halachic concerns. The following questions regarding experience, impressions of your specific case, and the best course of action can help you determine if this attorney is the right one for you.

- How much experience do you have with divorce and custody cases in general, and how much experience do you have with cases involving domestic abuse?

- How much experience do you have working with Orthodox women? Do you understand their special circumstances and do you feel comfortable with their special concerns, specifically working with *beis din* to maintain proper religious decorum and to obtain a Jewish divorce?

- Once you have heard about my situation and my goals, will you respect my decisions about how I want things to be done?

- Will you have time to see my case through to the end? Do you understand that divorce cases involving spousal abuse can be unpredictable and drawn out?

- Will you be accessible when I have questions? Will you get back to me promptly? Will you allow me time to ask a reasonable number of questions as necessary?
- What are your fees and policies regarding payment?
- What are your feelings regarding mediation? If a judge wants to order mediation and I feel uncomfortable with mediation, will you advocate for me?
- What course of action would you recommend for me at this point in time?
- What are your expectations with respect to custody and visitation?
- What are your expectations regarding financial awards and/or settlement? What is customary and what special circumstances do you see in my case that might impact the final order?
- How should the process work? What can I expect?

You need to have a clear idea of what you can expect from your attorney. In the case of a private attorney, you also need to know whether you can afford it. Attorneys typically work on an hourly basis, and it is very difficult to predict how difficult and time consuming a given case might turn out to be. However, an attorney with extensive experience in divorce proceedings should be able to recognize potential complicating issues that could make the matter more costly. Your attorney should be able to give you an estimate of how much you can expect a divorce to cost. If one or more of the attorneys with whom you consult mentions possible complicating factors that could result in drawn out proceedings, ask the others about this possibility as well. If it seems likely that the costs of private legal representation will become unmanageable, consider availing yourself of funded legal services for battered women. Referrals should be available at your local woman's shelter or domestic violence services center.

Be realistic. With all good intentions, lawyers, especially good ones, are very busy, and their time is not their own. They have to appear in court and follow up on multiple people and all of their legal needs — planned and unplanned. It can get very frustrating for a woman who feels a sense of urgency regarding a particular issue not to be able to get in touch with her attorney, especially if the court system scares you and you were expecting to be in *beis din*. On the other hand, if you feel your attorney really is dropping the ball, or putting undue pressure on you to agree to something you do not want to do, you may want to consider switching. You can also consult with another attorney to double check what you are hearing. You will have to be particularly patient when using legal services from a domestic violence program. Because women who are abused are often without funds, there can be long waiting lists in funded legal services organizations.

Exercise Caution

Any licensed attorney is free to accept a divorce case. As a result, attorneys who need work may claim that they are qualified to represent you, even though they actually have little experience in this area. If your husband decides to move the venue from *beis din* to court, it is critical that the attorney you hire has extensive experience and intimate knowledge of the specific court system in which the case will be decided. Check the level of experience of any lawyer you consider hiring.

In addition, be certain that the attorney you hire is familiar with the special concerns of Orthodox women and how these may affect your goals and strategies. The attorney must be willing to be flexible in accommodating your needs. Some attorneys are used to having cases follow a predictable course, and they may not be willing to listen to your needs or take the time to accommodate them. Some attorneys may be too focused on *winning*, refusing to concede on a detail that actually would accommodate your need to get it done and move on. Others may be too willing to make concessions, eager for the case to be over and not adequately safeguarding your interests. Only *you* know what your goals are, how hard you are willing to fight for them, and how much time you are willing to invest in the process. It is important that you and your attorney be on the same page in this regard.

MAINTAIN REALISTIC EXPECTATIONS

Your legal advocate should be able to anticipate likely outcomes with respect to custody, visitation, and financial support and settlement. While every case is different, and it's impossible to accurately predict every detail of the final resolution, an experienced *toan* or attorney should be able to use precedent and prevailing guidelines to give you a rough estimate of what to expect.

Women often experience disappointment when the realization sets in: Even though they have suffered so much, they still will have to share their children with their husbands, and will often end up with financial concerns despite the fact that he has plenty of income. But the disappointment and frustration regarding the ultimate settlement are worse for those women who have spent time and money to fight battles that are not winnable. Knowing what is likely to happen and what you should realistically expect is very important to your peace of mind.

Ask your *toan* what is realistic to expect in *beis din*.

Ask your attorney what is realistic to expect in court, if you find yourself there.

Ask your therapist to help you emotionally process the outcome you have to face, which many women feel stop short of their initial expectations. When you fight for unrealistic goals out of hurt and anger, it ultimately depletes you in ways that aren't good for you.

The decision to divorce is a very serious one that women should and do take seriously. There are many frightening, complicated, and stressful aspects to the process. Before proceeding, think carefully about everything. Take your time in gathering your information and making any decisions. If you feel you have no choice but to get divorced, please know that it will be very difficult, but with your own firm resolve, the right support, and the proper professional guidance, you'll get through it.

Chapter Eight

❧

Living Through Divorce

You've decided that, unfortunately, you must get a divorce. You've done your research and obtained the necessary information, supports, and representation. These steps were difficult and exhausting, and you're hoping that the worst is over.

You will almost certainly discover that the divorce process itself is a very trying period. The time between the initiation of the divorce and the finalization of the process will probably be much longer than you expect, regardless of the forum in which the matter is being settled. There can be multiple delays in the process caused deliberately by the spouse who does not want the divorce, or because terms continue to be disputed. The process can be grueling and usually takes the minimum of a year, usually two — and sometimes more.

Some women do get divorced more quickly. This can happen when there is unequivocal proof of wrongdoing, or when no one is fighting the process. More commonly, however, it's best to be prepared for a protracted divorce process that involves many different hurdles along the way. Women who go into the process with the awareness that it can take a significant amount of time and effort fare better emotionally than those who expend all their strength or resolve *before* the process is fully underway.

Stresses in the Divorce Process

Contesting the Divorce The first hurdle a woman may encounter in the divorce process is a husband who contests the divorce. The abusive husband may tell the *beis din* or the court (in states where "grounds" for divorce is required) that he does not want a divorce, there is no reason for a divorce, and that you and he should be trying to work on the marriage. The woman will have to prove that she should be given a *get*, or in court, that there are grounds for divorce — and this is not necessarily easy to demonstrate.

This tactic is often used by controlling husbands to drag the process out, seemingly endlessly. It can be extremely distressing to finally come to a decision, only to be completely stopped in your tracks.

Being completely prepared means finding out from your *toan* how to demonstrate that your husband is *chayev* to give a *get*. Alternatively, if your husband is contesting the divorce in secular court, your attorney should work with you to establish how to demonstrate to the court that there are grounds for divorce.

Refusing to Give a Get Many women fear the possibility that their husband will withhold a *get*. This *is* something that happens, and this is incredibly painful for those who are left in limbo. The husband may refuse to give a *get* until all other issues are settled, and he uses this as leverage in the settlement talks. He may demand a huge sum of money. He may refuse to comply with the *beis din's* ruling that he is *chayev* to give a *get*. He may refuse to come to *beis din* altogether.

Under any of these circumstances, you need to work very closely with your *toan*, lawyer, and *beis din* to see what alternatives you have. In the final analysis, you will have to decide what you can do and what you are willing to do, based on your individual situation.

Keep in mind that for an abusive, controlling man, the more he thinks you are worried about a *get*, the more powerful the *get* becomes to him — because he knows he can use it to continue to control you. Women who avoid speaking about a *get* or making it a focal point in any way, especially at the beginning of the process, have seen some success in mitigating a controlling husband's use of this tactic. Most men do know that this is important to their wives, however, and that the fear of not receiving a *get* will make her vulnerable.

Needs, Goals, and Negotiation

You have your resources in place. You've determined your needs, goals and objectives, and you have communicated this information to your advocates. But the negotiation process is just beginning.

While the divorce is being worked out, the process of negotiation continues to take place. This involves give-and-take, which means that you will be required to continuously discuss and be asked to modify your objectives in the light of proposals made by your husband.

You will not be doing yourself any favors if you seek unrealistic goals, make demands, or hold out for scenarios that are out of line according to *beis din* or state parameters. On the other hand, you don't want to be rushed into a deal that is extremely one sided — and not on *your* side.

It's almost certainly going to seem unfair to you. You will have to live on a more modest budget, and despite his abuse, he will get to spend Shabbos with his children on a regular basis, while you remain alone. But while your feeling that this is unfair may be valid, recognize that the process will probably end up "not fair" from your perspective.

This is an emotional process. Many women say, "Why me?" Every offer that isn't perfect — and nothing will be absolutely perfect — can end up seeming *outrageously* unfair. You look at a settlement agreement that sends the children to their father every other weekend, and you are likely to be consumed with how unfair this feels to you. This is why women wind up spending time and effort fighting battles that they probably won't win.

It's important to discover and accept, both on a practical and emotional level, that there will be a large chasm between what you *think* you are each entitled to, versus what you *actually* are entitled to. But while you can't control whether your husband will fight battles he can't win because he feels entitled to certain rights, *you* can choose not to dig into an untenable position. Listen to what your advocate (*toan* or lawyer) tells you is reasonable. Sometimes, when women insist on fighting for more than is reasonable, they don't realize until it's too late that they've wasted their time, energy, and money.

> *Lori's husband had mistreated her for years and he had barely paid attention to their three children. Then she had discovered he was unfaithful to her. When she confronted him, Mark told her he wanted a divorce.*
>
> *In the middle of the divorce process, her husband's lawyer proposed joint legal custody and extensive visitation. Lori thought this was outrageous. Her husband had an abysmal track record in terms of his involvement with the children. Why should he get liberal visitation?*
>
> *When her own lawyer suggested that she should accept these terms, Lori decided to switch lawyers and fight. There were hearings and evaluations and everything dragged on — and in the end, Lori ended up with not much more than she had been offered under the terms of the original negotiations.*

Lori's anger had drowned out her lawyer's advice and pushed her to find a lawyer who would let her play out her anger in court. There might be short-term satisfaction in the fight, but most usually regret this in the long term.

On the other hand, if you are being told to accept certain conditions and agree to parameters that really don't seem normal or typical, or if you are told to accept whatever you're offered without fighting harder in *beis din* or court, you can always get a second opinion. Consider, too, the value of speaking to a domestic violence counselor. Talking through your feelings can help you gain perspective on whether you should feel outraged about a particular settlement, or if it's your general outrage at the situation which is is getting in your way.

Some people will try to coax you to give in to outrageous concessions. This may be out of fear for the possibility that you otherwise will never receive your *get*. There may be impatience at how long the process is taking and a desire to move it along. There are many scenarios that could lead to a woman being erroneously pushed to concede. In fact, a woman might push herself to accept certain things, just to end the process.

It's important to have someone with experience to consult with if you feel that this is going on, because once you've given in on certain concessions, you can't get them back.

People told Chaya that she shouldn't fight too hard, for fear that her husband would drag the process out and not give her a get. *They kept urging her to just agree to what he wanted financially, which was the main point of contention between the two of them. The couple had substantial financial holdings that he did not want to split. He felt that he had earned the money and therefore he was entitled to most of it. He agreed to give her some child support, and the house and tuition payments, but wanted her to relinquish all claims to their other, fairly vast holdings.*

Chaya didn't feel this was right, and she was nervous about what this would mean for her financially in terms of raising her children. On the other hand, everyone was encouraging her to just end this. Ultimately, that's what she did.

After the dust had settled, Chaya finally realized that she hadn't needed to give in so fast. There are men who give their wives a hard time or never give a get. *But deep down, Chaya knew that this wasn't going to be her husband. He was abusive, but he also liked his image in the community, and he wouldn't do anything that would damage it, especially because she knew he would want to get remarried. If she had stuck it out and let things go at their own pace, she would not have had to make the concessions that she ultimately made. But the negotiations were over, all the papers were signed, and there was no going back.*

Fortunately, she was able to work for her brother, so she could support her children without having to sell the house or change anything major in their lives. Still, she couldn't be there for them as much as she would have liked because of her work schedule. If she had fought harder for the financial settlement, she would have been able to put off going to work for a while longer, until her children were a bit older.

It can be hard to figure out when to give in and when to stay strong. In order to stay clear and realistic, you may have to combat feelings of anger, hurt and what you feel would be fair, so you don't fight pointless battles. You may also have to combat feelings of fear, intimidation, and the fatigue the process provokes, so you don't give in too much or too quickly.

Forensic Evaluation If you find yourself in court, and negotiations and settlement attempts do not lead to an agreement about custody, the judge will often appoint a forensic evaluator to make an assessment of the parents and their relationship with the children. This evaluation is used by the judge to make a determination in the matter of custody. There are also some *batei din* that will use a forensic psychologist to do an evaluation to make a recommendation for custody.

The forensic psychologist meets individually with each parent, meets each parent with the children, meets with the children individually, and confers with therapists and others who are familiar with the parents and children.

There are two roadblocks that commonly undermine an abused woman's presentation to the psychologist and the outcome of the assessment: being highly emotional, and focusing on the wrong things.

Many women report that court-appointed psychologists are not always as empathic toward the suffering of abused women as one would hope. Extreme display of emotion is often not understood as a byprod-uct of being abused and the divorce process. Instead, the psychologist uses that behavior to evaluate *you* and your ability to parent. One would expect that a psychologist would understand why a woman seeking a divorce because her husband has been abusive might sometimes come across as desperate, pushy or highly emotional. Unfortunately, many abused women report that the forensic psychologist was neither partic-ularly sympathetic nor particularly understanding. When this happens, women are often labeled in ways that are not complimentary or helpful in her attempt to seek custody.

A woman who is going through the forensic process should be pre-pared for the experience and understand how to present herself in the most favorable light possible. A woman who feels that she is fighting for the welfare of her children, or who feels her children will be in danger in her husband's custody, might sound desperate and push to be heard and understood. After all, you only have one or two sessions to get this person to understand years of abuse and mistreatment, and that can make you desperate to "get it all in." That desperation can lead to unap-pealing pushiness and extremely emotional presentation.

Making it worse is the knowledge that your husband is quite capable of coming across in a polished, favorable light; quite capable of hiding from others, as he has for years, what he is really like. This feeling of despera-tion is often compounded when a woman has not had any counseling. She may experience a watershed of emotion when she relates her history to the evaluator, which can make her appear incoherent, disjointed, and disorganized. The flood of emotion can also make the psychologist un-comfortable.

Women who have been to counseling with a mental health profes-sional and who have felt heard, understood and supported, can make another mistake. You may consider this mental health professional, the forensic psychologist, to be like your counselor — someone who is on your side. He or she is not! He is not against you, but he is not there for you, either. He is there to *evaluate* you. Your presentation is crucial.

To prepare for an effective meeting with a forensic psychologist, look back to the section in an earlier chapter about gathering your thoughts. If you haven't already done so, organize the facts of what's been going on in your marriage, emphasizing anything that the children witnessed or were affected by.

In addition to organizing the information you want to present, you need to give some thought to how you would like to present it. Rather than run the risk of coming on too strong, too pushy or too desperate, start the session by asking what the psychologist wants to know. Ask him or her where you should start, and if there is any specific type of information that she would like you to share. Approaching the meeting this way makes it clear that you are in control of your emotions. It also makes the psychologist's job easier, which in turn makes you more appealing.

You might want to use your notes to make your presentation complete. You may explain that a lot has gone on and you didn't want to forget anything. If you feel like everything is coming out in a too matter-of-fact way, explain that you're feeling a little overwhelmed and need to read from the papers to make sure you cover everything. Clarify that you are keeping the feelings at arm's length in order to get through the process, so he'll understand that this has affected you greatly, even if it isn't always apparent.

If you find yourself doing a lot of crying, don't be concerned — it demonstrates how much this has affected you. Ask to stop for a minute to collect yourself, and try to get back on track.

The second mistake that can prevent you from making the best possible presentation to a court-appointed evaluator is focusing on the wrong issues when describing the history of the relationship. This mistake seems to be made more often by women in our community than women in general. We might be outraged by behavior that is considered completely inappropriate in our world, but not in the world outside.

In addition to the fact that there had been a lot of emotional, financial and sexual abuse in their relationship, Rifkah's husband had been watching hours of pornography on a regular basis on his computer. In fact, her husband's use of pornography was something that terrified her when she thought of the possibility of her son living with her husband.

To Rifkah, her husband's inappropriate obsession was an obvious testimony to why her husband was not good for their son, and why she should get custody. This was what she emphasized when she spoke with the forensic psychologist. She spoke very little about her husband's emotional abuse toward her and their son, and the abuse which was directed at her and witnessed by their son.

Rivkah hadn't realized that the forensic psychologist cared very little how much pornography her husband was viewing. Since her husband had been careful not to allow his son access to the pornography, this did not overly concern the court. The forensic psychologist should have been told about how infrequently her husband cared for their son — he was never involved in his day-to-day care, leaving homework, school events, medical issues, and teacher consultations to her. Because Rivkah spent her time and focus on details that had no bearing on the recommendation the psychologist would make regarding custody, she lost an opportunity to demonstrate why she was the better choice as custodial parent.

Rifkah's experience makes it clear that a woman who is describing her marriage to a court-appointed evaluator should be aware of the factors that the court considers relevant to custody decisions, and she should focus on those aspects of her story. Factors that are crucial to her because of her upbringing and the accepted standards of our community may not be considered very important by the court. In a case where this is particularly relevant, she should be prepared to explain the importance of these issues within her community, and the potential adverse impact on her children.

If there are other issues that are distressing to you, find out if they are relevant in this evaluation before making them a focal point. Ask your lawyer which items are important to mention to the psychologist, and which events are not as significant, however appalling they may be to you. An unfaithful husband is a good example of this. However hurtful this is, however much it may have weighed in your decision to end the marriage, it will not affect custody or how the court assesses the parental fitness of your spouse. This is, in fact, one reason your husband may want these issues settled in court and not *beis din*, which would take a much dimmer view of this behavior. Understand that in matters of custody, it is important for you to demonstrate why and how you make the better custodial parent.

Stresses in the Separation Process

Being on Your Own If you are separated from your spouse during the divorce process, expect some adjustments. You may be happy and relieved about your new situation, but be prepared for the negative as well.

For starters, just because his abuse was intolerable, it doesn't mean that he did nothing. Maybe he paid the bills and balanced the checkbook. Now you must perform this role. Maybe it was yard work and household repairs that you don't know how to do. Maybe it was having him available to drive the kids places from time to time. Maybe he did the grocery shopping — even if it was out of his desire to have control, it was something you didn't have to do. Although the relief you feel may be tremendous, it can be overwhelming to have to handle everything. On the other hand, once they get into the routine, most women feel that the ability to control their own lives far outweighs the loss of an extra pair of hands. This is especially true for the woman who felt that extra pair of hands was constantly undermining her.

You might have enjoyed some positive interactions with your husband, at the times he wasn't being abusive. You might have appreciated his presence sometimes — at least you were not alone. This may be the first time in your life that you are alone, if you moved straight from your parents' home into marriage. You might be confusing the general feeling of loneliness for feeling alone without him.

As part of the healing process, it's human nature to push away negative experiences as soon as they are no longer right in front of you. This can make this period very difficult. The divorce process can be unbearable in many ways — financially and emotionally. The children may start acting up. If you are feeling lonely, you may start thinking about the good times and mitigating the bad ones.

Recognize that when you separate following the decision to divorce, you separate from the entire package, not just the abuse. Remember, one question to ask yourself in making the decision to divorce is: "Would I rather be alone, than live with this man?" Even if you answered yes to this question, you might not have been fully aware of all the ramifications of this decision.

You may still feel certain that you've made the right decision. But the absence of a spouse is a different type of loneliness, and there will be times when it gets to you. Maintaining a positive social network will help you get through this process in a way that maintains your dignity and the dignity of your children.

Continued Attempts at Control

You may be separated and divorcing your abusive spouse. But that doesn't mean he's given up his attempts to control you. On the contrary — for many women, the attempts at control often increase. Fortunately, your new status also offers you some new options.

> *Zeldy was in the middle of very contentious divorce proceedings. She was separated from her husband, had moved into a garden apartment — but she was wondering when she was going to feel relieved. She still felt so frightened and very much on edge.*
>
> *As Zeldy spoke about her feelings, she began to describe the visitation arrangements. Her husband would play games with visitation dates, often calling to reschedule or change the time. He also insisted on picking the children up at her apartment. Inevitably, he would use the time when he picked up the children to try to manipulate her, harass her or insult her.*
>
> *Zeldy had been living with her husband's abuse for so long that she didn't realize that she now had choices. When they were living*

under the same roof, she needed to tiptoe around him and avoid his anger. But now things were different. She didn't have to give in to what he wanted. She actually had options.

Zeldy could refuse to allow him to pick the children up at her apartment. In fact, they didn't even have to be there at visitation time — they could be at her sister's house. Alternatively, she could allow him to pick up the children at her apartment, but she could lock the door so he couldn't simply walk in and start insulting her. She could have someone there with her (mother, sister, brother) when her husband came for visitation. And she could stay firm with scheduled visits: if he could make it, fine; if not, he'd have to wait until the next scheduled visit.

It turned out that Zeldy had many options. She hadn't been aware of them, but they were available to her, and now she was able to take advantage of that.

Divorcing Without Separation

It may be difficult to imagine divorcing while under the same roof as an abusive spouse — but it does happen sometimes. This plays itself out in various ways. Sometimes things stay exactly the same in terms of where each person "lives." Or one spouse may move to a different bedroom or a different floor of the house. Don't expect the abuser to agree to make this move, however, without outside intervention. And if you feel it is unsafe to continue to live under the same roof while getting divorced — then get help! Find a way to change the situation so you do feel safe.

Even if safety is not a concern, there are many complications in this arrangement. With the close proximity, the conflict can be more intense, along with the escalating pressure to get you to change your mind. And while you may be prepared to deal with it, don't forget about the effect this can have on your children. There is a broad consensus among professionals who deal with divorce that the strongest predictor of the children's adjustment is how much they are exposed to the conflict between their parents. Try to shield your children as much as possible.

The best way to do this is to have areas of conflict managed by your representatives in the appropriate forums. You do not want your children to observe you arguing with your husband about the settlement or any other aspect of your relationship or your relationships with the children. Do not discuss any of these issues with him in front of them, because you never know when discussion will lead to argument, and argument can lead to verbal and/or physical aggression.

In the service of avoiding conflict, you may want to make arrangements to avoid your husband during this time. Some women have a family member sleep over during particularly acrimonious periods. With the advent of text messaging and e-mail, it is possible to have all necessary contact without directly communicating. While your ultimate goal may be to be able to have direct communication for the sake of the children, right now anything that reduces the contact, and thereby the conflict, is helpful.

Of course, while you may be interested and invested in keeping contact to a minimum, your husband may be attempting to do the opposite. Be on your guard. If he tries to start fights or discuss negotiations in front of the children, leave the room. If he tries to pull the children into the negotiations, you need to firmly and clearly get them out. It's important to convey the message that, "I know this is hard for you, and I know Tatty asked you to ... but children don't belong in the middle of issues between parents. Tatty and I need to work this out ourselves, or with the other adults who are helping us." Don't try to convince them to be on your side, either. Your primary goal is to shield them and let them be kids.

This can be particularly difficult to resist if your husband tries to use the children as a bargaining ploy. He may act as if he's willing to give in regarding a specific issue, as long as you allow the children to become involved. Consider this carefully — even if he is sincere, how will this affect the children? And what is the likelihood that he *is* sincere? Isn't it more likely that this is just another ploy to manipulate you?

New Stresses for Your Children

Intense Attention   When the divorce process begins, it's not uncommon for the husband to begin focusing intensely on the children — either negative or positive attention. This may be because he is losing control of you, so he decides to exercise control in an area where he still can — the children.

It can be quite disturbing when this comes out in negative ways: He uses them to get to you, to appeal to you, to manipulate you. However, it can be just as disturbing to some women when suddenly there is an intense amount of positive attention showered on the children, particularly if he had essentially ignored them before the divorce process began. Now he is demanding time with them, is attentive to them when they are with him, and making sure the time spent with him is extra fun.

Exacerbating your frustration is that most children will not look at this objectively. They will be appreciative of having their father in their lives in a positive way, regardless of the reason. They will often not see it as a loyalty issue, as you might; they usually will not decide to reject their father because it's "too little, too late."

This may be difficult for you to handle emotionally. Perhaps you stayed in the marriage, suffering for as long as you did, because you were trying to work things out for the children's sake. Perhaps you finally decided to divorce because you felt the children were negatively impacted by the situation in your marriage. Now, if they are so easily accepting of their father's newfound attention, it may feel like a slap in the face.

Always remember that this does not diminish their love for their mother. It is also important to remember is that children do best during and after the divorce process when they have *two* loving parents. Even if your husband is being loving because he wants to get at you, or prove something to you, or look good to the community, his *rav*, the *beis din* or court, you should actually hope that he'll continue to want to prove this for the rest of their childhood. It may offend your sense of *emes* (truth) and hurt, but it is still in your children's best interest to have their father in their lives in a positive way.

All the same, if he is acting the good guy, and you are stuck with all the discipline and chores, your children can be left with a negative feeling. Try to institute some fun time when they are with you. Schedule a game night or baking night or art night. It can be low cost or homebound. As long as it's positive, you won't get pigeonholed as the difficult or downer parent.

Don't fall into the trap of trying to show the children your point of view. If they can't see it, it's because it isn't obvious. If you try to point it out, *you'll* lose. On the other hand, if your husband is *actively* undermining you, as we discussed previously, making a concrete, direct statement to illuminate your point of view is important.

If your husband does things that you feel may be harmful to the children, such as activities that you perceive as dangerous or unhealthy, seek immediate guidance on how to handle this in an appropriate way. However, keep in mind that certain aspects of your husband's conduct that you regard as inappropriate or harmful may not be viewed in the same manner by the court.

Using Children as a Go-Between

As a general principle, avoid placing your children between you and your husband. Do not use them to convey messages back and forth. Do not vent to your children about how difficult their father is being or how difficult it is for you to cope with the process of divorcing. You are entitled to vent, but do so to your trusted friends or adult family members.

Some mothers talk about wanting to protect the family name and keeping the details very private. That's fine, but not if that leads you to decide that the only ones you can vent to about your husband are your children. This applies even if they are now adults.

The Stigma of Divorce

The issue of stigma associated with parental divorce, and how your children handle it, may come up now or at any time during and after the divorce process. Encourage your children to share what they are feeling regarding the impact of the divorce on their friendships.

Consistency and self-esteem boosting activities help children stay grounded during this difficult time. If your children have been involved with extracurricular positive activities, make sure he or she sticks with them. Their self-consciousness and desire to "hide out" until the storm blows over may be understandable, but it really isn't in their best interests. The questions will come eventually — encourage them to get them out of the way sooner rather than later. Maintaining consistency, with as little disruption as possible, is always a plus for children (and adults too).

Let your children know that if anyone asks a questions that makes them uncomfortable, or if they're asked a question they don't know how to answer, they can come to you to brainstorm how to handle it. Ask if they have some questions of their own, or if they have some in mind that they are worried about answering. Ask if they'd like to practice now. Answering their own questions might help, but what they need to know and what they will share can be two very different things.

Let them know, too, that if a question they don't know the answer to comes up unexpectedly, they can always tell the person, "I don't know," or "I'll have to think about that," or "I don't want to talk about this right now." This is a helpful tool that prepares them to deal with any encounter that might make them uncomfortable. Help them understand that they don't have to have an answer ready, or have to share what they don't want to.

> *Shelly had separated and divorced her extremely abusive husband. After a while, her former husband fled the country, rather than pay child support.*
>
> *When Shelly first talked to her daughter Molly about the impending divorce, she was worried about her reaction. She knew teenagers could be difficult, and she was concerned that Molly would be uncomfortable at school as a result of the divorce.*
>
> *Molly surprised her, though. She reassured her mother that she would be fine. She knew other girls at school whose parents were divorced, including one of her friends, and didn't see anyone treating them differently.*

For a while, it did seem that the divorce hadn't impacted Molly's social interactions. One day, though, Molly came home extremely distraught. After some coaxing from Shelly, Molly explained that when the divorce news first come out, it really was no big deal. What had now become an issue was the fact that her friend Miriam, whose parents were also divorced, had started talking to Molly about how often she sees her father, what they do when they spend time together, what Shabbos is like with her father, and so on. When Miriam asked Molly to share details regarding her experiences, Molly became completely mortified. She didn't know what to say or how much she wanted to let anyone know. She now told her mother that she had become completely flustered and didn't want to go back to school — ever!

Preparing your children for possible uncomfortable situations will be a tremendous help in their adjustment. Whether they can anticipate questions that might make them uncomfortable, or they need you to come up with general scenarios and how to handle them, the key is to offer to role play until they are comfortable.

Let the appropriate individuals at your child's school know what is happening. Ask them to keep an eye on your children and let you know if anything seems to be troubling them. Being proactive by letting the school know sooner rather than later will enlist the support of your children's teachers in advance. This increases the likelihood that they will interpret any problem behaviors on the part of your children as by-products of the situation, rather than indications of a poor character. It may also guide them to make the decision to give your child some leeway where appropriate, should they need it.

And of course, if one or more of your children appears to be taking the divorce particularly hard and manifests anxiety, depression, or angry acting-out behavior, you might want to seek professional help for the child.

Changes in Relationships

Following your disclosure of your decision to divorce and continuing through the divorce process, you will encounter changes in many of your personal relationships. People may treat you differently from before. Some reactions and changes will be easier to handle than others.

Your Closest Support/Confidants: Parents and Friends

Some people are blessed with the emotional intelligence and ability to completely put themselves aside in order to listen to your needs. More likely, however, is that your closest allies — parents or friends — will struggle, as you will, with your decision and your process, and there will be times when what they want to give in the way of support, advice, and direction is not what you want to get. They may think you should take a certain course of action, compromise on issues, or strategize in ways that you disagree with.

There may be times that you want your parents or friends to be more involved, and times when you would rather that they are not a part of your divorce process. Because they are not you and cannot read your mind, the likelihood of anyone being perfectly in sync with what you need at each stage of the process is highly unlikely.

> *Paula's mother was extremely distraught and emotional when she found out about the abuse her daughter had been subjected to by her husband. After Paula separated, her mother would call every day to find out what was going on, what her husband was saying or doing, what she had heard from the lawyer or the rabbi, what her therapist had said, and so on.*
>
> *At first Paula appreciated her mother's involvement. It felt good to have her mother be so validating. She had hesitated for so long in telling her parents for fear of their reaction, worrying that they might not believe her, or even blame her. When her mother reacted by being horrified and supportive, Paula almost couldn't get enough of that support.*
>
> *But the daily barrage of questions soon became overwhelming.*

When Paula, after much thought and consideration, agreed to cer-
tain concessions on visitation and financial issues, her mother hit
the roof. Paula realized that if she wanted to pursue this course of
action, she would have to relinquish the constant support from her
mother. If she kept her mother involved by giving her all the details,
her mother would react by insisting that Paula should never give in
on anything. It was hard to give up the support, but at some point,
the negativity outweighed the benefits.

While the above scenario involves a mother and daughter, it could be a woman and her close confidants. You might need their care, their involvement, and perhaps their connections. You certainly don't want to hurt their feelings by appearing to ignore their advice and suggestions. The situation will be complicated further if they are helping you financially, perhaps at the expense of sacrificing their own needs. You may be concerned about pursuing a course of action that *you* feel is right, and they don't — if they will be required to pay for it. Trying to be mindful of their feelings while making the decision that is right for you can be agonizing at times. Having an open and frank discussion might mitigate some of the negative fallout you hope to avoid in this most important relationship.

At the other end of the spectrum is the ambivalent or non-supportive parent or friend. Some people respond to divorce with disapproval or even blame. There may be attempts to get you to change your mind, try something else, or even intimidation in the event that you don't reconsider.

If it's your parents who are having this reaction, ask yourself why. Is it because they just don't believe in divorce, no matter what? Is there some rift between you that would make them less supportive? Are they limited emotionally in some way, which might make them very self-centered and worried about this will affect *them*?

It can be difficult to go through this process without your parents' support, or the support of your good friend who you assumed would be there for you. Although stressful family support can be hard to manage, as was the case with Paula, when parents are completely rejecting of your decision, it is even more stressful.

If your parents or friend(s) are reacting negatively, consider whether you have fully allowed them into your process. If you have been suffering in silence so as not to distress them, and sought help and intervention without involving them (perhaps for their own benefit), it's not surprising that you might encounter this reaction to your announcement that you are getting divorced — even from very loving parents. While you may have had good reason to shield them from all or most of what has been going in your marriage (perhaps you were even afraid of what your husband would do if he found out you had disclosed), now would be a good time to sit down with them and catch up. While you may prefer not to re-live all the details, without a full disclosure they will have a very difficult time being there for you. You've run ahead, and if you want them by your side, it's necessary to give them the opportunity to catch up.

Keep an open dialogue — but not too open, if they are becoming interfering. Even if your parents are not supportive now, allowing them insight into your process might eventually bring them into the supportive role that you want for them.

Your Husband's Family

Change is the operative word when it comes to relationships with members of your husband's family. Family members who have supported you in the past, and perhaps even made efforts to get him to change his abusive behavior, are likely to become more supportive of *him* once the decision to divorce has been made. This is especially true if he has been getting progressively less observant, in addition to being abusive. His family members may feel that a divorce will hasten his move away from *frumkeit*, and as much as they might have felt for your plight, they fear what will happen to him if you let go of the reins. To compound matters, they now feel that they have to support him to keep him *frum*. This may be very misguided, but it is typical of how many families in this situation react.

Sometimes the previously supportive family member — aunt, sister-in-law, cousin — realize that while you are leaving the extended family, they are not. They might feel that as long as they were helping you and you were staying in your marriage there was not a conflict. But to support you *leaving* their brother, husband's brother, nephew or son would demand too high a cost to their own family relationships.

Of course, the manner in which relationships with the various members of your husband's family will change is related to the nature of these relationships prior to the decision to divorce. Some women have been very close with one or more members of his family. Others had a decent but superficial relationship, while there were those who had a contentious relationship. You may have felt that his family members could have intervened, made things better, forced him to get help, and because they didn't, you are resentful and angry toward them. Some members of his family may have had little or no knowledge of his abusive behavior, while others may know the entire story.

Some women find that their *best* relationships were with his family members, since he didn't feel threatened by them and therefore allowed that relationship to develop. Perhaps you had a good or even a close relationship with your mother-in-law or sister-in-law (this may be his sister or his brother's wife), but you didn't actually confide what was going on in your marriage. You might have enjoyed being a part of his larger family, and a close relationship may have developed despite the fact that this person had no idea what you were going through with your husband.

In this scenario, when you decide to divorce it is quite likely that his family will cut you off or turn on you. They may say negative things about you to others, or work to undermine you in your attempt to get divorced. Such a response may leave you feeling hurt and angry. Remember, though, that your abusive husband is their son or brother, and they are not aware of the full extent of the abuse. While you may still feel the loss of the family that you enjoyed, it is easier to accept it.

In another scenario, you may have had a close relationship with a member of your husband's family who was aware of the abuse. She may even have been one of your supporters during the period in which you were trying to get him to change. In this scenario, once you have initiated the divorce process, it is less likely that your confidant will turn on you actively or start saying negative things about you to others. Nevertheless, it is very likely that your relationship with her will undergo a considerable change.

Through five years in her abusive marriage, Simmi's mother-in-law, Dahlia, had been an incredible source of support. Simmi had confided in her mother-in-law, sharing even the most odious aspects of her husband Michael's behavior with his mother.

Over the years, Dahlia had not only provided an empathic listening ear, but had also slipped Simmi some money when she could. Throughout this entire period, Simmi's mother never told her son that Simmi had shared his abusive behaviors, because she knew that letting on would cause Simmi more trouble. Both she and Simmi were careful of keeping Michael from finding out.

Given the closeness of their relationship and Dahlia's long history of lending a helping hand, Simmi assumed that her mother-in-law would continue to support her after she decided that divorce was the only alternative. She was convinced that her mother-in-law would understand the necessity of this action, having been privy to all of the gory details. She also felt certain that her mother-in-law would continue to help her out.

But when Simmi began talking about actually leaving the marriage, Dahlia started to slowly change. In the past, when Simmi would tell her about an incident in which her husband had been abusive, her mother-in-law had always been validating. Dahlia had often reassured Simmi that her husband's behavior was wrong, and how dismayed she was that he could treat his wife this way.

Now, though, Dahlia seemed to be more willing to make excuses for her son's behavior. Dahlia began suggesting that there could be an explanation for his abusive actions, that her husband wasn't really a bad person, and perhaps there was something Simmi could do to keep things together. Simmi felt terribly betrayed at the loss of support.

Your decision to divorce can often result in a shift in the direction of more support for your abusive husband, and less support for you. Even when the family member is aware of how abusive your husband is, she is still likely to feel sympathy for him at the prospect of the impending divorce, or a responsibility to keep the marriage together regardless.

This can take a lot of getting used to, both emotionally and practically. Emotionally, it can be quite hard to lose a primary support, and this extra loss — which is in addition to the loss of the dream of saving your marriage — can be quite devastating. On a practical level, you need support to go through this process. If you've lost one of your primary supports, it's important to get others.

Women who have had only superficial relationships with members of their husband's family usually have no particular expectations regarding how they will respond once the divorce process is underway. If you have formed no particular emotional ties with his family, once the separation occurs and the divorce process is initiated, you presumably will not have very much contact with his family — and this probably will not disturb you. Your children will likely have continued contact with them during their time with your husband, but your own interactions will be minimal.

Some of how this plays out will depend on what you want and what they want.

Sheila had been in the divorce process for a couple of months when she ran into her husband's cousin at the yeshivah where they both sent their boys. Sheila actually liked Debbie. They lived in the same community, and when she was still married they sometimes had a Shabbos meal together. Their boys, while a year apart, got along when they were together.

When Sheila ran into Debbie, her initial reaction was to be pleased. But then she felt cautious. She didn't know how Debbie would react to her and the fact that she was divorcing Debbie's cousin. Sheila didn't have hard feelings toward Debbie, but she didn't know how Debbie felt.

Debbie was actually warm, and suggested that Sheila and her son come over for a Shabbos meal. Sheila said she would let her *know when. But then she started having second thoughts. Could she feel comfortable at Debbie's, while knowing that anything she did or said or shared could go back to her husband? Her husband was looking for anything he could use to fight her for custody, **and he would certainly grill Debbie for details if he found out she had been there.** In the end, she decided she would rather keep her distance.*

Of course, this is just the beginning. There will be the "after the divorce" situation. There will be family *simchas* where interactions aren't avoidable. Some of these encounters will be easier than others. If you can keep civil when they are, and avoid them when they aren't, keeping things free of overt conflict will always be in your and your children's best interest. If the relationships are closer than that, and it's what you want and feels safe — all the better.

Acquaintances and the Community at Large

As mentioned previously, one of the most difficult things to deal with can be the intrusiveness of community members and acquaintances. When people find out that you are getting divorced, they probably will not be aware of the abuse you have endured and will not understand why you are seeking the divorce — since you have reserved that information for your innermost circle of friends. That will not stop others from coming over to ask questions, offer advice, make suggestions or even accusations. This can be extremely difficult and draining to deal with. Prepare yourself, much as you have prepared your children, for answering these uncomfortable or intrusive queries. Most important, give yourself permission not to respond when it is not in your best interests.

There may also be people who reach out to you because of their own situation. Perhaps a woman is unhappy in her marriage, and views you as someone who can help her or give her the strength to do what *you* did. There are those who are divorcing, or have divorced, who may reach out to offer support or caution you based on their own experiences. Be cognizant of how these outstretched hands are affecting you — are they lifting you up, or dragging you down? At this difficult time, your primary focus has to be on you and your children. You may be able to be there for others in the future, but now your primary goal is to have your support people close at hand so you can get through this in the healthiest possible way.

Chapter Nine

After
the Divorce

The final settlement has been reached, the *get* is given. The no man's land of separation is over. Life after divorce begins.

The divorce process can be very different from one situation to another. But once that is complete, the struggles women contend with afterward are fairly universal. Some of these issues may have begun while separated, especially if there was an extended separation period. Most, however, feel that there is something different about being divorced. There's a definitive quality that changes things.

There are various difficulties, challenges, and adjustments that need to be made after divorce. There are also triumphs and fulfillment that women experience. This chapter addresses the challenges, because you probably don't need help figuring out how to enjoy the good stuff!

Many women report that, at this stage in the process, along with a sense of relief often comes the time and space to feel much of what they have been holding in abeyance. In the relative quiet after the divorce, memories of their marriage and the accompanying feelings of pain, humiliation, and betrayal can resurface. Each woman will need to work this through individually.

In terms of the more common challenges women face, there is a lot to be gained from listening to other women who have been through this situation. In this chapter, you will hear directly from women who have insight born of experience to help you negotiate life after divorce.

Common Challenges

"I'm Divorced — Go Ahead, Say Whatever You Want"

Do you feel like there's a sign written on your forehead announcing this to the world? You're not alone. Many women report how unbelievably insensitive, ill informed or downright rude others can be, and how difficult it is to believe that people can sometimes say such things.

Unfortunately, there are those who believe they are entitled to simply insert themselves into the situation, without recognizing how inappropriate that might be. The shock of these intrusive comments may leave you feeling paralyzed or defensive.

To ease that feeling, it may be helpful to see some of the comments others have had to contend with, along with their responses. This list is by no means exhaustive, but it should be enough to reassure you that it's not just you!

WHAT WAS SAID	WHAT YOU MIGHT BE THINKING	WHAT WAS SAID/DONE
(from a casual acquaintance) "What happened?"	*"Do you really think it's appropriate to ask me the personal details of my life?"*	"I really think it's best/I was told not to casually discuss the details."
"Did you really have to get a divorce?"	*"No, I just thought it might be fun to go through the trauma, I'm weird like that."*	"Yes" and just walked away.
"Have you thought about what effect this is going to have on your children?"	*"How dare you — that's all I've thought about and agonized over!"*	"Yes" and just walked away.
Not to you, but in your presence, "Second marriages are so weird."	*"Don't mind me, I'm just over here hoping for a second marriage."*	Nothing.
Not to you, but in your presence, "It's so nice to have your children close together. Too far apart and it's like two different families."	*"My child is already three and I'm not re-married. Best case scenario is that I have more children, however far apart they may be."*	"I'm glad that I'm so well-adjusted that you don't think of me as divorced, but could you please think before you speak?"
(At a *simchah*) "Where's your husband tonight/which one is your husband?" or "What's your maiden name?" (when you've gone back to it) or other comments that force you to either hide or say you're divorced.	*"AAAAARGH!"*	"I'm divorced. Don't feel uncomfortable, people stumble on that all the time." (Even if you do feel uncomfortable, taking control of the awkward situation will make you feel better.)

WHAT WAS SAID	WHAT YOU MIGHT BE THINKING	WHAT WAS SAID/DONE
"So, why are you still covering your hair?" OR "Who said you could stop covering your hair? Do you think that's really the right thing?"	*"Do you actually think that's your business?"*	"I didn't make any decisions by myself."
"You know, I was really nervous when you got engaged to him, I mean there were things going around about him," OR "I knew he had issues, but I was hoping marriage would help," OR "I didn't want to ruin his chances."	*"Is that supposed to make me feel better: that you knew before and didn't say anything?"*	Some felt better about saying, "Oh," and just walking away. Others did feel the need to say, "I hope you re-think this strategy in the future."

In all likelihood, you could add a few of your own insensitive comments to this list. There is no great way to answer these types of comments. Most women report that they felt best being brief and simply ending the conversation. The women who shared their experiences above said they felt good afterward, even if at the moment they were angry or felt humiliated.

Those who became defensive, or shared a lot of information in order to explain things, felt worse than when they kept silent or brief. Saying more usually means you have to expose more information. And since these comments usually provoke strong emotions, there's a greater chance of "losing it" if you engage in an in-depth conversation.

Shabbos and Yom Tov

Shabbos and Yom Tov can present practical and emotional challenges. From a practical perspective, everyone's situation will be somewhat different in terms of the custody and visitation arrangements, family support and proximity, and whether there are children or not.

Without exception, every woman will need to figure out how to manage emotionally. Women without children acknowledge that while this can be easier in many ways, it also leaves them feeling as if they're in a no man's land. They aren't married, but they aren't single. They feel their parents shouldn't have the same rules or expectations regarding what they do on Shabbos or Yom Tov as they did before they were married. But their parents may slip back into that way of thinking, since these women don't have the status of being parents. Being around your married siblings or friends can also be difficult. Some women choose to alternate between spending time in a family environment and being with other singles. Everyone has to figure out what works and feels healthy.

When there are children involved, the challenges are different. How can you remain in a healthy state when you don't have your children for Shabbos or Yom Tov? How will you manage to meet their and your emotional needs when they are with you? There are differences in each person's situation, but there are also a lot of commonalities. Hearing how others have learned to cope in a positive way can be extremely valuable.

Here, Sarah provides good advice on how to handle a wide range of the emotional issues associated with Shabbos and Yom Tov, while providing for yourself and your children.

> *Yom Tov can present a particularly difficult emotional challenge. I want to be happy and enjoy Yom Tov, but of course it isn't that simple. When I have my children with me, I worry about where we're going to spend Yom Tov and how it will work out. I love my family and I want to spend Yom Tov with them, but I have one sibling who doesn't understand. One of my brothers resents the fact that I'm divorced, feels embarrassed by it and is judgmental. This makes things uncomfortable, especially when I feel that he looks at my children with pity and contempt, and then blames me.*
>
> *But I don't have a better alternative. I don't want to be alone at*

home with the children for Yom Tov. I want them to have a full family environment. I want my boys to go to shul with someone.

Some divorced women I know go to other families because their own is not an option, for a variety of reasons. I just don't feel comfortable with that right now. So I try to ignore the looks or insensitive comments that come my way.

Eventually, I figured out that it's really important to prepare for Yom Tov in advance. When I have my children, I find out who is coming and for which meals. I arrange things so I'm busy when that brother is going to be around, and make myself scarce when he tries to start a conversation with me, or when he talks about divorce in general, because I know he'll bring the conversation back around to me and my divorce.

To make Yom Tov a great experience for my children, I go to the library and take out books they like. If I have the extra money, I buy a new game. If not I ask friends or neighbors for a game we could borrow. On nice days I have at least one outing to the park. If the weather doesn't cooperate, I find someone they'd like to visit. Sometimes it's a sister who wasn't coming over, so we could go there for a meal or dessert. Sometimes it's a married friend with children their age, and we go for a meal or two. When the time is filled with activity and warmth from friends or family members, we all feel better for it.

Of course, if my children expressed a desire to spend time alone, with just us in our home, I listen. Even if this is harder for me, I know I need to hear what they have to say. I also make sure that I don't use being home as an excuse to stay in bed or in my pajamas. The children need to feel that even if things aren't how they "should" be, they are going to be the best they can be. I get dressed, we go to shul, the table is set l'kavod Shabbos, and we have Shabbos meals like any other family.

The older ones can sense who treats them the same, viewing them as "normal," and who treats them as if they are different. They sometimes comment that they prefer spending Shabbos or Yom Tov with people who make them feel like they're still the same kids they were before. I respect their invitation requests as well.

It's harder when I don't have the children. I admit I sometimes look forward to the break, but mostly I dread the empty feeling that comes from just thinking about Yom Tov or Shabbos without my children. There were times, early on, when I could get physically ill thinking about being without them. And my worry over how they were doing with my ex — don't get me started!

But for my children's sake, I had to figure out how to give them the sense of security that only I can provide. It was my job not to dwell on my worries about what might happen, or how much happier they say they are when they're with me. If I didn't put that somewhere, I just couldn't manage.

At first, even when I didn't have my children for Yom Tov I still went to my family. I always thought, "That's what Yom Tov is all about — being with family." And they were great (okay, except for that one brother), but it was still very hard. Because it seemed to amplify my situation — here I am with my family for Yom Tov, but my children aren't here!

I eventually realized that it was best for me to go to a family for Yom Tov, but not my own family. I needed a different routine for the times when I didn't have my children. It was just less painful that way.

I have friends with families, an aunt, family friend or other relative who I felt comfortable going to. This gave me the best of both worlds. I had change, but I was still part of a family structure that is so important to maintaining stability and spirituality, and keeping me strong and whole. Occasionally, I would stay home alone for a Shabbos, to re-charge my batteries and just decompress, but I never let that become a pattern, and never for Yom Tov.

It's important to note that if you have concerns based on actual incidents that your children report upon returning from their father's home — seek immediate guidance. If your worries or anxieties are a byproduct of being separated from your children, on the other hand, be assured that this is extremely normal. But it's important that you work these through so you can be there for your children in the best possible way.

If You Move Back Home

When I first walked into my parents' home, I knew just one thing: I needed them. I wasn't sure what was going to happen, I just figured that my father could fix it. I mean, that's what fathers do, they fix things.

Not everything is so easy to fix. This time, he couldn't just tighten a screw or change a battery, but he did the smartest thing he could under the circumstances: He called a rav. From that point on, until I got my get, *we did exactly what we were told to do, we tried what could be tried. But here are the results: I was spending the rest of my* shanah rishonah *in my parents' home, pregnant and newly divorced.*

Some women move back to their parents' home when they separate, and stay if they have to divorce. Some go through the divorce process while still in the marital home, and then move back to their parents. Some move back because they feel it is the right place for them to be, some because of financial considerations, some for the support or help with their young children.

Moving back into your parents' home after you have become accustomed to running your own home can be a difficult adjustment.

All my parents (and siblings) wanted to fix things, take care of me, help me with the obvious pain. But they were going about it in a way that was making me feel overwhelmed, even suffocated. I needed them, but I also terribly needed my space.

It was really difficult to get it at first. I had a brand new baby, Baruch Hashem, *whom they loved to pieces, and they wanted to spend every moment with her. But there went my privacy. Even after they renovated the basement for me so I had my own little apartment, that didn't stop my family members from walking in whenever they wanted and staying as long as they wanted.*

I tried really hard to remember that I am under their roof and show the proper hakaras hatov, *not to mention* kibud av v'em. *I tried to remember, too, that everything they were doing was out of love and concern. But I also felt that I needed more boundaries — the type I would have if my apartment was down the block, instead of in the basement.*

I tried to explain things to them and help them understand my perspective, that my needs for boundaries and independence were not an insult or a rejection. I wrote a letter, which is very helpful when you want to say things just so, and then we talked.

It didn't change things overnight. But over time we have come to a place of understanding and appreciation for each others' needs and perspectives, and I know how grateful I am to have all of them in my life.

For those with parents whose natural parenting style allows for more independence, this type of conflict will be somewhat less common. It will be more difficult for those whose parents are more overprotective, but who themselves crave independence. On the other hand, some women feel needy and traumatized and crave extra support, and that type of situation would work well for them.

Sometimes the combination of needs and types work well for a while, but then the needs change and the transition hits a rough patch. For example, perhaps at first a woman needs her parents to be very overprotective, doting on her and her process, but eventually she'd like to stop talking about it so much. Or she begins to feel more confident in her ability to manage with parenting, or contacting her ex. But her parents have come to assume a certain role and style of helping her, and they want to keep giving to her that way.

In any situation where there is strain between the current reality in your family relationship and how you prefer things to be, it's important to address the issue sooner rather than later. First, determine what it is that's bothering you, why this change is important to you, and what can be done to make this change. Next, find the best venue for presenting this to your parents. Do you want to write them a letter, as in the example above? Do you feel okay about discussing it with them? Or would talking about it with a third party be helpful? Coming together with a third party can increase the chances that the conversation will stay constructive.

Some parents do stay focused on *their* need to give, as opposed to what their child says she really wants. For the most part, however, I have found that when you can clearly talk about your needs and the changes you'd like to see, while being open to hearing their hesitations or difference in perspective, families can usually come to a place where they can live together happily. This is particularly true when you remember to have respect for the fact that they are your parents — they are also in pain, and they have needs, too.

Family and Childrearing

When you move back home with your children, one common area of difficulty is differences in childrearing styles and expectations. Here's what Shaindy had to say:

> *I felt it was important for my children's chinuch for them to see me being respectful to my parents. I was living in their home, and I needed to respect their standards. When we differed on how strict to be in a specific situation, if they stepped in to discipline, I didn't contradict them in front of my children. If they were being more permissive, I tried to step in with the discipline before they could permit something, so I wouldn't have to step on their toes by contradicting them. If there was a specific thing that they kept allowing that troubled me, I would talk to them at a quiet time and ask them to please respect my standards.*
>
> *If they disciplined a child, I would not double discipline. I let them know that although I respected their right to discipline my child in their home, I didn't think it was fair to my children to "get it" twice. Showing them respect and keeping the lines of communication open helped things stay smooth — for the most part!*

Being on
Your Own   Yes, in many ways you may have been on your own for a while. But when the divorce is final, there is something much more real about this status of *being on your own.*

There is a lot that is new and frightening for a woman when she gets divorced, especially a woman who doesn't move back home and is now navigating life and making decisions completely on her own. Even for those who do move back to their parents' home, there may be things you never had to know how to do before — but now you're the one who has to do them. Perhaps it's health insurance, or car insurance, or other particulars that you have to take care of. Perhaps it's figuring out how to fill in your financial picture; you may need to get on public assistance, or get items or funds from a *gemach.*

If you run your own home, you might need to have things fixed, make an improvement, deal with service or maintenance people either through your building manager or on your own. There may be details you never had to manage before, and having to deal with it all can be very overwhelming.

Here's what Miri had to say:

> *Some of the responsibilities I now have I never had to worry about before, and I just didn't know where to start. There were other responsibilities I had been taking care of all along, but they didn't seem as overwhelming when I had the illusion of having a partner. Being completely in charge of my life sometimes left me feeling as if I was drowning.*
>
> *One of my parents would occasionally want to rush in to rescue me. It was so tempting to let them, and there were times that I did. But I realized this was not a great solution. It felt good in the short term, but it was also a confirmation that I <u>was</u> helpless. So while that particular thing might get done, my overall sense of myself and my new life didn't get better.*
>
> *Then a friend of mine suggested that I get a notebook and create sections for each technical item that kept coming up — and always felt like a mountain I had to climb. She told me to research possible*

solutions. Ask other people who they used, how they got it done, how much it cost, or what made something work out easily.

It was a lot of work at first, and not really my style to call people and ask for these details. At first I only called people I was comfortable with. When they said something like, "You know who knows a ton about this? My uncle Shmueli, and I'm sure he would have no problem answering your questions," I made up some excuse, or ignored the offer.

After a while, though, two things happened. First, I got more comfortable with asking strangers questions. Second, I found that I had a handle on most typical problems or issues. When they came up again, I just referred to my notebook of resources, and it was no longer something that required a lot of time or effort.

It is not uncommon for someone newly on her own to find it challenging to face the issues of managing everyday life. This is both an emotional and practical challenge. Miri's suggestion of organizing, researching, and creating your own resource book is an excellent one. There will be different categories of people to whom you might go for guidance. There will be personal contacts, such as a neighborhood friend or family member who can refer you to a reasonable and reliable plumber. There will be agencies or organizations in the community either for divorced or battered women, or those struggling economically, which might be a resource for you. Once you have organized your issues and started tackling them in a systematic fashion, things should feel a lot more manageable.

It may not be your style to ask and research and pursue, but it really is the only way to get a handle on things and start feeling in control of your life. When women defer to others when they feel overwhelmed, two things can happen. With Miri, the main concern was how it kept her feeling helpless. In addition to that, sometimes the others who step in make decisions that *they* deem appropriate. These decisions won't necessarily be in line with what *you* want done, but since you relied on them to take care of it, you will have to accept their decision. When *you* take charge of the decisions and are prepared to take care of the details, you'll start to feel as if life is under control.

Figuring Out Your Finances: One of the most difficult areas after divorce is managing financially. Most women really struggle. Figuring out how to make ends meet can be extremely overwhelming. This is especially true if you were a stay at home mom, and not already in the work force. And for those who are working, often it was to have something extra, not to provide fifty percent of support. The financial responsibility changes significantly after a divorce, whether or not you already have a job, or if your job will provide the amount you need. Consequently, even though you were abused and controlled in your home, from a financial perspective you may feel more desperate and destitute *after* the divorce.

Your ability to figure out how to manage financially will largely depend on how you manage your expectations. Before, you may have done some part-time work for pocket money, but that was "on the side." Now you realize that you *need* to work. This change represents a major adjustment, because it involves not only a major change in thinking, but also a number of major decisions. It is devastating when a woman's dream of living happily ever after in a healthy marriage ends in divorce. There may be a second feeling of devastation when she can't be the stay at home mom she had always wanted to be, because she can't manage financially without going to work.

If there is an immediacy to your need to earn money, you might have to start something right away, regardless of what it is or how much it pays. If you have help to tide you over for a short time, you may be able to engage in job training that would help you get a better paying job when you go out into the workforce. If you have already been working, but your job only provided extras in your marriage and is inadequate to support you and your children, you need consider different options. A flexible boss in a job that doesn't pay you enough to get by needs to be weighed against a better paying job with less flexibility. You may be able to stay in that job and find other ways of filling in. Are you eligible for additional sources of support or income? Are there some creative ways to make up the difference?

Here's what Sima had to say:

> *There were many new realities in my financial situation. I was completely ignorant about some of the basics, such as how to balance a checkbook, how to save money and budget effectively, how to figure out what I spend, what I make, and how to fill in the gaps. I literally had to ask my friend and her husband to sit down with me and teach me this stuff. It was a little embarrassing, but I knew that this wasn't my fault. My husband had never allowed me to know anything about our finances, so I had never learned.*
>
> *Next, I had to get used to accepting help. Sometimes this meant applying for government programs that I never dreamed I would have to resort to. Going down to the public assistance offices felt completely degrading, and I can't say that I felt much better about utilizing community resources. Don't get me wrong — the kavod and discretion that the gemachs exercise is awe inspiring. The tznius way that Tomchei Shabbos made deliveries to my house was amazing. But it was a good long while before I stopped walking around with my head hanging low, even though no one knew anything about how I was managing. I had to work hard on changing my perspective on accepting necessary help, and being more realistic about my goal of becoming completely self-sufficient. Ultimately, I was proud that I was providing for my children's needs in a perfectly respectable way, even if I needed some help.*
>
> *I also had to work on my anger, and how I was going to handle my children's issues in a healthy, balanced way. You see, my ex wasn't having financial problems. He had plenty and gave me very little. Yet he had the chutzpah to tell the children that he gave me plenty of money, and if they needed an extra nine dollars for a school trip they should go to me. This was just one of many ways he would rub my financial hardship in my face. I really didn't have the extra nine dollars, and pulling a ten dollar bill out of his wallet would have meant nothing to him.*

I had to learn not to be bitter in front of my children, telling them that I would manage somehow, while also letting them know in simple language that what their father provided in no way covered our expenses. I didn't want to keep talking about the financial situation and make him out to be the bad guy. But I also wanted to make sure they knew enough so he couldn't make me into the bad guy, while I sat by quietly.

The financial situation for a woman post divorce can be very messy and complex. It complicates matters if you are struggling emotionally with your feelings about your ex and how he seems to be just fine in that department. Rather than staying stuck in your feelings, it is in your best interests to get active in making a plan.

Decide whether you are able to go straight to work, or if you will need education or training so you can provide a salary that allows you to make ends meet. What training do you need, and how much will be necessary to accomplish your goals? How will you finance this training? Will you need to work full time, or can you get by with part-time work? You will need to balance your own aspirations and long-term goals against the immediate needs of your family.

Each of these decisions can be difficult, involving many variables. If you are not accustomed to making decisions of this nature, the task can seem overwhelming. You might benefit from the experience of other women who have gone through a divorce and faced the same decisions.

Use the yellow pages, shul bulletins, or online searches to find groups or organizations that provide job counseling and training. Job counseling services are provided by many colleges and universities which offer special help for adult learners. There may be scholarships and grants that are available to you. There may also be child care services available while you are attending classes. You will need to seek out the specific information you need. Find local sources of support who can help you understand your options better.

Hindy wrote:

I was so overwhelmed and bitter over how much I had to provide. The time and energy it took out of me made me feel like a slave to the process. Don't get me wrong — even during the most difficult times, I didn't fantasize about going back to that marriage! It was just that it was so hard, and there didn't seem to be any end in sight.

But then I realized that, unlike my marriage, here I really did have choices. I could determine the course I could take — yes, within limits, but still, the options were there. With my new perspective, I could slowly take the time to look around and think about what I saw other people doing that I might like to do to support my family. Right now I had to take the job I could get, but I could work toward something that would be more fulfilling. Now I'm on a path that is definitely long, but it is taking me somewhere that I want to be.

It's common for a woman who has lived for a period of time with an abusive spouse to lose sight of who she is as a person, what her likes and dislikes are, and what she wants to achieve. Even when you have the time and space to think about it, ideas might elude you. If you're trying to figure out what job would appeal to you, one possibility is job counseling. Another way to start your self exploration is to look at classified ads for job opportunities, and magazine ads for classes. What would you enjoy? Is it realistic for you to think you could get that job, to have the time for that course? Would it pay enough? Thinking in terms of possibilities can shift your perspective, even if your job doesn't change any time soon.

Negotiating Friendships, Building a Support Network, and Moving On

Old Friends Your old friends probably fall into a couple of categories. There are those with whom you interacted, maybe enjoyed the occasional outing, but did not share what was going on in your marriage. As far as they can tell, you're getting divorced out of the blue. It can be very difficult to figure out how to handle this.

Here's what Tali had to say:

> *I didn't believe it was respectful to my children or to myself to tell my story all over town. There were those who had to know — my lawyer,* toan, *and one close confidant who helped guide me. Beyond that, I didn't want to spread things around needlessly.*
>
> *Some friends knew me well enough to recognize that if I wasn't sharing details, it was because I didn't want to. There were those friends who asked what happened, but when I said I didn't want to get into it, they respected that and we moved on. And there were those who could not let the questions go. With the latter group, I let the friendships fall by the wayside, and reassured myself that* baruch Hashem *I had at least a few who fit in the other two categories. That is really all I need — and have time for!*

Another type of friendship may exist. It preceded your divorce, kept up throughout your divorce process, and is someone you still value afterward. This is the friend you confided in and has seen you through the entire experience. Every detail was discussed, every move reviewed. She was there for you all the way.

Now you are divorced. Some things still come up, but most have definitely settled down. You still want this friend in your life, but you're bothered when conversations between you keep coming back to *him.* This friendship has become uncomfortable, and you don't know why.

When a relationship is forged over something this intense, it can be hard to shift gears and turn it into a regular friendship. It's important to do this if you want to retain the friendship, though, because if you're trying to move on, but the friendship doesn't, then the relationship that was so helpful to you is now starting to hold you back.

Here's what Melanie had to say:

> *Naava was amazing. She helped me through everything. I finally got my* get *and my divorce, and I couldn't have done it without her support.*
>
> *Things settled down. There were still parenting issues, and*

frustrations over my ex's financial shenanigans, but eventually I felt like I was getting settled in my new life post divorce. I realized, though, that Naava and I hadn't moved on. We kept talking about it, about him, about all the stuff that I had gone through.

Yes, I had needed that for a while, even after I was out, but now I wanted to stop talking and thinking about it. But Naava was my best friend, the person I talked to a few times a day, and because she couldn't let it go I ended up talking about the old stuff far more often than I wanted to. So much of our friendship had been about planning and strategizing, and it seemed like Naava couldn't stop, even though I wanted to.

Eventually, I told Naava that her friendship meant the world to me, but we had to develop a new relationship — one that didn't necessarily include venting to her about my marriage, or being so dependent on her, or talking about my ex and the injustices that went on during the marriage or the divorce proceedings. It took a little doing, but eventually we figured out how to have just a regular friendship.

This type of shift in friendship is usually possible once you notice and discuss it, though it might take some willpower not to fall back on divorce/ abuse discussions. Once in a while, however, a friendship that really served a woman well during her divorce process can't make the transition to normal life. Usually that happens when the friendship was actually formed around the crisis of the abusive marriage and divorce. In the cases where the friendship doesn't last, it's because the women realize that, without all that stuff to talk about, they don't actually have much in common. Moving on in life might mean moving on from the friendship.

New Friends After a divorce, many women seek to connect with others who have "been there." The goal here may be twofold: to forge new friendships, and to create a network to help with financial resources, parenting resources, or other issues best addressed by someone who has gone through the system.

While this can be very helpful, women who have moved on in a healthy way often have a common message: Don't let your whole world, or your whole social network, become about divorce or be restricted to divorced friends. Here's what Shayna had to say:

After my divorce, I joined a Tehillim group specifically for divorced women that met once a month. I was eager to meet others who had been there, because although I had some great friends, no one had experienced what I had. I thought it might be nice to be around women who could relate more closely to my experience. On the other hand, I was a little hesitant. I didn't want to sit around talking about my situation — that didn't seem to be a healthy way to move on.

The Tehillim group was just the right mix. Everyone was reminded (or in my case told, since I had never been there before) that this was a gathering about tefilah *and enjoying each others' company. The rules of the group were no venting, bashing, dwelling, and so on. I was surrounded by women who were sharing information about a new* gemach *or other financial resources. I could ask questions without shame or embarrassment, but I wasn't going to get stuck in the muck of talking about the whole sordid situation. It was the perfect balance.*

Others, like Shira, didn't have such a good experience.

After my divorce, I was contacted by another young divorcee in the community, asking if I wanted to get together with a couple of girls who were in a similar situation. It sounded ideal. Most of my friends were married and not going out much. When I was around those who hadn't been through what I had, there always seemed to be an insensitive comment, or something said out of a lack of awareness, that made me upset. I thought this would be a good solution.

I met with this group at a local café. I knew one of the women a little bit and was meeting the others for the first time. But as we sat and talked, I was disappointed that everyone just wanted to talk

about what they had gone through and what a terrible person their
ex was. Don't get me wrong, my ex was just as bad. But I had a ther-
apist, and I preferred confining my discussions to my sessions with
her and my sister. Yes, I was looking for friends who could "get it,"
but I wasn't interested in a support group where we talked about it
endlessly.

It was clear that this group was not for me. I wanted a fun outing
where I could learn a few things about resources, and not have to
worry about ignorant comments. Not this bitterness and negativity.

I've found, as I've watched other women struggle, that it's impor-
tant to have a balanced life with friendships of married friends and
singles. Though I sometimes feel offended by a comment my friends
don't even realize is inappropriate, it's better than being around too
much bitterness. Women who are healthy are those who find outlets,
such as a chesed *organization to join, which helps you remember*
that there is life beyond. You can remain a giving person. And being
part of an organization, a structure, or a family helps you stay away
from focusing on yourself too much. If you have your own family,
you may not have much time or energy, but it's still important to get
involved in something positive, so you can see a healthy future for
yourself.

If you know at least a few divorced women, you've probably noticed
that some "look good" after going through divorce, and others don't.
The difference usually is exactly what Shira and Shayna described. Yes,
there can be times when you feel down, but the only way out of that to a
healthy place is getting involved in positive activities, and staying away
from settings that might bring short-term relief, but ultimately will bring
you further down.

One final caution: Avoid overwhelming or burning out a friend. It's
to your benefit to have a friend who will be there for you if needed. But
don't push yourself on her; don't overstay your visit. If her husband's
coming home, it's time for you to go, even if you're still feeling needy.
Perhaps during the initial crisis, or in an emergency, it would be okay

to push the limits. But crises don't last for weeks and months. Now that you're moving on, make that subtle change to your relationship. It's not fair or smart to overburden someone. In the long run, you could lose out — because you could lose her.

Consider joining an organization, group or club with women who share common interests. This can help you develop new interests from which you may have been constrained during your marriage, and it will expand your social network. If you are not involved in a formal educational program or career-related training, consider taking some adult education classes. Perhaps you can develop an area of interest such as gourmet cooking or photography. The point is to get out, do things, and meet people.

Take advantage of your new status as the head of your household to invite new people over to your home. You now have the freedom to actively develop a social network. This may be a strange new reality for you. Coming from a controlling and abusive relationship, you may have had little opportunity to pick and choose friends or decide how to spend your time. Welcome these new possibilities. You may need to bolster your courage to make new overtures; you may need the support of old or new friends. Don't shrink away from the challenge. Consider this an adventure!

A Word About Boundaries

In all friendship situations, you will be exploring your new ability and opportunities to create boundaries. When you were married to an abuser, this decision may have been out of your hands. Perhaps the abuser didn't allow you to have friends at all, or you feared that a friend would find out what was going on. Alternatively, you may have been so dependent on a particular relationship that you didn't want to assert your needs out of fear that you would lose the person.

Now that your situation has changed, you can and should think about what boundaries and parameters you want in the relationships that you have. Boundaries in relationships are important and healthy.

Childrearing Issues

Children of parents who have divorced have the same needs as children from intact families. They require love, security, stability, and consistency.

You probably don't need anyone to tell you to love your children. Security, stability, and consistency may be more difficult, if your divorced spouse is not interested in helping you provide them for your children.

Divorce by definition challenges a child's stability, security, and consistency. Some couples can successfully work together to restore these elements, because they are able to put the children before themselves. That, however, takes both parents working together.

With most abusive husbands this is not possible. Some discover that their ex will use the contact necessary for true co-parenting to harass or manipulate them further. Others describe their husbands' active attempts to alienate their children from their mother, which does nothing to restore their stability.

If you are able to get to a place where you can work together to restore security, stability and consistency, that's great. In the likely event that you can't, however, these pointers can help you provide these things on your own.

Security   Following a divorce, most mothers with children typically cannot maintain the same standard of living. The amount of money you receive from your ex-husband for child support is not likely to be enough for the lifestyle you used to have. This decrease in economic status following divorce affects the sense of security felt by children. If you are clearly struggling to make ends meet, the children know it, and they tend to absorb your stress.

The changes in where you live, how you live, and which extras you can provide may be only marginally within your control. What *is* in your control is how much you allow your children to be exposed to your stress over the situation. While you may want to validate their feelings that it's difficult having changes in this area, you don't need to let them know how difficult it is for you. *You* need to be there for *them*, to let them express this to you.

When you need to express how it's affecting you, speak to friends or family members when your children aren't around. To provide your children with security despite losing financial security, be strong and positive when you're around them. This sense of positive confidence will serve them well.

Some suggest that when children spend time with their father as well as their mother, it is disturbing if there is a substantial discrepancy in the economic statuses of the two households. Children may feel conflicted if they want to spend time with their father to take advantage of items he has at his house that you don't: the big, flat screen TV, the state of the art computer system (what happens when this discrepancy presents *hashkafic* differences will be discussed later). It can also be problematic if their father can take them places and do things with them that you cannot afford. Some fathers spend their visitation on outings to toy stores or another money spending activity, which you either can't afford or aren't interested in doing.

Here's what Shifra had to say:

> *I made some serious mistakes at the beginning. I was so down about all the things my ex was buying my kids that I might have been close to a clinical depression. I was upset at the inequity, especially since all those years, I had worked so hard shielding my kids from his true nature; I always covered for him whenever he let them down or wasn't there for them. And now he was showering them with attention and exciting things, so he looked like the hero and I ended up the* nebach *in their lives. I was angry, and made my second mistake: bad mouthing him. They resented that, and that made them move further away from me.*
>
> *Once I realized those mistakes weren't helping me, I decided to do some reading, some talking and some thinking. I came to recognize one central truth, however difficult and unjust it seemed: it's good for my children to have their father in their lives in a positive way.*

Whatever his motivation, he was spending time with them, and not in a harmful way, however hurtful it felt to me. So I changed my approach. I started being positive about their time with him and the things he got them. I acted excited for them and their new acquisition.

When there was something he purchased that I disagreed with, or wasn't keeping with my standards, I wouldn't comment. I did feel like I was looking away sometimes, but I knew if I tried to convince them that it was wrong, it didn't change their outlook — it just made me the bad guy. Of course, if anything was severely out of line with our lifestyle, I would have objected, but nothing was quite that bad. Still, when they asked why we couldn't get whatever it was for our house, I would very unemotionally tell them that there were differences between their father's house and our house, and briefly tell them the reasons I had certain standards. I avoided sounding like I was trying to convince them or speaking negatively about their father. I wouldn't dwell, or complain, or attack.

I also looked for ways to make things positive in our house, whether it was games we would play together, less expensive but fun outings, or other bonding activities. Once I changed my approach and looked for resources to help me make things positive, I found that there were great ideas out there.

I actually think their father must have sensed that his spending wasn't bothering me so much anymore, because he seems to be spending less these days!

It's not uncommon for men who had been abusive to their wives, and not particularly involved with or attentive to their children, to suddenly become involved and invested after a separation and divorce. This may be genuine, or it may be an attempt to retain some control, or to demonstrate that he's really a great guy. Whatever the situation, if it benefits your children, try to put your resentment aside and allow it to help them. It may take time to get there, but it's a good place to get to.

Of course, not all ex-husbands shower their children with gifts. Some withhold from their children, sometimes telling them that he gives their mother enough money, so if there isn't enough for their wants and needs, she must be spending it on herself. The guiding principles of what is best for your children still remains the same:

Remain positive with them and vent to others.

If they challenge you with false information that they get from their father, explain the reality to them in an age appropriate manner, without emotion, simply and succinctly.

Infuse your home with positive suitable substitutes whenever and wherever possible.

Stability   Research shows that children in divorced families benefit when as many aspects of their lives as possible are not changed. It's best not to move if at all possible. It is also best to keep the children in the same school that they attended before the divorce, and to have them continue with extracurricular activities.

Of course, given new economic constraints, it may not be possible to keep everything the same as it was before. There may be a limit to what you can do, but you should be guided by the goal of keeping things the same, as much as you possibly can.

Another aspect of providing stability for your children is making sure they know that they have a mother they can always count on. Custodial single mothers have substantially higher rates of anxiety and depression than comparably aged women in other marital status groups. This isn't surprising, given the stresses a woman faces following a divorce. However, you need to be strong so you can provide for your children and be an effective parent.

It's understandable if you are feeling overwhelmed by your situation, and combating this can be quite the task. One strategy that many women have found to be effective is to use the time when their ex-husbands have visitation to take care of themselves. Too often, that time is spent feeling down about the loss. Instead, take advantage of this opportunity to boost your energy levels so you can take care of all of your children's needs in a positive way when you have them back with you

Another important point is that you absolutely must remain a parent. You cannot succumb to the temptation of enlisting a child as a confidant on whom you can dump all of your frustrations and insecurities.

In single-parent households, there is a natural tendency for the custodial parent to turn to the children to perform some of the household roles that have been left absent by the departure of the other spouse. Since divorced mothers tend to have multiple responsibilities and very tight schedules, they are particularly prone to expecting children to get involved. The message is typically very clear that, "We are all in this together," and, "We all must do our part."

This is fine when it comes to chores that a child in any household might be expected to perform. It's problematic when a child acquires a greater voice in making household decisions than would normally be considered age appropriate. Don't confuse giving children a positive atmosphere with giving them inappropriate power in a household. It's also not appropriate to give in to their decision making simply because you don't have the energy to stand up to them. A positive, healthy household is one where the adult is in charge. Although children may fight against rules and boundaries, without them they are left feeling very insecure. Giving them age appropriate decision making and independence is very different from allowing them to run the show.

If you carry the idea of partnership too far, or if you try to balance all the things their father gives them by giving up parental responsibility, your relationship with your children may becomes less like a parent-child relationship, and more like a peer relationship. You may find yourself sharing everything with an older child, including financial problems, personal frustrations, and feelings of loneliness. Your child becomes a confidant, and she may begin to nurture and support you to a degree that is not healthy for her.

You are the parent. Your child cannot parent you. No matter how mature the child may appear, no matter how responsibly she may behave, she is still a child. She can't handle problems that are overwhelming you. If you allow her to try to do so, it will be at the expense of neglecting her own anxieties and concerns. You will be compromising her stability as a child.

Children who are allowed to assume this role frequently manifest their distress by developing somatic symptoms such as sleeping disorders or eating disorders. They may also consciously or unconsciously rebel against the assumption of the confidant's role by acting out. Mothers who share their feelings or adult decision making with their daughters sometimes find that these daughters develop a negative view of marriage.

You are first and foremost a parent. You are the one who is principally responsible for the economic viability of the family unit, the smooth running of the household from day to day, and the emotional well-being of the family members. This is a unique role. It cannot be delegated. You want to be positive and fun, but you are still the one in charge.

Consistency

Your parenting role also requires you to be consistent. This means knowing what you expect from your children in terms of proper conduct and behavior, performance in school, and responsibilities around the house. You then need to communicate your expectations clearly and unambiguously. You should monitor your children's behavior consistently to make sure your expectations are being met. Establish clear consequences for deviations from expected standards, and be prepared to enforce these consequences when the need arises.

Many divorced women worry that if they are too hard on their children, they will alienate them and drive them toward their father. The specter of your husband's household offering an inviting escape from your expectations may hover over you as you attempt to perform your parenting role diligently.

The complications of co-parenting will be explored in a later section. For now, recognize that the fear of driving the children into his waiting arms is typically much exaggerated. Children sense your love and concern. They understand that rules are based on your considered judgments regarding what is best for them. Even if your husband lets them "get away with murder," it does not mean they will run away to live with him. (There's also a chance he wouldn't want them living with him full-time anyway.)

There are some instances where children, particularly adolescent boys, may choose to live with their father for a time. If this occurs, it is often pointless to fight it. Often boys who do this stay for a time and then return to live with mom.

You don't need to transmit your expectations negatively, or like a drill sergeant. Try charts to encourage good behavior. An older child may be able to earn a special prize for doing chores, school work or respectful behavior. With younger children you may be able to turn chores into a game. Perhaps they can earn a chore pass, where they get a day off if they work for a certain amount of time without complaining. Perhaps there's an occasional mess day, when no one has to do anything.

There are many books on the subject that you can use to guide you. Find one that makes the most sense to you, and follow it *consistently*.

Co-Parenting Issues

This section examines some of the issues that you may face even after the divorce is final. Recognize that it's never really over when there are children involved. Being aware of what you may face, with some words of wisdom from those who have been there, may help you navigate your own issues that continue to come up.

Ongoing Conflict   In most *frum* divorce settlements, there are a lot of specifics included about who gets which Yom Tov, including first days and last days. Still, it is almost impossible to anticipate every eventuality that may arise during the childhood and adolescent years, so there will always be some potential for conflict or attempted control or manipulation. Issues may also arise over where the children should be at special times, such as an unplanned *simchah* like your sibling's *vort* or a cousin's *bris*.

If someone wants to create conflict, he'll find a way to play around with expectations and arrangements. Here's what Linda had to say:

> *It was less than a year before the bar mitzvah. The financial agreement specified how much each would contribute to the bar mitzvah, even though our son, Yoni, was only five at the time of our divorce. I thought things would go fairly smoothly.*

How naïve I still was! Every time I tried to reach out to my ex to discuss where the bar mitzvah would take place, he completely ignored my overtures. He didn't seem to realize (or maybe he did) that details had to be taken care of in advance for a bar mitzvah. Halls get booked, shuls get booked, and caterers get booked. Time was passing, and plans had not been made.

The fact that he had already committed to paying a certain amount became less and less significant. Plus, hiring and paying the bar mitzvah teacher had not been included in the settlement, and I knew if I took care of it, he would undermine it, or never pay me back for his half of the lessons. We were back to negotiations and mediators, long after I thought I was done with all that.

As you can see from Linda's anecdote, even when it seems like your agreement has covered all eventualities, it probably has not. In the case of an ex-spouse who is looking to play games or make trouble, there are ample opportunities — even with an agreement which, at the time, seemed to have covered everything.

It may be possible to have an informal go-between intervene to get things back on track. Many current settlement agreements include the name of someone who the parties agree to go to in the event that a dispute arises. Sometimes this person is a *rav*, sometimes an *askan* or sometimes a formal or informal mediator. If you don't have this in place, and you and your ex can't agree on who to go to, you may need to resort to formal channels.

Sometimes issues arise with respect to the transfer of the children from one parent to the other at the assigned times. If you find that when the children are being dropped off or picked up, their father cannot resist starting an argument, seek to arrange it so transfers occur with the two of you not present at the same time. A friend or relative may drop the children off, or receive them when your ex-husband drops them off. If your husband is erratic or inconsistent in getting the children back to you when he is required to do so, seek guidance as to how you can get relief from this.

Differing Parenting Philosophies and Lifestyles You and your ex-husband may have had some different ideas about raising children, but there probably was a consensus regarding what *type* of religious life you led as a couple and family. One of the most difficult things for a woman to contend with after divorce is when her ex-husband changes things drastically in terms of how he parents, behaves, or conducts himself religiously after the divorce. It's very painful for a parent to watch her children exposed to conduct that does not fit what was "supposed to be."

Most people believe that there is an unspoken contract that if they get married with this set of religious standards, they agree that the children will be raised in those ways. What happens when one parent changes his religious standards, and maintains those changes during his time with the children?

To make matters worse, an abusive, controlling man who never paid much attention to the children may now derive great (and perverse) joy out of behaving in ways that he knows you would disapprove of or object to. These behaviors may be as simple as refusing to supervise the children so they complete their homework, or they may be as pernicious as allowing the children to view what you consider inappropriate television shows or movies, play violent and inappropriate video games, go on outings or participate in activities which are outside of your religious standards. If the school does not allow these activities, it will force the children to lead a double life, which is very damaging. At the same time, you may be loathe to solicit the school's help to intervene for fear of the repercussions for your children.

Unless your ex-husband's behaviors with the children deviate quite substantially from accepted social norms or general Orthodox religious standards, there is very little you can do. And even in those extreme cases, the court often won't take that into consideration. Your marital environment may have been a good deal more religious than the way your husband is now living, but the courts often do not understand the nuances that can be so critical and which establish the differences between the original standards and your husband's new lifestyle.

Here's what Michal had to contend with:

He took me to court, refusing to go to beis din *to settle the custody issues — since he knew that a* beis din *would have a very negative view of how he had changed. But in court, a* hechsher *was a* hechsher, *a haircut was a haircut,* davening *at home for a bar mitzvah boy was still* davening, *and all children watch TV — what in the world was wrong with that?*

And that's all true. But both my husband and I were raised a different way, with different standards. We got married living those standards, with the understanding that we would raise our children with those standards, as we did while we were married. But now he wants something different. To spite me? Because he was never really sincere in his frumkeit? *I don't know. All I know is that the courts didn't see the big deal in the shifts he had made, so now, whatever my husband wants to do when the children are there is fine.*

It's difficult — they come back to me and want the same life here. I daven *to Hashem to help me handle things right: to balance being clear about my standards with my desire to keep them close. I let them know that Tatty's house and Mommy's house are different, and that's just the way we live.*

There are times when you might have to take a stronger stance on a particular issue. Also, if your husband is doing things that are clearly inappropriate, such as drinking excessively, taking drugs, or exposing the children to completely inappropriate stimuli such as graphic sexuality or images of extreme violence, you will have to discuss the matter with your attorney and seek remedy from the court. The same is true if you suspect that your husband is actually being abusive toward the children when they are in his custody.

Protecting your children might mean some upheaval in your life, and being believed when there are custody issues at stake can be difficult. However, if there are real dangers it's imperative that you get guidance on how and what to do to keep your children safe.

You and Your Child's School

School can be a very hard place for you and your children. Today, many schools have experience and know how to deal with divorce in a way that doesn't further scar your child. But every individual is different, and you will want to maximize your child's ability to have a positive experience.

Here are some words of wisdom from Esther, a teacher who is divorced:

Here's the truth: In the school system, single mothers are scrutinized, so it's up to you to go above and beyond and make sure the kids are always put together. Do they have their snacks, clean clothes, are they bathed, are their projects/homework done? Volunteer, show your face — and make sure the face you show is a woman who has her act together; you never know when you will need a good word from teachers or the principal. Write positive notes to teachers: "Love the project", "My daughter's reading is soaring!" When you give off a positive image, it will affect the teacher's attitude toward your kids and you.

Some teachers (and people) assume that children from a divorced home are going to be trouble. If your child goes in unkempt, ill prepared, and you're never around, you'll be reinforcing a negative assumption.

Address the issue of divorce with the teacher. Definitely be up front! At first, it's uncomfortable just to be divorced, never mind discussing the situation with teachers who are strangers. If you have multiple kids, you can ask one to spread the word about the situation, or ask the principal to let the teachers know that if any teacher has a question, he or she can call you.

Be in touch with the teachers a couple of times a year, and go to conferences. It's good for the teachers, and good for your children's sense of stability. They are there to help children, and generally, teachers are special and wonderful people. There are many who will call and discuss the best ways to handle things once the door has been opened. They will exercise care in how they teach seder, family units, and so on. It's hard to open up and be vulnerable, but it can be tremendously important for your children.

As much as possible, keep the teachers and the principal out of the conflicts you may be having that involve your child. If your ex seeks to drag them into the middle of a dispute, tell the school that you want to avoid this and you are trying to get a different intervention. It may be tempting to have school personnel intervene — there are situations where they appear to be the perfect choice. You have to really think about how this will affect your children in the long run.

He's (Getting) Remarried

There are a lot of issues that come up for women when their ex remarries. Women worry how the new wife will treat their children. They worry that the new wife will be competition for their children's affection. Some women are concerned that people will assume that *she's* the one with issues, if *he's* able to get remarried without a problem.

Some are conflicted. On the one hand, there is a sense of relief that now her ex will have someone new in his life, so he will have less interest in torturing her. On the other hand, she doesn't wish him and his abusiveness on anyone. There is also the hope that her ex will be less involved with her children, together with concern over how her children will feel about this — even when she doesn't believe him to be a particularly good influence in their lives.

The best strategy is to keep your head out of the particulars, while continuing to remain attentive to how your children are doing. If you see a shift that concerns you, don't dwell on the reason it's happening. Focus instead on what you might do to help your child. If you haven't yet had to deal with an ex who tries to buy your children's love, and now you do in the form of his new wife, research how other women have handled this. But as much as possible, keep your attention away from his new marriage. This will be the healthiest approach.

Dating

After divorce, the subject of dating inevitably comes up. Women have different feelings about dating and different challenges when contemplating their return to the dating world.

Not Yet   Some women feel so scarred that they don't even want to think about dating — but everyone around them keeps push, push, pushing them to go out, regardless of how they're feeling. Why is this so common? Many of the caring and concerned people in your life are convinced that your healing will only be complete when you are successfully remarried. You, on the other hand, might be thinking, "I'm not ready to get remarried until I feel that I've healed." Women often find that they have to expend a lot of energy fending off people's efforts on their behalf until they are ready to move on.

Gitty wrote:

> *I was really quite amazed when the comments started so soon after my separation. "I know a very nice man who's recently divorced." And it wasn't just one person who approached me with similar comments. I tried to focus on the fact that people were thinking of me, but I had a hard time moving away from the thought that people had lost their minds. I wasn't even divorced yet!*
>
> *Unfortunately, the process dragged on for me, and I didn't get my get for years. When I had been separated for a while and people would call to set me up, I understood that they just assumed that I must have gotten my get by now. But that reminder was still painful, though I knew they meant well.*
>
> *When I finally got my get after eight years, it was a big simchah and big news. And naturally, the next comment I heard was, "So now we can tell you about somebody, right?" People refused to understand that I needed some time. "Time? You've had eight years' worth of time."*
>
> *For them it was simple and basic. But for me, the time spent waiting and worrying and planning and re-planning, hoping and*

davening *and not knowing, was not the same as the time I needed now to recuperate, to process, to settle in and enjoy my new reality. Maybe even to make sure that it was real, before counting on it and jumping to the next thing in life.*

Yes, I wanted to experience a true marriage, with a healthy, fulfilling relationship with my spouse. But first I needed time to let it all sink in.

What's Taking So Long?

Other women are eager to move on right away. They face a different challenge: finding the appropriate person seems elusive. Perhaps there aren't that many names suggested. Perhaps you look into someone, but the details you discover are not encouraging.

It can be very distressing to want to go out and have no one to go out with for months at a time. As a result, a woman can fall into the trap of getting into a relationship with a man who knows how lonely it can be to be divorced, and will prey on your vulnerability. He may cause you to believe that the relationship can lead somewhere, when in fact he has no intention of having it go anywhere real. Although the temporary reprieve from loneliness seems like a relief, many women talk about the damage they did to their self-esteem by allowing themselves to be treated or used so shabbily.

In their desperation, some tune out the lessons they learned the hard way in their first marriage, and get remarried to fill the void.

There's a woman I know in my community who got divorced the same time I did, and it's killing me to watch what she is going through. Sometimes I ask myself, "Was there something I could have done for her?"

Whenever we ran into each other, she would talk endlessly about her situation: what her ex was up to, what was happening in court, how she was destitute and desperate... Maybe I should have been more supportive, but I didn't want to talk about divorce and ex's and court minutia all day long. Instead, I encouraged her to go to a counselor. I thought if she had professional help, she could get out of that rut and start moving forward.

I don't know if she ever did. In fact, considering what's going on now, I highly doubt it. You see, she's going through a second divorce. Not long after the first divorce was finalized in secular court, and shortly after she told me how destitute she was, I heard she was engaged to a man with a lot of money. A year after the marriage, when I heard she had filed for divorce, I did wonder if her lack of financial stability and her loneliness had caused her to disregard the signs that might have indicated that he wasn't the right one for her. On top of the trauma of a second divorce, she had uprooted her children and moved away from her family to marry this man — and now she was going to have to uproot them once again.

There are women who leap into getting remarried without spending enough time investigating, for fear of being alone. On the other end of the spectrum are those who are so terrified of being fooled again that they don't allow themselves to move on.

These are common concerns. There are ways to handle these concerns, to learn to date smart. Women can learn how to look for important qualities in a spouse, and how to detect if a specific individual isn't right for her, or isn't likely to be a good spouse.

Trying On the Relationship

To help women understand how to date smart and really get to know someone during the dating process, I like to use the metaphor of the wedding dress. There are two facts that we can say about all *kallahs* and their wedding dresses. The first is that they all attend their weddings in a wedding dress. There may be different ways they got their dresses — from a friend, a *gemach*, a store, and even custom made. *Kallahs* also vary in how long it takes for them to find their dresses — some find the right one at the first place they shop, others look for months. But in the end, every *kallah* attends her wedding in a wedding dress.

The second truth is that all *kallahs* try the dress on *before* they decide that this is the right dress. No *kallah* see a dress hanging on a hanger and declares, "Great, I'll take it. Wrap it up, I don't need to try it on. I'll put it on the day of the wedding, it'll be fine." She'll try it on, see how it fits and how it feels, if she can walk in it, sit in it, how it looks from the back, front, and sides. She might show it to her mother or mother-in-law or sister for their opinions. It's unimaginable to think of a *kallah* walking around a dress while it sits on a hanger and deciding from that vantage point that it would be a suitable fit.

But consider this: Often a woman makes a decision about the person she's dating and whether the relationship should go forward from exactly that vantage point. This isn't referring to the length of the dating process. Different parts of the community have different norms. But if you are "dating smart," you should be able to determine how it would really feel to be in a relationship with this person, what kind of person he is, and if he is in fact for you. Problems usually arise when instead you try to decide whether it will fit from outside of the relationship.

Let's consider Shevy:

Shevy came in a few weeks after her second wedding. She had been divorced from a very abusive man several years earlier. Six months before her visit to my office, she had been set up with a widower by a friend whose husband knew this man from the community and thought it would be a good idea.

Shevy and Yitzchak went out several times. She really liked him — he had a great sense of humor, was very learned and intelligent, they could talk about anything, and he seemed very devoted to his four children.

During the course of their dating, Shevi did see some things that caused her concern. He had very definite ideas about certain matters that were actually quite different from her own. For example, Yitzchak once commented that when he came home from work, he needed to sit straight down to dinner — without waiting. This sounded a little rigid to Shevy. He was a widower with four children, and she was a divorcee with primary custody of four children. The household was going to be fairly hectic!

When these types of concerns came up, Shevy discussed it with her two close friends: the one who had set her up, and the third in their very close-knit group. Her friends had heard Shevy describe how wonderful and intelligent and fun this man was. They assured her that he must know how hectic a house can get, that a smart man would see that this was just not possible, especially at first. They insisted that the fun and intelligent side she described didn't match up with the concern that he would be too rigid. They concluded that it must not be a real issue.

For Shevy, asking her friends whether she should be concerned about this relationship was the equivalent of holding up the wedding gown on the hanger without actually trying it on, and asking her friends if they thought it would fit. How could she have "tried on" the relationship to see how it really felt? In Shevi's case, it meant asking Yitzchak if he literally meant what he said; it meant honestly telling him that she considered his expectation to be unrealistic, and seeing his reaction — would he be reasonable and reconsider, or was he really rigid about this, as well as other issues that came up?

Moments like this are an opportunity to explore how the relationship feels. When you ask the person if he really meant what he said, and share your concerns, how does he handle it? Does he belittle it, make fun of your worries, tell you that you're being ridiculous? Does he discuss it respectfully, concerned about your concerns, and able to shift *his* perspective? Check if the relationship "fits" by discussing these issues with *him.*

There *is* a role others can play — by sharing their advice on *how* to raise your concerns with him. But do not let them decide that these issues are or aren't a problem for you. How can they, or you, really know by looking at the relationship from the outside? When you engage directly with someone regarding the conflicts, opinions, or negotiations that come up, it gives you a much better chance to feel what marriage to that person will really be like.

On the flip side, an unexplored issue can lead to a break up that didn't have to happen. Negative assumptions could be made based on an unclarified interaction. This wouldn't happen if the two had talked directly with each other about it, as opposed to relying on the perspective of a third party who decides, "This is what he/she meant by that." This can be particularly true the second time around: you, your parents, and your friends are feeling extremely cautious, since you are naturally afraid of being hurt again. This may lead to issues and interactions being judged in a negative light. When these issues are not addressed directly with the other person, there is no opportunity to clarify the reality of the situation.

"Do you think he meant it when he said that? Do you think this means he's going to want that if we get married?" If you find yourself posing these questions to someone outside the dating relationship, and not to the actual person you are dating, it's a sign that you're deciding about the relationship without trying it on.

Your questions to those you consult for guidance should instead address *how* to broach an issue that concerns you. Ask, "How can I let him know that I'm concerned about what he said?" or, "How should I tell him that I disagree or I am uncomfortable with what he told me?" These types of question can help guide you so you can actually get into the relationship, to see how it feels to *you*.

What to Look For

To accurately assess whether a relationship is the right fit for you, you need to know what to look for — and how to know if it's there. You'll also benefit from the support of people around you, who will take your concerns seriously.

> *During the five times Rochel went out with her* chassan *before they got engaged, she noticed some issues that concerned her. In fact, there was one major incident that really upset her. But when she told her parents about it, they assured her that the incident didn't mean anything. The boy came from an important family, and he was known to be a good boy with a good reputation.*
>
> *The abuse, including physical abuse, started shortly after their marriage. When Rochel finally told her parents about it, they were horrified and guilt ridden at not having taken her concerns seriously.*

After going through an abusive marriage, most women (and their support networks) have learned the hard way the need to be thorough and cautious in determining that a relationship is right. What should you be looking for?

Many people search for compatibility, but you also want someone who is capable of having a healthy relationship. You might have a virtual checklist of the ideal spouse: he's smart, driven/goal oriented, *frum* but fun. Or maybe your list is a bit different — he's laid back but serious, he's *frum* and wants to learn, he's smart and dedicated.

But there needs to be another list — the qualities that need to be present to have a healthy relationship and marriage. When asked, most people would create a list like this one: trust, respect, honesty, care, support, good/positive communication, love, giving, and so on. These are the basic qualities for a healthy marriage, and need to be given by *both* people in the relationship.

A major mistake is when a person finds her "personal list" in a prospective spouse, but assumes that the basics are also included. Someone who's smart surely isn't dishonest. Someone who is fun certainly won't communicate in a negative way. Someone who is *frum* won't be disrespectful.

During dating, the indications that someone might not have the proper attitude or qualities to make a healthy spouse are often very subtle. These subtle indicators can be hard to see. And if the prospective marriage partner matches your "personal list," you may be strongly tempted to overlook the little hints that could indicate issues in his ability to have a healthy relationship. You might tell yourself, "That's not the real him," as if his positive qualities can override these possible deficiencies. You could end up concluding that the negative isn't anything to worry about in the long term, so it's all good, and the search is over!

Yes, you do need to know what type of person you are drawn to and compatible with. But when you find that person, remember to take a separate look at the general list of qualities that are important in a healthy relationship, and make sure those are there as well. And remember, they are *not* automatically included!

Here is a list of some indications of potential concerns, and how to further explore the issue within the relationship should it come up. The column on the left is an example of "trying on the dress" and seeing how the relationship *really* fits. The column on the right offers an example of how women instead stay out of the relationship, allowing it to progress without effectively exploring if that's the right decision.

None of these alone should be taken as an indication that the person you are dating is abusive. When you do see an issue in one of these categories, though, it is pointing to a possible issue with one of the qualities that it takes to have a healthy relationship: respect, trust, honesty, support, care, giving, good/positive communication, and so on. Look into and explore it well, to determine if it is a real negative indicator or not.

He is jealous of the time you spend with others and/or tries to isolate you from family members and friends.	
Although dating and certainly a more serious relationship takes time away from other activities, do you feel free to keep up with your friends and family members and make it to the social engagements that you want to attend? Yes, you may want to spend time with him, but does it feel like it would be okay to tell him when you have a conflict?	If he shows hurt, anger or disapproval about an outing you've mentioned, do you feel pressured to change your plans to keep him happy — and does this happen often? Have you started to anticipate these times and avoid making plans you know he will disapprove of? Unless you're willing to live your life like this forever, you need to see how he will react if you make and stick with plans that are important to you.
He wants to know your whereabouts at all times, and gets angry if you're not available.	
Do you share your day because you want to, and feel like he does that as well? Do you act naturally in terms of checking in or getting back to him?	Do you feel pressured to let him in on where you are and what you are doing? Do you find yourself stressed about keeping him happy?

He gets angry when you don't follow his advice.	
Do you (at least some of the time) stick with a decision, an opinion or a request, even when he disagrees? Don't test this out just to be stubborn, but when you do feel something is significant, are you comfortable expressing that?	Do you find yourself acquiescing most of the time in order to get along, so you don't appear "mean" or unyielding, telling yourself that it's not really so important? Do you rationalize your discomfort by thinking, "Shouldn't I want to please him?" Yes, you do, but you should get the feeling that he cares about pleasing you as well.

He doesn't take responsibility for his actions — it's always someone or something else.	
Do you take note of this and consider it seriously and what it might be like to live with someone who doesn't take responsibility and is never wrong?	Do you just brush it aside without thinking about it at all?

He seems to have two sides to his personality — he can be kind, but also cruel at times.	
Do you confront the behavior when it's directed at you, and see change or elimination of that behavior? If you observe it as it's directed elsewhere, do you consider what it would be like if it would be directed at you? Do you talk to him about your discomfort with his attitude or treatment of others?	Do you avoid or change the subjects that get him angry or nasty, take on the role of trying to coax his "good side" out when he has gotten upset at you or someone else? Do you rationalize that his bad behavior was due to being upset, and minimize to yourself what it might be like to live with someone who reacts to things that way?

He has unrealistic expectations, or expects to always have things his way.	
Do you tell him your own opinions and thoughts about various issues? Do you bring up your differences or discomfort in the moment, so you can observe a more honest, immediate reaction, rather than later, during an intellectual discussion, where reactions can be edited? Do you behave in a way that reflects your opinions and priorities, so you can see if he respects you?	Do you allow these things to pass, make excuses for what he says or demands, ignore the fact that while he may verbally acknowledge your opinions, in practice, he ignores them in favor of his own? When he is dismissive or disrespectful, do you choose to believe that he didn't mean it, even when he says it outright? Do you always wait to discuss the differences that come up, allowing him time to cool off and figure out how to say just the right thing?
When there are differences, his attitude is "my way or the highway," without basic respect and attempt to come to a mutually acceptable compromise.	
With a couple there will always be differences. Sometimes we can resolve our differences or conflicts, but even in a good marriage there can be unresolvable issues. If you have a difference of opinion, does this person respectfully agree to disagree? (Hint: You'll only find that out if you don't always back away from conflict.)	Do you quickly acquiesce to calm the conflict down, thereby camouflaging how he handles conflict? If you do this effectively you won't know what he's like in the face of conflict until you're already married.

You're uncomfortable disagreeing with him.	
Disagreement seems impolite; you were taught to be "nice" to other people, and it doesn't seem "nice." But in fact, when you do disagree, he respects your opinion.	You're uncomfortable because when you've tried to disagree, he gets angry and upset. Perhaps he doesn't call as regularly as he usually would or mocks your opinion, pressuring you to acquiesce. Are you more concerned about losing the relationship than you are about being married to someone you can't express yourself to?
When he doesn't get his way, he pressures you either directly or indirectly by sending someone (perhaps an authority figure) to convince you to relent.	
Do you stand firm to see exactly how far he'll go to get his way? Do you talk to him about how he expects to get his way, that you don't feel your wants/needs are being considered? What happens when you have that conversation? Does he try to please you, make sure you're happy and comfortable, work on a compromise you can both live with — as you would do?	Do you excuse the way he focuses on his own wants and needs exclusively, telling yourself, "It's normal to go after something you really want," without acknowledging that it is inappropriate to refuse to consider the other person? Do you ignore the fact that he wants you to keep things private and not talk to anyone, but he feels free to discuss things with anyone he thinks he can use to pressure you?
There are consequences when he doesn't get his way — pouting, belittling your way or ideas, not calling for a couple of days, turning things on you to make you feel defensive.	
Do you stand firm and/or confront him on this? How does he react? Does he hear and listen to what you have to say?	Do you give in because you are worried about what he might do, or what this might do to the relationship? Realize that this doesn't go away after marriage — it usually gets worse.

There are contradictions in his religious observance that seem to serve his needs — when he can get what he wants by being more religious, he is, and when it serves him to be less religious, he's not.

Almost everyone has something to work on in their *avodas Hashem*. Still, there should not be serious discrepancies. When one person can seem very *frum* about certain things ("my *rav* told me we shouldn't have a long engagement") but more permissive about others ("I would like it if your skirt were a little shorter; you can take certain liberties to please your (future) husband") you need to look deeper. Do his religious stringencies and lapses always seem to support what he wants you to do? Then perhaps this is not a typical struggle in religious observance that people face when they seek to improve. Are you taking an honest look?

Do you explain things away, make excuses, decide or seek reassurance from others that these discrepancies aren't a big deal? Do you assume or accept at face value that he'll change after marriage, even though you have seen no evidence of that? Do you stay away from asking about or expressing your discomfort with these discrepancies?

He is pushing you into marriage before you are ready, or tries to have you express feelings he wants you to have, rather than the feelings you actually have.

Do you let him know that, while it's hard when one person in the relationship is ready for the next stage before the other, you want to be allowed to do things/express things in the time frame that's right for you?

Do you go along with what he says he wants to hear from you, or his time frame ("we should get engaged already, even if you aren't ready"), because you don't want to upset or lose him? Do you do things he says he needs you to do to show you really care about him, even if they make you uncomfortable?

He does or says things to change your mind, or get you to do things his way.	
His tone remains respectful, even as he states his preference. He might say, "Can we talk to someone together who we both feel comfortable with to help us resolve this?" or, "Is there a compromise that will make us both comfortable?"	He says he wants to resolve this with you, but when you're not won over by his arguments, he starts telling you, "You should do it my way because..." The "because" may refer to a conversation with his *rav*, which you did not participate in. Perhaps he shuts down the argument by saying, "I think we need to have better communication," meaning that *you* should listen to *him*.
You are afraid of his reaction when he is angry.	
Think of specific times you've seen him get angry and what that has been like. How do you feel about living with this behavior? Consider it carefully.	Do you brush it aside and make excuses, denying to yourself that you were scared, hurt or intimidated by his anger, and felt intimidated into giving in?
You are uncomfortable or concerned with certain behaviors that you've experienced or witnessed in your relationship.	
Have you discussed this with him directly, only going to your support network (parent, friend, teacher, therapist) to seek advice on *how* to talk to him? Has he been responsive and respectful of what you need to tell him?	Have you given over decision making to other people by asking them what *they* think of the behavior, without ever addressing it directly with him?

No two people are going to think exactly alike, want everything exactly the same, or see things the same way. With that as a given, the important question to ask in every potential relationship is — how does he handle the differences? Is he respectful to you, even when you disagree with him? Is he respectful of your right to have your own opinion?

The discussions you have are not just to determine that you have similar goals, *hashkafos*, and so on, though that is important. It's equally important to see how he handles the differences. And this has to be seen in action, not just as part of an intellectual discussion. Someone might *understand* that it's important to apologize or say the right thing — but does he actually behave that way?

It's in real life situations and interactions that you see what someone is really like. If you have reached the stage where you are avoiding unpleasant or uncomfortable or frustrating situations — if you are already giving leeway for someone to behave badly in these situations — you will have a very hard time seeing him for who he is and feeling what it will be like to be married to him. Without making sure you have this information before the *chasunah*, you are really gambling with your future.

Pursuit Is Not Predictive

Sometimes a young man wants to date a young woman so badly — he pursues her, travels to see her, apologizes or tries to explain away issues that disturb her — that she's convinced that he can't possibly be controlling. This young woman is projecting her own way of thinking onto the other person: "If I was so interested in someone, I would certainly cherish him and treat him well." Perhaps she is right, and this is what he is thinking. But the existence of pursuit does not *prove* that this is what he is thinking.

This is because his efforts to win her over do not indicate anything about his attitude regarding control or his feelings of entitlement in a relationship. He may be seeing her as something he wants very much to possess, as opposed to a partner in a relationship. People go to great lengths and expense to have certain things, and yes, they love that object and want it to be just so. But they don't expect to have to consider its opinion. They also expect perfection — after all, they've just gone to tremendous lengths to get it. If there is a flaw, it will be fixed to their specifications.

The fact that he seems to be pursuing you, and perhaps is even willing to speak with someone to straighten out any issues, does not tell you that he will treat you with respect. You need to explore this as a separate issue.

Carol was dating Jeremy again. She had gone out with him a couple of times a year and a half ago and didn't really think he was for her, but he had recently called the shadchan *and told her that he kept thinking about Carol and really wanted her to give it another chance.*

This time they became close very quickly. They were able to talk about everything, they enjoyed each others' company, had a lot in common, and overall things seemed to be going very well.

There were, however, a few things that worried Carol. Jeremy sometimes seemed oblivious to her reactions to things. He could be insensitive, making assumptions about what they would do when they went out, not seeming to care that she wasn't interested in or sometimes uncomfortable with what he had planned. These things did seem small, and they didn't really make sense — because he really wanted to be with her, wanted to go out all the time, even telling her that he wanted to get engaged. When this picture didn't seem to add up, Carol assumed the negative aspects must be a mistake or misunderstanding on her part.

When they were close to getting engaged, they started discussing some of the details. They disagreed about one in particular: when to get married. It was April. Jeremy said there was no reason they couldn't get engaged in the next couple of weeks, and he really wanted to get married in September. Carol explained that her elderly grandparents were already planning to come from England in December, and since it was expensive and hard for them to travel, she would really like to wait until December to get married.

Jeremy's response: "I thought you were more caring than this. I thought you had the sensitivity to be a good wife. That's what marriage is all about."

Suddenly, the little things that had been bothering Carol seemed much bigger. The fact that he seemed to want to be with her so much finally became separate from the way he treated her on occasion. Carol was able to see that Jeremy actually did want her — but on his terms.

Carol decided she had to take a hard look at how he actually treated her, separate and apart from the fact that he seemed so eager to be with her.

Carol was at risk of failing to perceive what Jeremy was really like, because she didn't understand that pursuit is not predictive of how she would be treated by the person doing the pursuing. She had also assumed that the presence of a positive behavior meant that a negative behavior couldn't be present as well.

I'm Changing/I'm Working on It

Sometimes the other person seems to be taking your concerns seriously. He is not disagreeing or defending. In response to whatever the issue or problem is, he says, "I'm changing," or, "I'm working on it."

This can be very confusing and misleading. After all, he's agreeing with you, because he says he is working on it. This in fact may be completely true — that he also sees it as an issue or problem.

The trouble is that change is really hard! Yes, he might be sincere, and really mean what he's saying. But talk is relatively easy. In what way is he working on it or changing? Do you see actual changes? Do you see demonstrative movement, from point A to point B, in changing the problem?

Sitting in one's home thinking or even talking about change is not change. You don't necessarily need to see *complete* change to believe there is effort, but you do need to see a *progression*, one that is in forward motion. You should be ready to move forward with the relationship when you see enough change to believe in his commitment to the process — not because you're counting on additional change taking place.

It's never a good idea to marry someone based on the belief or assumption that something will be different after marriage. As my father-in-law, Rabbi Abraham J. Twerski, MD, says, "Marriage is not a hospital."

In Summary

It is my hope that this book provides some education, some guidance and some solace for you in whatever stage of the process you are in. And, with Hashem's help, I hope that you (and your children) have health and happiness, under whatever circumstances, in every stage of your life.

Counseling and Helpline Resources

The following is a list of resources assembled by surveying fellow mental health professionals. Inclusion on this list is not intended as a recommendation or approval by the author, and the readers are urged to conduct their own diligence with respect to any resource which they may utilize.

CHICAGO

Shalva Domestic Violence Program
  Phone: 773-583-4673
  info@shalvaonline.org

LOS ANGELES

Jewish Family Services of Los Angeles (JFSLA) family violence project: Nishma
  Crisis line for referrals and support 818-505-0900 / 310-858-9344

Aleinu Family Resource Center
  Phone: 310-247-0534

MARYLAND

Project Chana
Resources for victims of domestic violence

Phone: 410-234-0023

NEW JERSEY

Project S.A.R.A.H. Domestic Violence Program: providing services statewide
Contact Elky Stein, Director of Domestic Violence and Sexual Assault Services, Project S.A.R.A.H.

Phone: 973-777-7638 x154
e-mail: e.stein@ProjectSARAH.org

LCSC (Lakewood Community Services Corp.)
415 Carey St. Lakewood, NJ 08701

Phone: 732-886-6964

NEW YORK

Shalom Task Force
They have a hotline providing referrals in New York, New Jersey, Pittsburgh, Washington D.C. and Maryland area, Detroit, and Massachusetts

Phone: 718-337-3700 / 888-883-2323

Ohel Domestic Violence Services and Shelter
The contact person is Esther Katz, LCSW, coordinator of the program, who can be reached at 718-851-6300.

Jewish Board of Family and Children's Services Domestic Violence unit in Brooklyn
Intake- 718-435-5700 ext 222 or Faye Wilbur (coordinator), ext. 209

The Takanot Program at the Mount Sinai:
Sexual Assault and Violence Intervention (SAVI) Program: Manhattan, NY serving the tri-state area

Phone: 212-423-2147

Project Eden
Project Eden is a collaborative program bridging the criminal justice system and the Orthodox community, based out of the Kings County District Attorney's office.

www.brooklynda.org/project_eden/project_eden.htm
Phone: 718-250-2005

Met Council Family Violence Services serving all of New York
Phone: 212-453-9618 / e-mail: family@metcouncil.org

TEXAS

Jewish Family Services
Serving all of Dallas Metroplex and surrounding counties and Fort Worth

Domestic violence program coordinator: Ariela Goldstien, LCSW

Phone: 972-437-9950

WASHINGTON D.C.

Greater Washington Jewish Coalition Against Domestic Abuse (JCADA)
Serving the Greater Washington DC area including southern MD, Northern VA and D.C.

1-877-88-JCADA (52232)

AUSTRALIA

The Jewish Taskforce against Family Violence and Sexual Assault
Melbourne, Australia: provides services for the Jewish communities throughout Australia

Administration: 613-9523-6850
Support Line: 613-9523-6850
e-mail: admin@jewishtaskforce.org.au

CANADA

Auberge Shalom pour femmes: Montreal, Q.C. Canada
Phone: 514-731-0833
website: www.aubergeshalom.org

Jewish and Family Services — Women's Abuse Program — Toronto
Phone: 416-638-7800

ISRAEL

The Family Institute of Neve Yerushalayim
Har Nof, Jerusalem, Israel serving Jerusalem and its surrounding neighborhoods

Domestic violence unit: 02-652-7893

Crisis Center for Religious Women 24 hour hotline
Phone: 02-673-0002

Bat Melech
Comprehensive network of social services for victims of domestic violence

Phone: 1-800-292-333 (in Israel only) or 972-2-651-6103
e-mail: office@batmelech.org
http://www.batmelech.org/index-english.html

Yad Sarah: Mercaz L'Mishpacha

Frum female and male social workers, trained and experienced in the domestic violence area. Hebrew and English speaking staff.

Phone: 02-644-4566

UK

Jewish Women's Aid

Phone: 020-8445-8060
Website: www. jwa.org.uk

Glossary

aishes chayil: woman of valor; dedicated wife

akeres habayis: lit. "pillar of the household," the wife

askan: community activist

assur: prohibited

aveirah/aveiros: transgression/s

avodas Hashem: Service of Hashem

baal chessed: person who performs acts of kindness for others

baalas teshuvah: one who turns to a religious way of life

beis din/batei din: Jewish rabbinical court/s of law

baruch Hashem: "Blessed is G-d"; thank G-d

bashert: pre-ordained

ben Torah: lit. "son of Torah," one who dedicates his life to Torah

bentching licht: reciting the blessing over the Shabbos candles

blech: a metal sheet used to cover stovetop burners on Shabbos

bris: covenant (circumcision)

chassan: bridegroom

chasunah: wedding

chayev: obligated

chinuch: Jewish education and/or upbringing

chutzpadik: brazen

daas Torah: Rabbinic guidance; Torah viewpoint and perspective

daf: scheduled daily learning of a Gemara page

daven/davened: pray/ed

d'var Torah: words of Torah; Torah thought

eitzah: advice

emes: truth/honesty

emunah: faith, belief in G-d

Erev Shabbos: the day preceeding the Sabbath — until nightfall (Friday)

frum/frumkeit: (Yid.) religious, Torah observant

gemach: a free-lending organization

get: certificate of Jewish divorce

hakaras hatov: gratitude

halachah/halachos: Jewish law/s

hashkafah/hashkafic/hashkafos: Jewish ideology/ies; moral outlook/s

hazmanah: summons

hechsher: Rabbinic supervision, certification (generally on food); kosher

kallah: bride

kavod: honor, esteem, respect

kehillah: community, congregation

kesubah: marriage contract

kibud av v'em: honor of parents

l'kavod Shabbos: in honor of the holy Shabbos

lashon hara: derogatory speech, such as gossip, slander, talebearing

maggid shiur: lecturer of Jewish Studies

mashgiach: dean of students of a yeshivah who acts as an adviser and guidance counselor

mechalel Shabbos: violator of Shabbos

mentsch/mentschlich: A person with integrity and concern; a refined person

mesirah: informing on or turning a Jew over to non-Jewish authorities

middos (tovos): (positive) character traits

mikvah: ritual bath-house/s

minyan: quorum/s of ten Jewish men, required or preferable for certain religious obligations

mitzvos: commandments

mussar: rebuke or the study of Torah ethics and personal discipline

mutar: permitted

nebach: pitiable person

niddah: a woman in a state of ritual uncleanliness

nisayon: spiritual test or challenge

parnasah: sustenance; livelihood

parshah: the weekly Torah reading

pikuach nefesh: the obligation to save a life in jeopardy

psak: a halachic ruling

rabbanim: rabbis

rav: Rabbi

rebbi: male Torah teacher

seder: order

seruv: a declaration that a person is in contempt of a beis din

shadchan: matchmaker

sheitel: wig

shaliach: messenger

shalom bayis: marital and/or family harmony

shanah rishonah: first year (of marriage)

she'eilah/s: halachic question

sheva brachos: seven blessings recited at a wedding and during the following week; celebratory ceremony at the end of festive meals honoring the newlywed couple for the week after their wedding

shidduch/shidduchim: match/es (usually used both matrimonially and in business)

simchas: happiness; joyous occasion/s of

taharas hamishpachah: family purity

talmid: student

tefilah: prayer

teshuvah: repentance/return

tikkun: an occurance that has been pre-ordained by Hashem which purpose is an atonement

toan: a person who function as a lawyer or pleader in the rabbinic court

tznius: modesty

vort: (Yid.) engagement party

yeshivah gedolah: post high school Torah learning institution for boys and young men

Yeshivishe: yeshivah-style

yetzer hara: evil inclination